THE SEVENTH VOLUME

2,000 INTERNATIONAL IDENTITIES by LEADING DESIGNERS

1. 2. 3. 4. 5. 6. 7.

VOLUME 7 OF THE WORLD'S MOST COMPREHENSIVE LOGO DESIGN SERIES

JURIED BY EIGHT IDENTITY DESIGN LUMINARIES, each LogoLounge volume represents the zeitgeist of the world of logo design. This volume is a collection culled from the logo entries on LogoLounge.com since the last LogoLounge publication. The selections span across all categories and are organized for efficient research and study. To own a LogoLounge volume means much more than just owning a book – **IT MEANS OWNING A PIECE OF DESIGN HISTORY.**

bill gardner 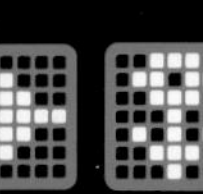  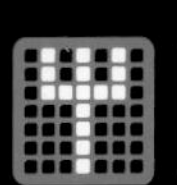  anne hellman

logolounge 7

2,000 International Identities by Leading Designers

Bill Gardner and Anne Hellman

ROCKPORT

Rockport Publishers
100 Cummings Center, Suite 406L
Beverly, MA 01915

rockpub.com • rockpaperink.com

First published in the United States of America in 2012 by
Rockport Publishers, a member of
Quayside Publishing Group
100 Cummings Center
Suite 406-L
Beverly, Massachusetts 01915-6101
Telephone: (978) 282-9590
Fax: (978) 283-2742
www.rockpub.com
Visit RockPaperInk.com to share your opinions, creations, and passion for design.

10 9 8 7 6 5 4 3 2 1

ISBN: 978-1-59253-727-3

Digital edition published in 2012

eISBN: 978-1-61058-410-4

Library of Congress Cataloging-in-Publication Data available

Production Coordinator: Jessica Hansen, Gardner Design
Design: Gardner Design
Cover Design: Gardner Design
Layout & Production: *tabula rasa* graphic design

Printed in China

To my twin (the other half of my identity), my family, and a special thank-you to Tad Crawford.

—Anne Hellman

Every night I pray that clients with taste will get money and clients with money will get taste.

—Bill Gardner

contents

Portraits

Sketches

Collections

introduction

Great designers of logos tend to have a huge passion for the craft. Part of the success they achieve is based on their draftsmanship and ability to create visually captivating and succinct images. I'd argue that the larger part of this gift is due to a diverse education, one that allows for a deep understanding of symbology and its origins. A personal well that I frequent is mythology, as it lays the foundation of much of modern-day storytelling.

I have a coin on my desk that was minted in Greece circa 300 BCE. It bears a picture of Athena on the face and an owl on the reverse side. This owl, known in mythology as Glaucus, was often depicted sitting on Athena's shoulder and was considered symbolically to be the source of her great wisdom. This is where most folks will jump to the "wise as an owl" cliché and be done with this story without asking, "Why?"

Many different attributes of the owl have given way to legend. The owl is a symbol of vigilance because it is capable of seeing in darkness and stands watch at night. It is a symbol of philosophy because it spreads its wings at dusk, like a curtain closing on the day, which from then on can only be viewed in retrospect. The wisdom attribute came from the owl's ability to turn its head 180 degrees and see as easily into the future as it can into the past.

Anyone can look to the future, but no one can forecast where he is going unless he knows how he got to where he is today. This mythological owl had predictive capabilities, not because it could look forward or backward, but—like the creators of brilliant brands—it did both at the same time. Now you know the real genius behind today's prophets of design.

The logos selected for this book were culled from more than 33,000 submissions from the very largest branding firms in the world to one-person studios in the hinterlands. The eight masters of design responsible for judging and selecting this amazing content have just made life much easier for you. They have selectively created that prophet's vision of the best of where we are and where we are going.

Absorbing the trends and reviewing these logos is made all that much easier by meticulous organization. The brilliance of these 2,000 marks is magnified when shown in context with other similar logos organized by topic and style. Members of LogoLounge.com can view every logo submitted to past, present, or future books as well as receive unlimited uploads of their own logos for possible inclusion in future editions. At the time of this writing, LogoLounge has a database of over 170,000 logos, contributed by members from more than 100 countries. Each of these logos is searchable by keyword, industry, designer, date, client, and style.

New ideas, along with old ones brought back to life, come pulsing through identity design on a daily, if not hourly, basis. *LogoLounge 7* not only showcases the most exceptional logos of our time, but it also provides dozens of case studies that give readers a peek behind the scenes of recent identity projects from around the world. Designers will recognize some of the same trials and processes both peers and idols work through to arrive at solutions for their clients. They will also undoubtedly come away with inspiring new approaches they have never encountered before.

The nine portraits and twelve sketches in this book reveal both the challenges and the ah-ha moments of a full range of visual-identity creations made by multinational branding firms, small design studios, and one-person shops. From world-famous fashion brands to start-up clothing lines, prominent food organizations to local restaurant chains, car brands to online companies, global corporations to art schools, all of the identities highlighted in this edition were created by designers seeking both to customize and to simplify so that the brands could speak more directly to their audiences. Many take customization one step further and create systems that are anything but fixed—fluid and flexible identities that can change and adapt to evolving environments and users.

While this book is rife with the works of leading identity designers, I can assure you it is also home to the next wave of name-brand designers because, just like the mavens of our industry now, they look both ways before designing.

—Bill Gardner

jurors

Tom Andries

Branding Today, Leuven, Belgium

Japan Garden, by One up

"I always look for a good idea in a logo. I love the Japan garden logo because it is simple and smart. The designer uses the image of a Japanese rock or dry garden, in which gravel or sand is raked to symbolize the ocean, a river, or lake. The act of raking the gravel into a pattern recalling waves or rippling water has an aesthetic function, and the use of type and color are in perfect balance with the mark. The idea of the rake drawing the initial J is just genius!"

Tom Andries studied graphic design, advertising, and typography. He started his career at Marketing Design Brussels and later founded the creative hotshop Vulcan. He became creative director of Redstar Design Antwerp (the design department of LDV United, a WPP company), where he created a number of well-known logos and brand identities (City of Antwerp, Veritas, Sony Center, and the Brussels airport). He then set up Branding Today, his own brand-design agency, which features companies such as Thomas Cook, Ecover, Vmma, and bpost on its client list. Tom won a gold Effie Award for his "A" logo for the city of Antwerp.

Photo © Christine Navin

Ken Carbone

Carbone Smolan Agency, New York, New York

Hill Elementary PTA, by dandy idea

"This playful logo represents one of those 'ah-ha' moments, in which two seemingly unrelated elements dovetail nicely to convey new meaning. Even before I Googled it, I suspected that it was for a school in Texas. This adds to its communicative power and clarity. I really like its simplicity and color, which is a relief from so many digitally tricky logos. It's very kid-friendly, and the designers were lucky that the letters in the school's name could be integrated so well into the drawing of the armadillo. This is an admirable piece of graphic design."

Ken Carbone is a designer, artist, musician, author, and teacher. He is the co-founder and chief creative director of the Carbone Smolan Agency, a design and branding company in New York City. For more than three decades, CSA has integrated content, strategy, and art to create comprehensive 2D, 3D, and digital design solutions for an impressive roster of brands, including W Hotels, Morgan Stanley, Taubman Centers, Mandarin Oriental Hotels, Canon, Carnegie Textiles, Chicago Symphony Orchestra, Corbis Images, Architectural Record Magazine, and the Musée du Louvre. Carbone is the author of *The Virtuoso: Face to Face with 40 Extraordinary Talents* (Stewart Tabori & Chang). He is a professor in the MFA program at the School of Visual Arts and a featured "Expert Blogger" on *Fast Company* magazine's Co.Design blog.

Louise Fili
Louise Fili Ltd., New York, New York

Alabama Folk Art Exhibition, by wray ward
"The handcrafted rusticity of this logo was a refreshing change."

Louise Fili is principal of Louise Fili Ltd., specializing in food packaging and restaurant identities. In 2004 she was inducted into the Art Directors Hall of Fame. Fili has taught and lectured on graphic design and typography, and her work is in the permanent collections of the Library of Congress, the Cooper Hewitt Museum, and the Bibliothèque Nationale. She is co-author, with Steven Heller, of *Italian Art Deco*, *Dutch Moderñe*, *Streamline*, *Cover Story*, *British Modern*, *Deco Espana*, *German Modern*, *French Modern*, *Typology*, *Design Connoisseur*, *Counter Culture*, *Stylepedia*, *Euro Deco*, and *Scripts*. She teaches every summer in the SVA Masters Workshop in Italy.

Cesar Hirata
FutureBrand BC&H, São Paulo, Brazil

The Great Tea Road, by Denis Aristov
"I am attracted to this logo, to the path with the leaves intersecting it in perspective, floating in free form and in luminous color. It looks fresh and ethereal and is very sophisticated in its execution. For me, it communicates easily, in a simple and witty way."

Cesar Hirata joined BC&H Design in 1991 and became a managing partner in 1995. He has been developing and consolidating long-term relationships with corporate and consumer clients since then. Since 2002, following the acquisition of BC&H by Interpublic, he has focused his role on bringing all of FutureBrand's global branding expertise to its local and regional clients, leading important relationships and a large, multidisciplined, creative team. Major clients include Ambev, Bradesco, BRF Brasil Foods, Cielo, Grupo Boticário, GM, Grupo Pão de Açúcar, Itaú, Medley, and Nestlé. Cesar is a founding partner of ADG Brasil, the Brazilian Association of Graphic Designers.

jurors

Paul Howalt
Tactix Creative, Phoenix, Arizona

Star Power, Insight Design
"Each of the final logos I considered possessed an obvious visual concept, but in the end, I eliminated the ones that lacked the rendering polish, boldness, and personality that this one possesses. I couldn't ignore that his mark works on so many levels: it performs when broken into one-color iconographic components, and even better when brought together as a single composite concept. The positive to negative space ratio is consistent throughout all the component pieces and does not detract from the readability of the star in the negative space of the assembled four-piece composition. I can see this logo being sold through to the client with no explanation needed."

Paul Howalt has worked as a designer and illustrator since 1991. He is the creative director at Tactix Creative, a design studio he co-founded in the Phoenix area. His bold graphic approach has evolved from an unusually voracious appetite for comics and trading cards when he was a child. His clients include *The New York Times*, MTV, Disney, HBO, The NFL, *Sports Illustrated*, Target, Hasbro, Mattel, and many more. Howalt's work is on permanent display at the Cooper-Hewitt Design Museum in New York and has been awarded in numerous shows, such as The One Show, Print, Communication Arts, ID, AIGA, New York Type Directors Club, HOW, and Graphis.

Gyula Nemeth
Budapest, Hungary

Tango de Tightrope, Double A Creative
"I immediately fell in love with this mark. Its elegance, movement, details, and use of positive and negative contrasts make it effective. Even the colors communicate the heated and slightly erotic atmosphere of tango. This work could be used in so many beautiful ways, with so many appropriate type treatments. It's a standout."

Gyula Nemeth has worked as a graphic designer and illustrator since 2000. He has been working behind desks, on rooftops, on beaches, in beds, in bathtubs, on crowded buses, in moving cars, local trains, and planes above the Atlantic. During the last ten years he has switched back and forth from in-house to freelance while living in the United States, Hungary, Mexico, and the Dominican Republic. Nemeth currently lives in Budapest and works from his home studio. His client list includes Coca Cola, General Electric, University of Mexico, and Ironhead Canada.

Regine Stefan
venturethree, London, England

Read Aloud, Brittany Phillips Design
"This logo stood out from all the other logos because it is simple and playful. Rather than just representing the library's name, it has a lovely idea at the heart of it—to express the love for books. It is nicely composed and drawn in a confident, simple way. The two vibrant colors add to the playfulness. The logo is bold, unusual, and refreshing—especially in the library context, where logos can look stuffy and traditional."

Regine Stefan has been at venturethree since 2002. She is an award-winning designer with extensive experience in building brands. Most recently, she has been reinventing Liberty Global, one of the world's largest media companies. Stefan also leads the creative team on UPC, one of Europe's fastest evolving entertainment and communication companies. In 2009, she helped launch Sky in Germany and Austria. She was also instrumental in launching Sky Italia, Ono in Spain, and Parc1, an exciting development in South Korea, designed by Richard Rogers and Partners.

James Strange
Bailey Lauerman, Lincoln, Nebraska

Summit Series Conference, Indicate Design Groupe
"I picked this logo for its pure simplicity and concise execution. It says 'summit' and 'conference' without explanation. Brilliant."

James Strange is design director for Bailey Lauerman. He has more than twenty-five years of experience creating brands for companies, including ConAgra Foods, BassPro Shops, Bombardier, and Disney. His main focus is corporate identity and holistic branding. He has been recognized in numerous award shows, such as Communication Arts, Graphis, One Show, Logolounge, and Effies. He enjoys painting, eating lunch, and spending time with his family. He has received no major awards for the family part except a scrawly picture of an airplane from his three-year-old son and a few kisses from his wife.

portraits

Design Firm Turner Duckworth

Client Levi Strauss & Co.

Project Logo Redesign

There are few logos in the world as recognizable as the Levi's logo. The sharp white lettering on a red shape has existed for almost half of the brand's 150-year existence, and in that time it has spanned generations as well as continents. Like the clothing it represents, the brand mark had the potential to get better with age.

This was part of the thinking behind Turner Duckworth's renewal of the legendary Levi's "batwing." Levi's came to the firm with a particular challenge: with the brand's global growth had come inconsistency in its brand mark. Different countries used different variations. Although the vertical red tab has been predominant for some time, especially in the United States and the Far East (it graces the side of the back right pocket of every pair of Levi's jeans, and a graphic version has been used as the brand's logo), various batwing-shaped marks with the brand name in them were also in use.

Levi's wanted to distill its identity into one strong mark, to be used consistently around the world.

Levi's wanted to distill its identity into one strong mark, to be used consistently around the world.

The Turner Duckworth team, headed by founding partners David Turner and Bruce Duckworth and creative director Sarah Moffat, put the marks that were in use before them. The batwing shape is based on the shape formed at the top of the jeans' pocket by the brand's trademarked "arcuate" stitching pattern. It first appeared in the 1950s, and Landor Associates created a version with the brand name in it in the 1970s that was used for many years before the vertical tab replaced it.

The Levi's leadership team had decided to return to the word inside the batwing shape, but they wanted to ensure that they used the ideal version. This was a visual identity project that was limited in scope: The task was not the invention but the reinvention of a world-renowned brand mark and its applications.

"Levi's came to us with what was in a lot of ways a crafting project: how to make the mark look right," says David Turner. The brand's creative director, Len Peltier, wanted the mark to be the best it could possibly be. The design team quickly spotted the batwing shape's potential cool factor and even noticed that, occasionally, it had been used on its own, without the word *Levi's* in it.

Turner Duckworth took the word *Levi's* out of the logo altogether, creating a mark simply called the "batwing." They also crafted a house mark to help transition in the new icon.

The batwing shape is based on the "arcuate" stitching pattern at the top of the jeans pocket. Stitched into the left-hand edge of the pocket is the red tab, with its tiny, cut-off circled *R*.

The designers always placed the circled *R* so that part of it was cut off, because that is how it appears on the tab, and it gives a fitting sense of imperfection to the logo.

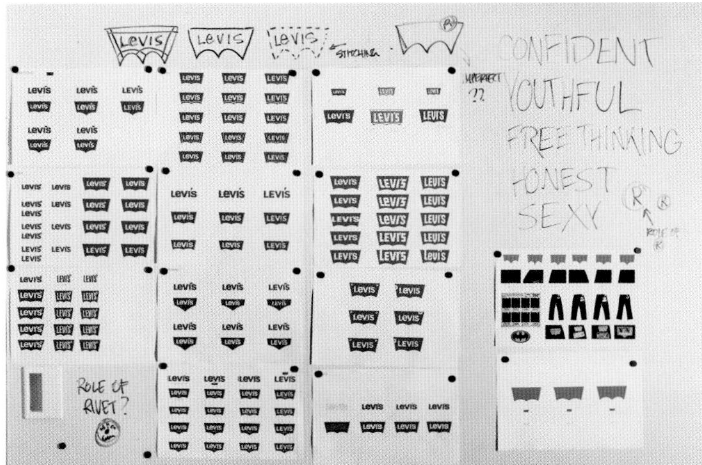

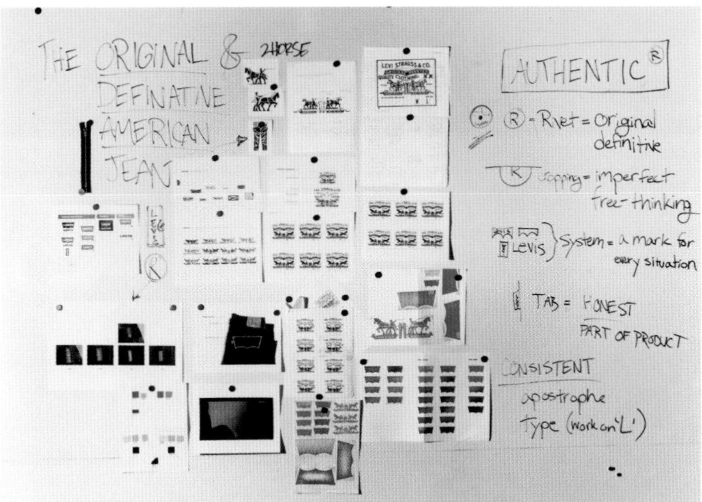

Turner Duckworth put the marks that were in use before them. The team quickly spotted the batwing shape's potential cool factor.

The designers became interested in a unique feature on the tab: the treatment of the registered trademark symbol, or "circled *R*." The woven tab applied to jeans was so small that only part of the circled *R* was visible; the rest of it was folded out of sight on the back of the tab. This quirky detail was unique to Levi's and had been replicated on the graphic version of the tab that had been used as the brand's logo. The designers added the cropped circled *R* to the batwing shape and the word to create a visual connection between the marks.

The team created a suite of marks that would look good together as the brand gradually transitioned to a single mark, all united by the circled *R*. But they also had an overriding hunch that Levi's was the kind of brand that didn't need a name in its logo. This helped them take the next step: They took out the word *Levi's* altogether, creating a mark they simply called the "batwing."

"In fashion especially, it is important that brands speak confidently, and being able to say your name without words is one way to do that," Turner explains. "Global brands like Apple and Nike have achieved iconic status, partially by having the confidence to represent themselves with an icon rather than a word. The absence of a word also means no need for translation." It was this aspiration to global leadership that convinced the brand's president, Robert Hanson, to support the new iconic mark.

Turner Duckworth worked on version after version to get the size and placement of the circled *R* right. At one point it was too big and overtook the batwing, which was potentially confusing since consumers might think it referred to a brand name beginning with *R*. When it was too small it became hard to reproduce. The designers always placed it so that part of it was cut off, because that is how it appears on the tab.

Jeans are the only type of clothing that gets better with age. As imperfections accumulate over time, a pair of jeans looks better. Part of the design team's recommendation then was to steer clear of a slick, corporate logo. They thought the mark should have a roughness to it, like a good pair of Levi's. The half-cropped-off circled *R* gave the mark this imperfect quality in a way that was unique to Levi's. Also, the presence of the circled *R* highlights the fact that the name isn't there.

Another element of the new identity was a redrawn "two-horse pull" image—the engraved picture of two horses attempting to pull apart a pair of jeans that one still finds on the leather patch on the back of Levi's men's jeans. Created to advertise its original patent of riveted seams back in 1873, many versions of the image had been used over the brand's history. But the drawing had become degraded and needed an update.

The designers created a bolder image, complete with stronger-looking horses, pulling hard against jeans that looked more like actual jeans to accentuate the brand's attributes of extraordinary strength and durability. They also updated the art for the leather patch itself.

Turner Duckworth proposed a transition strategy and usage guidelines for introducing the new iconic batwing to the world market. Levi's would begin to implement the logo slowly, over time, because in some places, such as

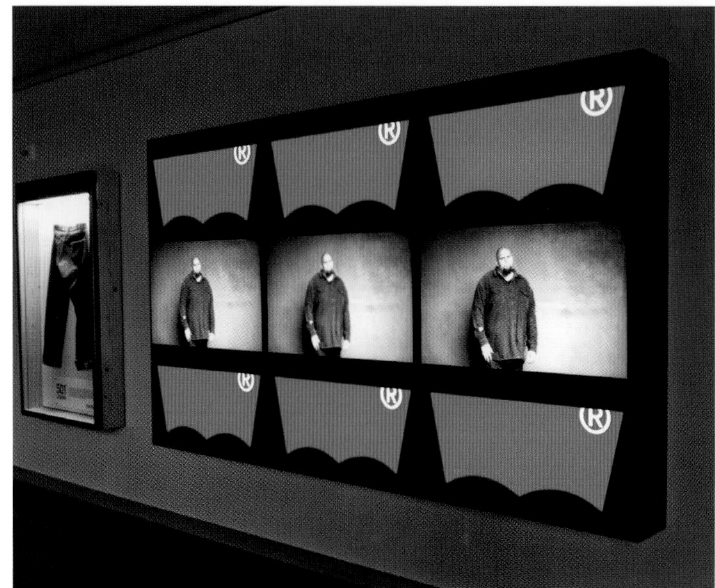

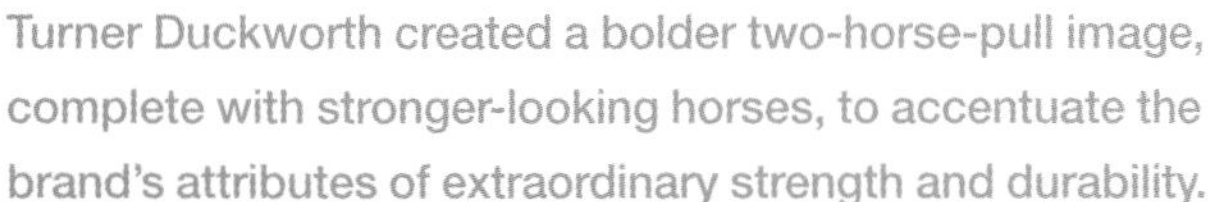

Turner Duckworth created a bolder two-horse-pull image, complete with stronger-looking horses, to accentuate the brand's attributes of extraordinary strength and durability.

The new wordless logo appears in interior signage and as a shop sign in Europe.

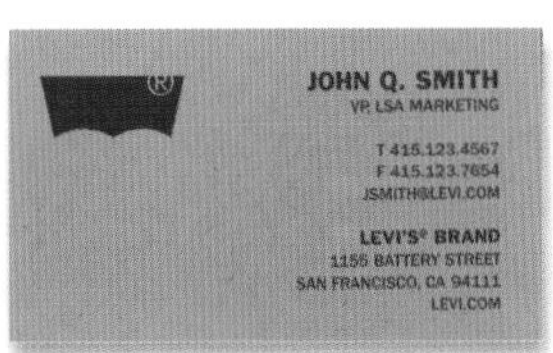

Turner Duckworth fashioned letterhead with the new batwing as well as merchandise that combines the heritage of the Levi's brand with its cutting-edge icon.

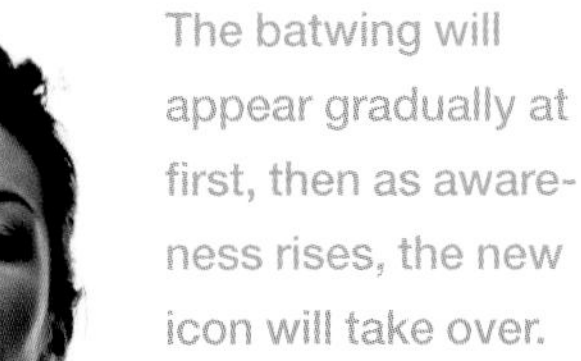

The batwing will appear gradually at first, then as awareness rises, the new icon will take over.

> The Levi's logo is modern and fresh, but it also has a sense of heritage, and I think that's a powerful combination.

China, the brand was still young. Consumers in the Far East were not used to the batwing because it hadn't been used as a logo there. Since its launch in early 2011, the new batwing has appeared around the world alongside a house mark that does include the Levi's name. For a while there will be a mixture of both across all markets. Then, gradually, as awareness rises, the new icon will take over.

Turner says, "The Levi's logo is modern and fresh, but it also has a sense of heritage, and I think that's a powerful combination. It's simultaneously exciting and reassuring, and great brands need to be both in a fast-changing world."

Tassimo
Identity Redesign

Turner Duckworth, London, England, and San Francisco, California

Left: Turner Duckworth based its redesign of the Tassimo identity on the "T disc" that makes every Tassimo beverage.

Above: The previous identity incorporated a coffee cup image, drawing upon the traditional imagery of other coffee makers.

Kraft-owned Tassimo is a leading provider of easy-to-use discs that fit into a Tassimo "T disc" brewer to quickly make an array of coffee, tea, and other beverages. Tassimo offers a full range of popular brands, from Maxwell House to Mastro Lorenzo coffees to Twinings tea to Milka or Suchard hot chocolate, among many others, in tidy packages that pop right into a Bosch-designed home brewing system.

Tassimo's original visual identity did not express its huge selection of consumers' favorite hot-drink brands. The company brought Turner Duckworth in to define and enhance its look, including the corporate logo, packaging, and brand identity. Whereas the previous identity communicated the traditional atmospheric qualities that so many other coffee makers convey, they wanted to disrupt the formula and break away from the competition.

The Turner Duckworth team, led by founding partner Bruce Duckworth, researched the competition as well as the everyday lives of consumers who used the Tassimo system in their homes. For inspiration, the designers went to the source itself: the teardrop-shaped disc that produces every Tassimo drink. They explored its visual possibilities and how it could form the basis for the entire identity system.

"The 'T disc' shape inspired everything: the icon and the typography, which we designed specifically for the logo," says Duckworth.

In early trials, the team experimented with a wheel made of the different brands Tassimo offers. This image became known as the "choice wheel," as it signifies the brand's main offering of a variety of well-loved beverage brands. As the design progressed, the brand images morphed into vibrantly colored disc shapes twirling around a center to symbolize a multiplicity of choices.

Turner Duckworth designed a "T disc"-inspired typeface for the logo. The word *Tassimo* now appears more contemporary, with the distinctive *a* mirroring the teardrop and the lettering overall sharing a rounded quality that ties in to the shape.

For the packaging, the team drew from the clean, sharp look of stainless steel found in contemporary European kitchens. Explains Duckworth, "We based the package on modern European furniture and interior design so that it would sit well on the kitchen counter and look right at home."

The teardrop shape has been implemented across all applications including exhibition stands, and the identity has begun to reach the world market as Tassimo expands outside of Europe to the United States and beyond.

The team developed a wheel icon representing the different brands Tassimo offers, which became known as the "choice wheel." The new aluminum foil packaging stands out from the competition while fitting in with contemporary kitchen design. Each package is highlighted with the color that represents the drink brand it holds.

Design Firm	**Branding Today**
Client	**Primus**
Project	**Identity Redesign**

The identity for Primus, a leading brand of one of Belgium's top breweries, didn't represent the rich heritage behind the name. Consumers across Belgium, and even the Netherlands, were very familiar with the story of Jan Primus, the thirteenth-century Duke of Brabant, as he was not only a powerful landowner but also an infamous lover of life. However, his personality was not represented by the standard typefaces and illustrations used in the old system.

Branding Today set out to steer the brand's image back in time in order to strengthen the package design and make it look more authentic. This entailed a great deal of research into the life and times of the legendary duke. The exploratory phase drew upon imagery and historical details from the past in order to create designs the brand could "own."

> Our goal was to refine the whole identity by designing each element separately and then bringing it all together into a harmonic brand.

The figure of Jan Primus, Duke of Brabant (1254–1298) is a perfect fit for a beer brand. "He was an epicurean, a music lover, a generous and happy personality who loved being amongst simple, hard-working people," says Tom Andries, creative director of Branding Today in Leuven. "He enjoyed good food and drinks. Before designing, we did some research on the era that he lived in—the clothing, the Brabant coat of arms, swords, and helmets." This thirteenth-century world would play the leading role in the ultimate solution.

"Our goal was to refine the whole identity by designing each element separately and then bringing it all together into a harmonic brand." The team felt it needed an original illustration. They researched Brabant's coin, its decoration and type design, as well as his signature, for a more "personal" touch. An image of the coin, front and back, was screened behind the signature on the final bottle label.

Branding Today's redesign of the Primus bottle label for Haacht harkens back to the brand name's rich thirteenth-century heritage.

"The illustration of Duke Jan had to be powerful and dynamic, reflecting a hero personality with a lot of movement," explains Andries. The emblem of the knight harkens back to Jan Primus's lifetime and performs well as an icon on its own, as an illustrative logo for the brand. Each element of the identity is equally strong, allowing it to be used separately throughout different kinds of applications, from labels and bottle caps to signage, crates, and advertising communications.

The logotype used on the label also had to be reworked. The previous font was a heavy and robust slab serif. Branding Today took the existing logotype and refined it specifically for Primus by using lettering with elegant spiky serifs. The letter *M* makes an interesting break after its first leg, adding detail and appeal to the name.

The firm was also commissioned to design various packaging applications, including a new mini-crate. The main objective was, above all, to be as creative as possible with each item, and to make them more modern. Whereas the previous packaging concept did not convey the high quality and centuries-old back story behind the brand, the new packaging had to incorporate history, quality, and craftsmanship along with modernity in order to help the brand live in today's world.

A sketch for the knight icon illustrates Duke Jan Primus as powerful, dynamic, and heroic and expands upon elements of thirteenth-century heraldry, including sword and shield.

Design trials for the armored knight on horseback play with different helmets, shields, as well as the balance of positive and negative space.

To this end, the Branding Today team chose black as the background for the mini-crate, which they designed to be smaller and more convenient, adding power to this element of the packaging and making the label shine.

Instead of launching an ad campaign simultaneously with the new packaging, Primus has introduced it to the market in stages. Primus wanted to switch out the old materials in circulation—the bottles, glasses, crates, etc.—with the redesigned materials before it embarked on a major relaunch. Reactions to the new identity have been extremely positive, and not just from beer enthusiasts or café proprietors. The Primus redesign won a 2010 Rebrand Award.

The final knight appears in the new Primus logo and as a stand-alone icon on the bottle cap. The designers lightened the heavy slab serif of the previous logotype and gave the letter *M* an appealing break.

The Branding Today team chose black for the mini-crate, adding power and giving the label a dramatic backdrop.

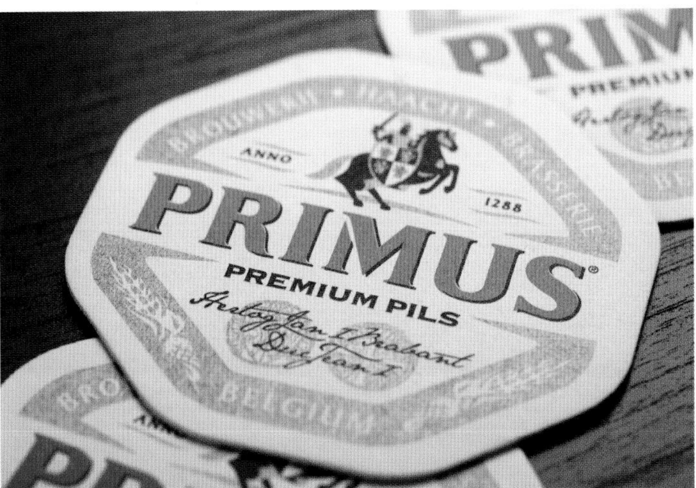

Applications of the renewed identity include glasses and label-shaped beer mats.

The illustration of Duke Jan had to be powerful and dynamic, reflecting a hero personality with a lot of movement.

i.materialise
Identity Design

Branding Today, Leuven, Belgium

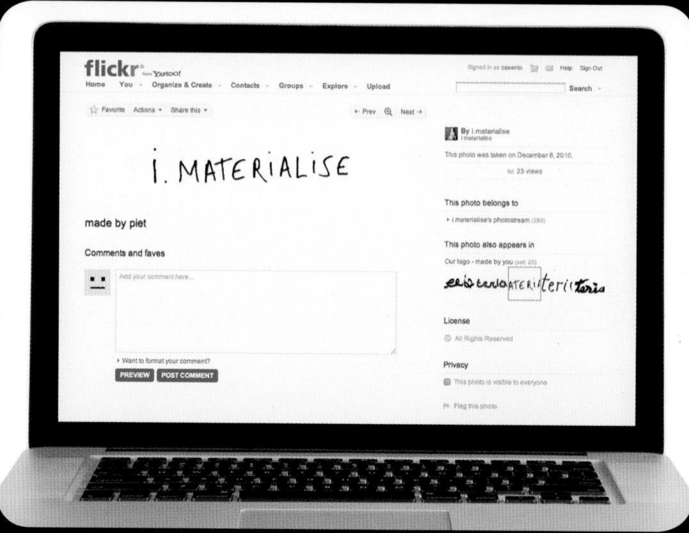

The forever-growing collection of i.materialise logos is posted on Flickr.com for everyone to browse and enjoy.

The notion of user-designed logos is one sprouting up across the branding landscape these days. The conceptual identity, rather than the hard-and-fast, black-and-white mark, makes perfect sense for a company like i.materialise, a 3-D print company that works with artists and graphic designers, and even hobbyists, to make their own custom creations.

When it met with Branding Today to initiate the project, what i.materialise wanted most was a brand identity that reflected its unique business proposition. And because creating one's own image or product is a deeply personal, often emotional experience, the logo design especially would have to express this.

The Today team narrowed down the solutions to three possible paths for the logo, each one more "customized" than the last. The first used the initials *IM* ("I am") as a reference to how personal these individual expressions are. In a second solution, the logo image unfolds into a 3-D letter *M* that can be used as a canvas on which to "paint" different customers' designs, veering further toward customization.

Ultimately, the Today team decided to go with a solution that allowed for even greater user participation. The logo would be the word *i.materialise* handwritten by different customers and uploaded to its website. Therefore, the logo would always be changing and reflecting the teamwork that happens between company and customer.

"It totally fits the brand," Monique Vanhumskercken, managing director at Today, says of the logo concept. "In a sense we are working to make the core strengths of 3-D printing available for everyone, not just designers."

At first, the i.materialise leadership team was taken aback by the proposal. They had expected to get a fixed logo that they could sign off on. But very quickly they understood the innovative aspect of the design, and the ways in which it mirrored their core offering. After getting a second opinion from their communications agency, True, they gave it the go-ahead.

The handwritten submissions are collected on the site and stored, and whenever the company needs a logo for its website, for an event, or as a signature on email communications, it selects one from its trove and uses it. "Next time you see an i.materialise sign at a design exhibit, the logo used might be yours," continues Peels. "My new business card might have your logo on it."

i.m
i.materialise
i.m
i.materialise
i.m
i.materialise
I.M
i.materialise
i.m
i.materialise
i.m
i.materialise
I.M
i.materialise
i.m
i.materialise
i.m
i.materialise

The first of three directions Branding Today explored for the i.materialise logo used the initials IM ("I am") to reference the personal nature of customers' creations.

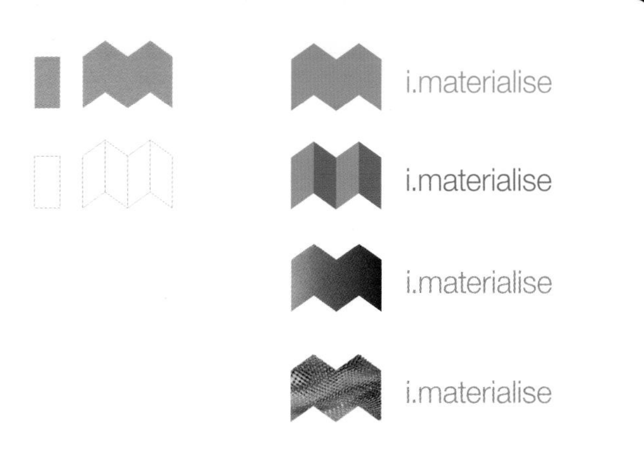

In a second direction, the logo image unfolds into a 3-D letter M that can be customized with individual designs.

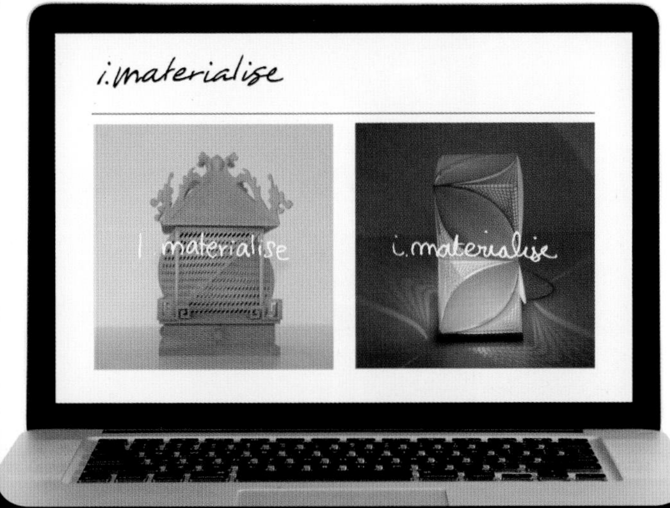

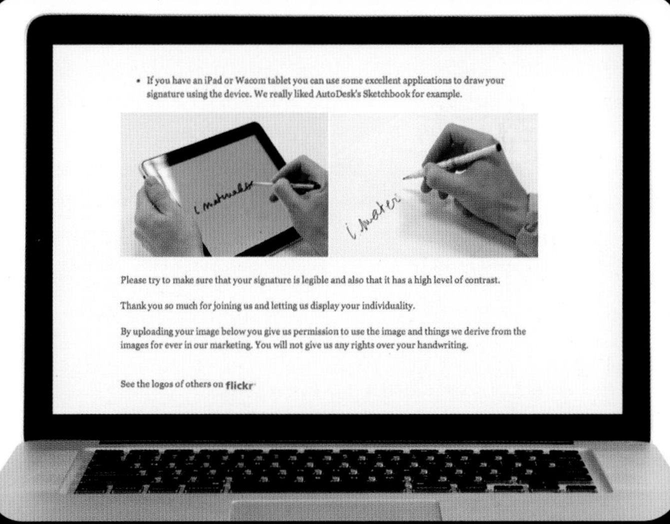

The final direction allowed for total user participation. The logo is simply the word i.materialise handwritten by different customers and uploaded to the i.materialise website. With an iPad, customers can write their logo directly onto the screen.

The i.materialise website rotates the logo constantly. The concept works especially well for individual designers, providing them with a handwritten logo to use on everything from products to business cards. The identity system has also extended to product packaging.

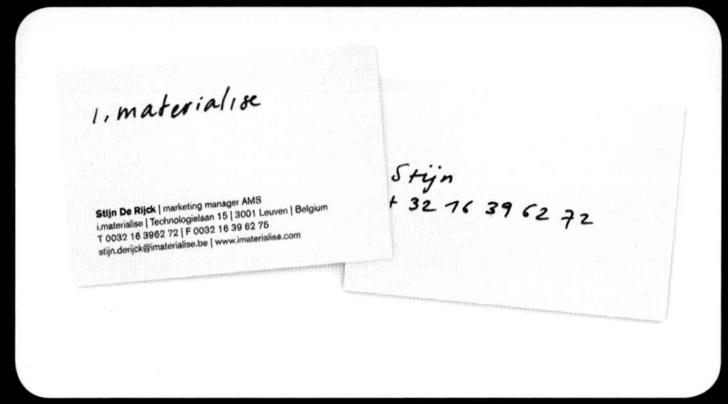

Business cards for i.materialise employees use logo versions designed by customers.

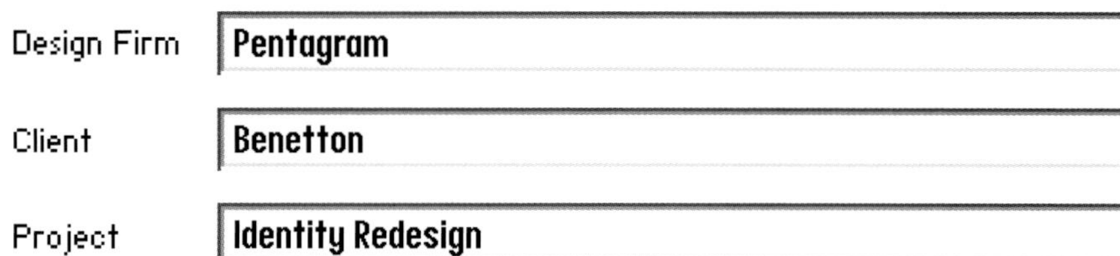
Design Firm: Pentagram

Client: Benetton

Project: Identity Redesign

Luciano Benetton's commitment to design has been well established for decades all around the world. Not only does the Benetton clothing label produce 150 million garments per year and sell them in 120 countries, but the founder's vision has also encompassed groundbreaking works of architecture by Afra and Tobia Scarpa and Tadao Ando, advertising by Oliviero Toscani, print by Tibor Kalman, and graphic design by Massimo Vignelli—to name a few.

In 2010, Benetton confronted an increasingly competitive marketplace and asked Pentagram to refine its identity system. As opposed to when it originally launched in 1965 with a single collection of colorful sweaters, Benetton now comprises a wide range of products and has accumulated multiple visual assets over the years. The question for Pentagram was, essentially, how can we identify and renew Benetton's truest elements in order to express its product lines most effectively?

> The question for Pentagram was, essentially, how can we identify and renew Benetton's truest elements in order to express its product lines most effectively?

The basis for the identity redesign as a whole was a shift toward consistency. Pentagram partners Michael Bierut, in New York, and Daniel Weil, in London, worked with Francesca Sartorato and team at Benetton to develop a set of guidelines for graphics on products, in advertising, promotions, and on storefronts, as well as online. They aimed for a new brand architecture that would tie together all of Benetton's entities.

At the heart of the brand was the most recognizable Benetton graphic of all: the white-on-green word mark, "United Colors of Benetton." Designed by Oliviero Toscani in the 1980s, the design broke from previous notions of what logos can and should do and instead stated a message using crisp, clean type against solid, saturated color, which would become known as Benetton Green.

Toscani chose Gill Sans for the typeface because of its sans serif authority and clarity. Over the years, however, as the company formed an array of product lines, Gill Sans had trouble speaking for all of them. The designers

Pentagram refined Benetton's world-renowned word mark, *United Colors of Benetton*, by commissioning a new font, Benetton Sans, that the brand could own.

UNITED COLORS
OF BENETTON.

A comparison of Gill Sans and Benetton Sans shows that the new font creates more space around the letters.

Pentagram determined the Benetton Green palette.

The signature Benetton graphic known as the "punto maglia," or "stitch," insignia had not been used since the early 1990s and the designers revitalized it.

The realigned logo gives both garment labels and hangtags a matching vertical orientation.

commissioned Joe Finocchiaro in New York to create a new typeface in multiple weights called Benetton Sans.

"Within Benetton, there was a long history of resistance to using Gill Sans as a supplemental typeface, since it was felt to have a bit too much personality, sometimes in conflict with the fashion direction for a particular line," explains Bierut. "Benetton Sans is intended to provide a more versatile, more neutral typeface, and one that could be proprietary to Benetton." The new font gives the letters more space and the mark has been realigned so that both garment labels and hangtags have a matching vertical orientation.

Bierut and Weil then turned to a signature Benetton graphic known as the "punto maglia," or "stitch," insignia. The icon hadn't been used since the early 1990s, and the designers thought that if revitalized, it had potential both as an independent graphic element and as a repeat pattern. They explored a range of variations using straight and dotted lines, then combined multiple symbols together, playing with positive and negative spaces to create patterns for garments, hangtags, and accessories.

Bierut and Weil took the punto maglia one step further and reconceived it as a redrawn Benetton Bunny, or "punto bunny," to sit as mascot for the baby clothing line. Rather than design a new bunny image, the designers used the negative spaces of the stitch symbol to form the arms and legs of the figure. And by recycling the insignia they upheld the new system of consistency: The Benetton Bunny was all Benetton.

The final design dramatizes the full breadth of Benetton offerings while at the same time clarifying them for customers at the point of sale so that they can find what they are looking for. Meanwhile, the redesign was so seamless, many customers may not have noticed a significant change when it launched in June 2011.

"This work was meant to support the company's marketing efforts," Bierut states. "It was meant to be a bit 'beneath the radar' with customers. The response from store owners has been positive."

The project was not a theatrical relaunch of an identity, nor was it a full-on rebranding. Instead, Pentagram stepped in and cleaned up, producing a more refined and effective word mark as well as a tighter identity system, so that the brand is better equipped for the next fifty years.

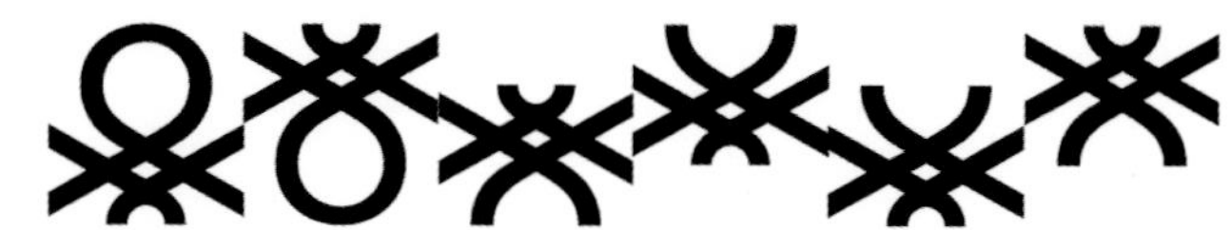

Pentagram explored a range of variations using straight and dotted lines, then combined multiple symbols, playing with positive and negative spaces to create patterns for garments, hangtags, and accessories.

Pentagram employed the negative spaces of the punto maglia symbol to form the arms and legs of the Benetton Bunny graphic.

> Benetton Sans is intended to provide a more versatile, more neutral typeface, and one that could be proprietary to Benetton.

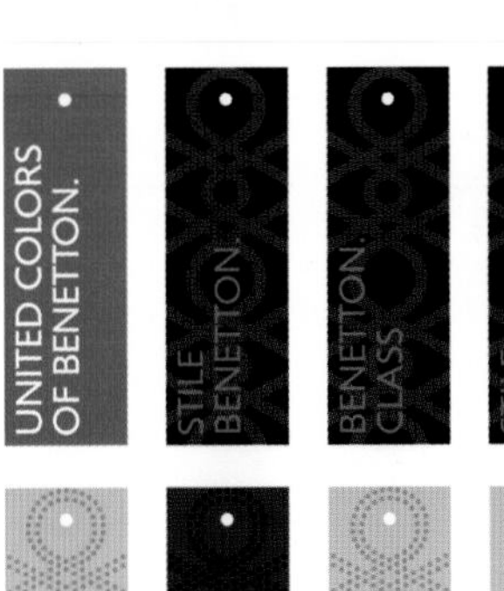

The punto maglia graphic now appears on hangtags, among other elements.

All Benetton product lines are tied into a consistent visual identity created by Pentagram, from Benetton Bunny to Benetton Vintage.

BENETTON.

BENETTON.

BENETTON.

BENETTON.

BENETTON.

BENETTON.

BENETTON.

BENETTON.

BENETTON.

BENETTON.

BENETTON.

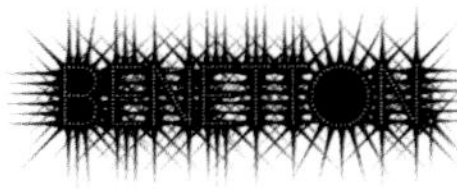

BENETTON.

Pentagram developed a series of logo variations based on the basic geometry of the new Benetton Sans typeface. Versions include stenciled, slab serif, stitched, distressed, hand-drawn, and even "exploded."

Bobby's Burger Palace
Identity Design

Pentagram, New York City, New York

Pentagram's Michael Bierut and Joe Marianek stacked the Bobby's Burger Palace name, and by applying a customized font and bright, bold colors, they created a logo that looks like a burger.

Graphics displaying Flayisms, such as "Bobby says we're goin' to the BBP" and "Bobby reminds you to get your burger crunch-ified," bring the restaurant's fun atmosphere onto menus and packaging.

When Bobby's Burger Palace opened in Long Island, New York, in July 2011, a different kind of burger also came into being. Michael Bierut and Joe Marianek of Pentagram, who worked with celebrity chef Bobby Flay throughout the creative process, designed a burger out of logotype for the new joint's identity system. Its logo is in fact a "logo burger," complete with bun, lettuce, and of course, meat.

Pentagram's main goal was to establish the restaurant as fun, accessible, and inexpensive, while making it a clear extension of the talents and enthusiasms of Bobby Flay, a chef cheered across America, as well as around the world, for his bold flavors and colorful cooking-show personality.

"We went to a few other burger restaurants, most of which came off as too 'boutique-y' and precious," recalls Bierut. "We wanted something that seemed really straightforward. Bobby was very involved and he was our main source of inspiration."

Using burger colors for the logo only made sense, especially when the designers stacked the three words and, harmoniously, the letters aligned—each word has exactly the same number of letters. With yellow-orange logotypes on top and bottom, a red one in the middle, and two crisp-green lines dividing the words, the logo burger came to life.

Marianek redrew letters from Hoefler & Frere-Jones's Knockout font to make them more "burger-like." For example, the *A*, like the *B*, has a rounded, cushiony feel, like a bun. The whole word mark looks edible.

Flay's team also wanted a sign that would help customers quickly order meat cooked to their taste, a unique touch to a fast-casual chain at this price point. Bierut masterminded a fun and easy-to-read color chart—easy to read because it is told through the color red. "Cool red" describes rare, whereas "warm with no pink" describes well done. With each color stacked like patties between two buns—as in the logo itself—the chart is accessible and ties back to the overall identity.

Rockwell Group designed the restaurant's interiors in reds, oranges, and greens, based on Pentagram's burger-color scheme. Many more locations have since opened.

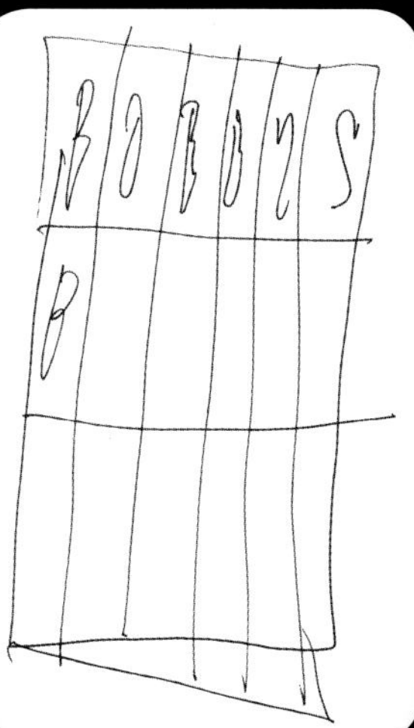

Left: Sketches for the Bobby's Burger Palace logo show the designers toying with typeface and stacking the name. Above: Design trials explored different concepts as well as color palettes.

HOW DO YOU WANT YOUR BURGER COOKED?
RARE
COOL RED CENTER
MEDIUM RARE
WARM RED CENTER
MEDIUM
WARM PINK CENTER
MEDIUM WELL
WARM WITH LITTLE PINK
WELL DONE
WARM WITH NO PINK

Left: Bierut's color chart makes ordering meat simple: Just choose a color. Above: The restaurant interior, designed by Rockwell Group, carries the color scheme of the visual identity into all aspects of the decoration.

Brand Illustrator	Chris Mitchell, www.epicicons.com
Client	Hulsbosch / Virgin Australia
Project	Illustrative brand identity icon: Virgin Australia Flying Lady

A logo's icon speaks without words. Very often it is the only "word" one reads. So important is the icon that it takes just the right hand to create it.

In 2010, Virgin Airlines commissioned Sydney-based brand and design consultancy Hulsbosch to spearhead a complete overhaul of the Virgin Blue brand, from positioning to naming to creating the visual identity. Virgin wanted Hulsbosch to take Virgin Blue upmarket and to remove its low-cost heritage from every aspect of its brand deliveries.

Renamed Virgin Australia to appeal to the corporate and leisure markets, the new airline needed a visual identity that communicated its shift in status. More specifically, in keeping with Virgin tradition, creative director Hans Hulsbosch and his creative team believed the identity required a "Flying Lady" icon that could speak across all applications. This is where brand illustrator Chris Mitchell stepped in.

Chris Mitchell crafted a new Flying Lady icon for Hulsbosch's rebranding of Virgin Blue. The Virgin Australia brand icon has a classic look, while the crisp gray-on-white color scheme elevates the image to the realms of contemporary luxury. "For me," says Mitchell, "using negative space as light is such a dynamic and creative ingredient in giving life and dimension to a design. I believe negative space is just as important to craft as positive space."

Virgin wanted Hulsbosch to take Virgin Blue upmarket and to remove its low-cost heritage from every aspect of its brand deliveries.

As the hand entrusted to create a large number of major illustrated corporate icons that serve their companies year after year, Mitchell specializes in capturing the essence of an enterprise within a singular image. Although Mitchell's Flying Lady was initially for the corporate identity design, Hulsbosch felt it appropriate to use Mitchell's version for the aircraft livery design.

The Flying Lady icon graces many Virgin travel brands around the world. The general public is familiar with the idea of figureheads ornamenting the bows of historic sailing ships. Traditionally a military custom, figureheads symbolized wealth, power, and good luck, and later appeared on the fuselages of military aircrafts as well as on the hoods of luxury cars.

Mitchell worked closely with the Hulsbosch creative team throughout the design process. During the initial exploration stage, he presented them with sketches to help determine positive routes for further work. Routes that were not worth pursuing were shelved early on to keep the development process as efficient as possible. In these early drawings, he provided a

Mitchell's sketches work toward a complex pose that best illustrates a feeling of flight while appearing simple and elegant.

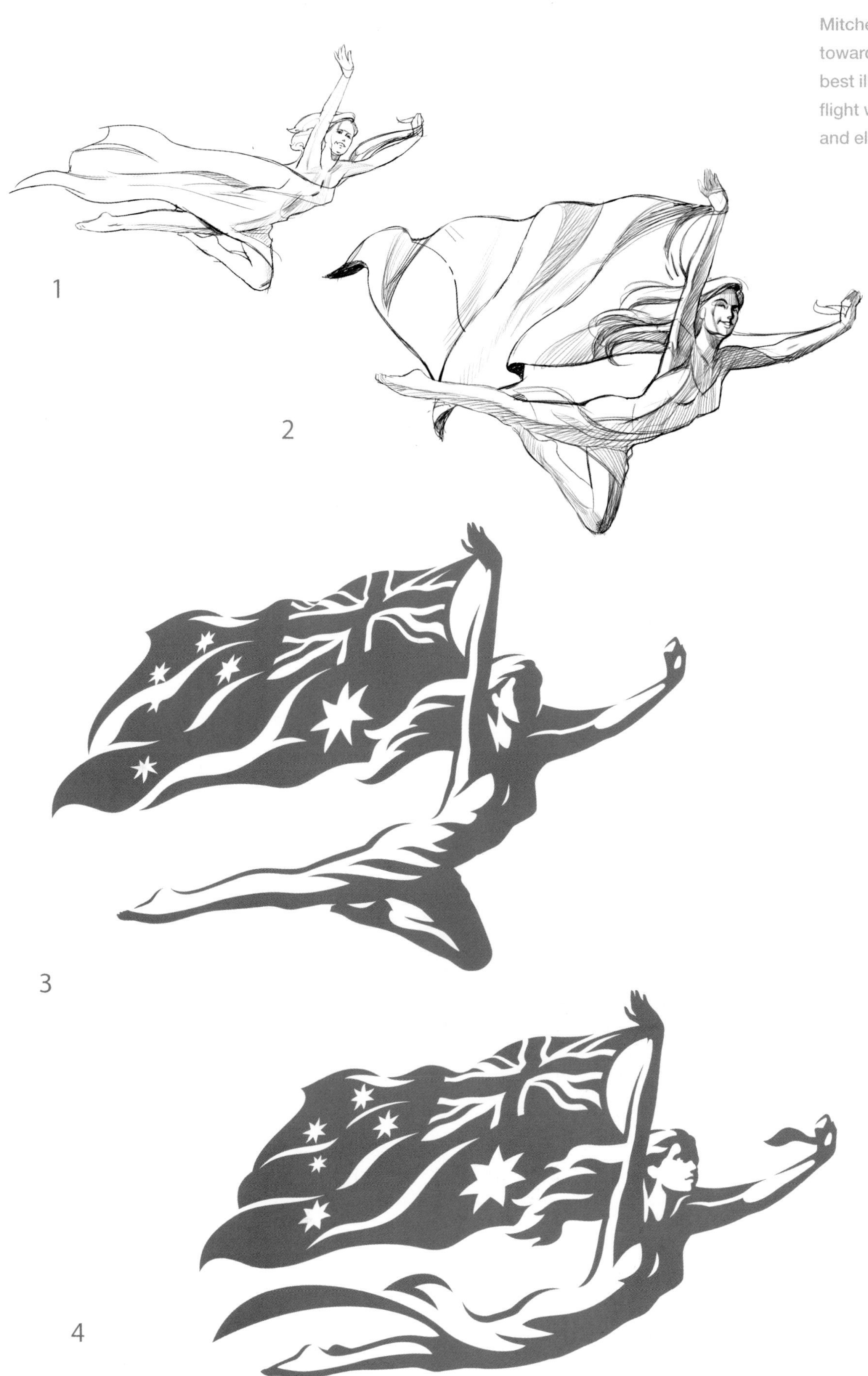

The Flying Lady appears on the aircraft's profile not far from where she would ordinarily adorn the bow of a ship.

range of pose and style options of the icon, as well as for the lady's dress detail so that the team could make important decisions from the outset.

"We wanted to find a pose that best illustrates a feeling of flight whilst holding the Australian flag majestically," Mitchell explains. "Being a complex pose, it had to appear simple and elegant."

Hulsbosch suggested that the Flying Lady wear a flowing dress to emphasize style and modernity—a big shift from the previous Australian Blue Flying Lady, whose hat and skimpy beachwear had to be replaced to make way for a more sophisticated image. There was also a danger in making the Flying Lady appear too characterful, which could restrict her appeal.

Hulsbosch asked Mitchell to work in one color from the very beginning to ensure simplicity and readability in all settings. This became critical in the design of the aircraft livery, which would virtually stand for the brand around the world. Mitchell simplified his line work throughout the development process to get it as clean as possible.

The Flying Lady appears on the aircraft's profile not far from where she would ordinarily adorn the bow of a ship, and thus joins the ranks of the company's illustrative icons, which have always projected a powerful visual statement endorsing the personality of the Virgin brand.

In pursuit of finding an iconic, crafted solution, Mitchell says, "I find inspiration from studying the way light falls on carvings and statues. For me, using negative space as light is such a dynamic and creative ingredient in giving life and dimension to a design. I also believe negative space is just as important to craft as positive space."

This philosophy, in combination with Mitchell's skills as an artist, made him a perfect fit for the project. The ultimate solution has a classic look and crafted feel, while the crisp gray-on-white color scheme elevates the image to the realms of contemporary luxury. Virgin Airlines and the Hulsbosch team were delighted with the design, and revealed it to the public in a press launch in May 2011. The Virgin Australia Flying Lady has been well received by the public ever since.

For me, using negative space as light is such a dynamic and creative ingredient in giving life and dimension to a design. I also believe negative space is just as important to craft as positive space.

Craft in Logo Design: An Interview with Chris Mitchell

AH: You are known for executing a high degree of craft in your work. Why do you feel craft is so important today?

CM: Keeping craft skills alive is more vital today than it has ever been. With budgets reduced and timelines shortened, the cheaper alternative can often be the first option. Without endorsing craft more readily, some creative heads, art-buyers, and designers may lose the ability to truly judge the finer points of crafted work, resulting in the execution of an idea becoming more fashion-led as a safe option or a hybrid of another crafted work.

Especially in the last ten years there has been a huge increase on the importance of ideas leading the way in design. "Ideas" people are heavily sought after in the process of hiring designers. This seems to be at a cost as the industry is losing craft skills, particularly in drawing ability, now not often a requirement for designers. I appreciate a good idea; this is crucial and is the obvious starting point for an effective design. The next problem, though, is how should that idea be executed?

AH: Why is an investment in craft particularly important in branding?

CM: Work that has a degree of longevity such as brand identity is an area where craft can excel if given the chance. The roll-out cost related to the distribution of a new global brand identity across all material can be huge, so the benefit of craft for the relatively small investment that it entails should be prioritized.

I appreciate a good idea; this is crucial and is the obvious starting point for an effective design. The next problem, though, is how should that idea be executed?

AH: When turning a great idea into an image, ultimately an icon, what sources of inspiration do you refer to in order to start sketching?

CM: For designers, often ideas are triggered by other visual material. Today there is a huge volume of material available online. Illustrators have historically contributed to the business of generating ideas. Their work has always proved to be a rich source of inspiration.

I am especially excited by seeing historic work, whether in sculpture, specifically statues, or painting. I have been lucky to have traveled quite widely and have been to some extraordinary exhibitions of beautiful, stylish work. It is not difficult to appreciate the wonderful use of pattern, flow, balance, and rhythm—all important ingredients of the most contemporary of work.

Black and white thumbnail sketch

With second tone. Thumbnail sketch.

Old Design

Early line sketch, character development.

Final Artwork

Mitchell was hired by Miller & Team Design to revitalize the logo for the Chartered Society of Designers. The previous design is in the lower left corner. Mitchell's development reveals how he turned the head to be forward-looking, raising the chin to make it more majestic and to align with the Chartered Society of Designers' brand vision of leadership and inspiration.

AH: What is your process when developing an image for a design firm? What steps do you follow in order to avoid going in the wrong direction?

CM: To visually communicate the idea uniquely I like to keep the process loose and simple early on to focus minds. The exploratory stage is most important and is best sketched quickly by someone who can draw instinctively (whether it be using a digital pen), either a designer or illustrator.

AH: Was there a moment in your career that steered you in the direction of making well-crafted designs?

CM: I was trained originally as a traditional illustrator, where learning different mediums and subjects was the order of the day. In those early days every thing was hand drawn. You could not avoid appreciating the traditional skill base around you. At the time, being a general illustrator, I worked on so many different types of creative jobs. Cartoons, book covers, advertising campaigns, story boards, packaging, film posters, even pet foods. What it did teach me was how important it was to interpret a brief, a skill that is crucial for developing major brand icons. And I always had a close association with designers, as my first job was to illustrate full time for a packaging design firm in London.

While on occasion a good idea can come in a moment, craft is an ongoing process of learning. It pains me when I see a good idea poorly executed, or on browsing through a design annual where craft can rarely be enjoyed for craft's sake. Let's hope it will not be left to the museums to display crafted talent in years to come.

Bulletproof / Football Association of Wales Crest Emblem Design

Chris Mitchell, West Sussex, England

Chris Mitchell turned the dragon's head to the right in his new crest emblem for the Football Association of Wales, giving it a forward-looking momentum.

The London branding-design agency Bulletproof faced a challenge: How could it provide a clear brand positioning and focus for its client, the Football Association of Wales, that would reinvigorate the Welsh passion for football?

A key feature of the FAW's identity was the crest emblem, and more specifically the Welsh dragon. Crests and emblems play key roles in visually projecting an identity, yet many are still entrenched in the past and follow traditional design guidelines. At the same time, more modern crests can appear bland, with little craft, excitement, or visual dimension. The existing crest appeared tired and old-fashioned, lacking luster and drama. The image needed more than an update but modernization to bring the club and its fans together behind a powerful new brand vision.

Bulletproof asked brand-icon illustrator Chris Mitchell, who has extensive experience in developing major sports logos, to bring vision, life, and drama to the new FAW crest emblem. Headed by design director Tony Connor, the creative team presented Mitchell with a loose concept to help in direction, and the development stages began. Mitchell presented sketch options exploring different elements of the dragon detail, shield design, and banner for Connor and his team to engage with and provide feedback.

"The Welsh dragon is a powerful and emotive historic symbol, universally recognized and loved by the Welsh nation," explains Mitchell. "There was good reason not to change the importance of this, as it was very much an historically relevant, integral feature of the FAW brand. To remove it could be likened to removing the lions from the England football emblem."

In answer to Bulletproof's directive, Chris drew the dragon's head so that it now turned to the right, as opposed to the left in the old design, projecting a forward-looking stance. He explored many alternative shield and banner shapes during the development process as well. It was important that all elements of the design work together in stylistic harmony so that the design could be seen clearly in all sizes. The color palette—red, green, and white—also had to be maintained to keep the brand portfolio consistent.

Although the new crest is a giant visual leap from the previous design, it retains the same elements of the old crest: a dragon featured within a shield and graced with a banner. However, this is where the similarity stops.

"The new Welsh dragon evokes passion and purpose at the heart of the brand," says Mitchell. "Even the dramatic banner design helps to visually give lift and focus to the now proud shield shape. The new crest visually projects the brand message, by revitalizing the renewable features of the old emblem, modernizing it, and turning it into something all can now be proud about."

Mitchell crafted two other identities within the FAW brand umbrella, for the FAW Premier League and for the FAW Welsh Cup. Bulletproof had thought through the concept development and application for these other two designs, so Mitchell's time was used efficiently for further development and craft, as it was critical that all three identity marks possess a visual consistency

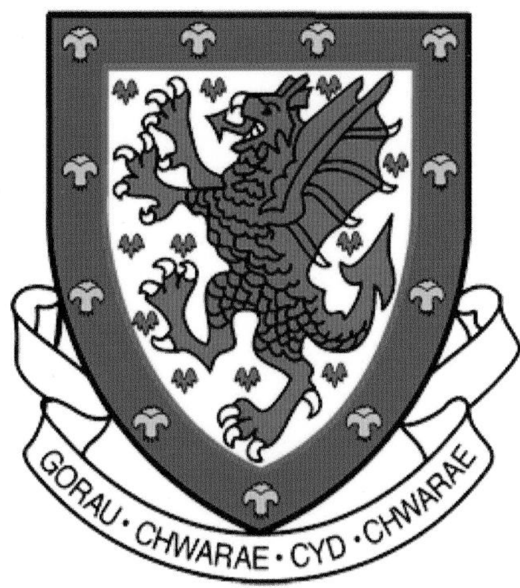

Above: The old crest appeared tired and lacked drama. London firm Bulletproof asked Mitchell to modernize it. Mitchell's sketch for the new dragon crest projects passion and movement. The designer even gave its tail a dynamic twist.

Right: Bulletproof commissioned Mitchell to develop two supporting identities to the FAW brand: the FAW Premier League and the FAW Welsh Cup. The marks carry attributes of the main crest emblem so that all three work as a collection.

The icon launched in September 2010 in time for the Wales vs. Montenegro Euro 2012 qualifying match. FAW produced prematch promotional assets, including posters, tickets, and programs, and in-stadium signage was supported by onscreen animations that used the core FAW crest. The mark was also applied to players' uniforms at a later date.

Design Firm	The Brand Union
Client	Alfa Romeo Mito
Project	Logo Design

By the time The Brand Union stepped onboard to create the logo for the Mito, Alfa Romeo's answer to the Mini, Beetle, and Fiat 500, the car had already been designed—the team was invited to Italy to see a prototype sculpted entirely out of clay—and the automaker was gearing up for launch.

Because much of the car's style and attitude were built in to its streamlined physicality and first-class engineering, the question then became, "What could the name, and logo, express that the car couldn't say on its own?"

The challenge was perfect for an agency renowned for marrying art with science in brands. The London team also happened to have an Italian creative director, Gianni Tozzi, at the time. To begin the process of developing the logo, the team consulted technical drawings of the car as well as early press shots.

Alfa Romeo was trying to tell too many main stories at the beginning. We narrowed it down to a choice between the cultural combination of Milan and Turin, or the meaning of the word *mito*, translated as "myth."

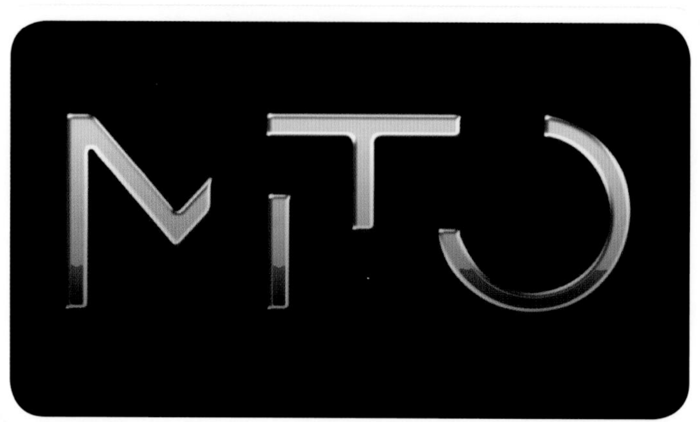

The Alfa Romeo introduced the Mito in 2008; at the same time it introduced a completely new kind of car badge. The Brand Union created a word mark that resists the usual language of automotive iconography. By giving only part of the word *Mito*, the logo encourages viewers to fill in the picture for themselves.

The designers found inspiration in three broad areas: "Il Mito Alfa," taking a fresh look at Alfa Romeo's personality and style in the context of Italian culture and motorsport; contemporary Italian graphic language linking back to 1930s typography, a route they dubbed "Futuralfa"; and "Urban Legend," which considered Italy's auto-racing capitals—Milan (Alfa Romeo) and Turin (Fiat)—and the concept of myth, both human and machine. They created mood boards to dramatize the three directions and ultimately chose the theme of myth (*mito*) as the route to pursue.

"Alfa Romeo was trying to tell too many main stories at the beginning," says Sue Daun, head of brand experience at The Brand Union London. "We narrowed it down to a choice between the cultural combination of Milan and Turin, or the meaning of the word *mito*, translated as 'myth.' We explored multiple options but chose to pursue the 'myth' theme as it became obvious it held the most emotional power and led us to more interesting places graphically."

The Brand Union team, together with Alfa Romeo, placed the badge on the rear within range of the long-established Alfa Romeo badge. While completely different, the Mito mark echoes the circular element of the original.

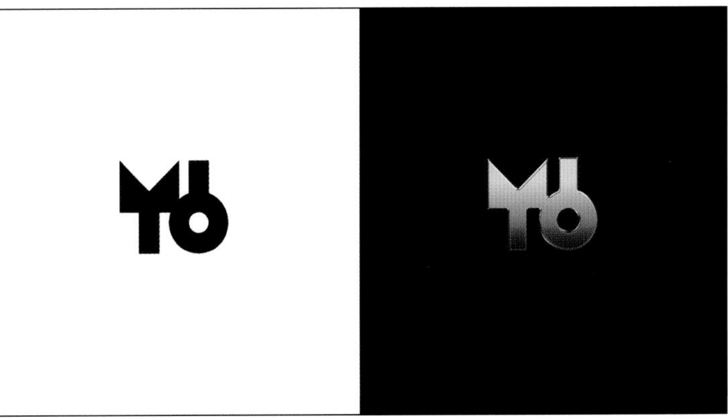

The Brand Union initially explored three different routes before settling on a final direction. These mood boards (for inspiration only) show the different concepts: "Il Mito Alfa," based on Italian motorsport and a new look at the Alfa Romeo personality; "Futuralfa," inspired by contemporary Italian graphic language; and "Urban Legend," focusing on a fascination with things that are incomplete and the link between man and machine. Each direction informed a potential logo design. "Urban Legend" became the chosen route.

Alfaromeo.com\ Models \ Mito
The 7 Logos 1 MiTo initiative is over.
ALFA MiTo
Alfa MiTo
"Brilliant, sophisticated, and fun logo. Matches the car's personality very well."
"WOW! I really like the logo it looks kwl..."
"As far as the badge goes, I love it. Great use of the gestalt, very modern."
"It is definitely the best looking logo from all 7."
"The winning entry is just as stylish as the car it's set to appear on."
"Your mind fills in the gaps since you already have enough information to go on. I think its clever."
"Wow, the logo looks good & individual."
"Well chosen!"

A selection of seven logo designs was published on the Alfa Romeo website and put to a public vote.

Before settling on a direction for the logo, the design team sketched out many possibilities. Once the "Urban Legend" direction was followed, the Mito word mark began to take shape.

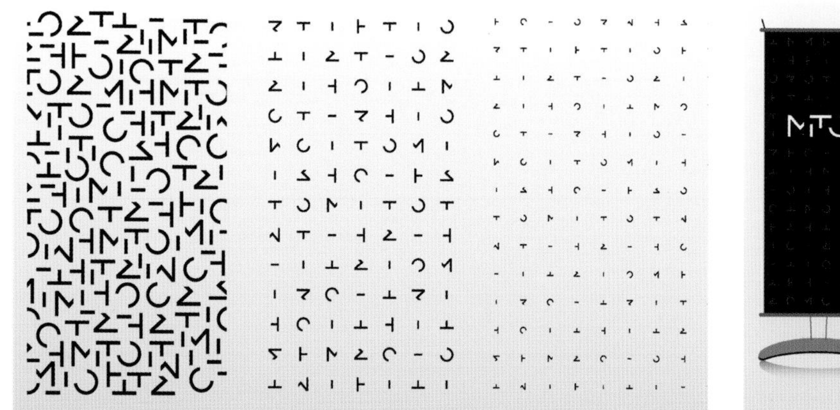

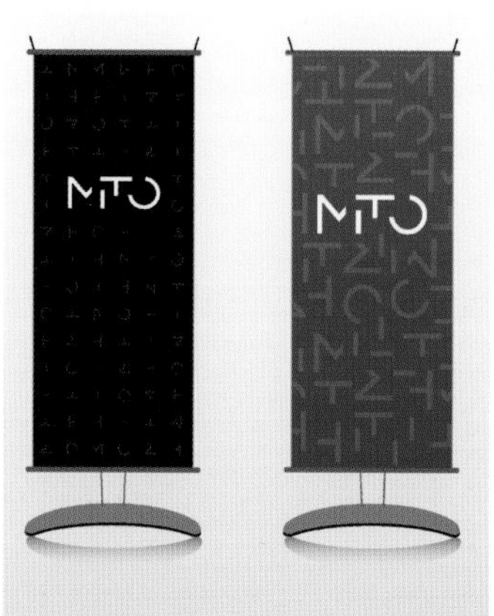

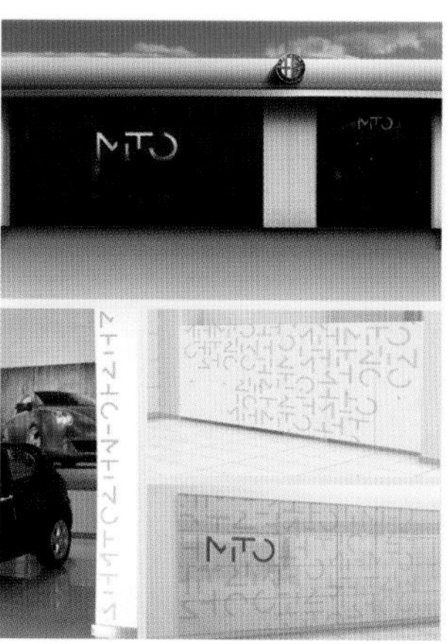

The Brand Union expanded upon the logotype to create a unique design language. The designers exploded the logo itself to make an abstract graphic pattern that could be carried into other touch points, such as point of sale and merchandising materials.

The Brand Union designed different logo concepts for each route. A selection of seven was published on the Alfa Romeo website and put to a public vote. Alfa Romeo aficionados who frequented the site made the final decision, and Alfa Romeo signed off on it without making any changes, a first for the automaker.

The solution was based on a contemporary version of the idea of mythology. The team worked with an overall design concept of "Urban Legend," exploring how information spreads and how a trend is passed on even without the whole story behind it being known.

Through many trials the team developed a typography for the logo inspired by the notion of the known and unknown, the real versus myth. The logo does not give the whole word *Mito*, but it encourages the audience to complete it visually themselves. What is equally interesting is the way in which the letters work to complete each other: They are interlocked and interdependent in order to be fully read. For instance, the *i* completes the letterform *M*, just as the *t* completes the *o*.

Ultimately, the logo resists the usual language of automotive iconography and embodies the fusion of style and engineering.

The Brand Union expanded upon the logotype to create a unique design language that could be carried into other touch points, such as point of sale and merchandising materials. The designers exploded the logo itself to make an abstract graphic pattern out of the different "pieces" of type, which, along with the overall metallic palette and toolkit, could be used for press, at dealerships, at events, and in product data sheets.

The cryptic nature of the logo has set the tone for Mito's marketing, but at the same time it was important that the Mito identity not rival the Alfa Romeo master brand. The entire identity system was inspired by the mark and then built to complement and reinforce the Alfa Romeo personality, not dominate it.

The logo launched along with the car at the Paris Motor Show in October 2008, and the reaction was mostly positive. Daun explains, "Obviously the logo is very different from traditional Alfa badges, being more contemporary, which was our intention. But even die-hard, traditional-script-loving Alfa fans, who initially took some winning over, have now embraced the mark, and we're incredibly proud to see it added to Alfa Romeo history."

Making the car badge was much like breaking up type on the screen and then putting the pieces back together, leaving some out.

The Mito at the British International Motor Show launch

Mauzan
Identity Design

The Brand Union, Dubai, UAE

Mauzan is the name designer Rafia Helal Bin Drai gave to her fashion label devoted to creating handcrafted yet contemporary abayas for her chic clientele. Twenty years after opening her first store in 1990, her retail presence has spread across the UAE, with customers ranging from royalty to students.

Rafia's designs uniquely incorporate the finest fabrics from all over the world, including nontraditional ones such as velvet and leather (she was the first fashion designer to incorporate pure silk chiffon into an abaya design), along with sophisticated embroideries, to make a traditional garment into a fashion statement.

However, in 2010, Mauzan was yet to be widely known as a premium brand. The designer worked with The Brand Union team in Dubai to create a logo and visual identity that captured this essence and communicated it to the world.

"We started with a simple truth: Every woman wants to look and feel beautiful," says creative director Simon Parkinson. "She wants what she wears to portray her unique femininity and empower her with confidence." Based on Rafia's statement, "My inspiration for designing the abaya is always the woman who wears it," the team developed a brand story that became the template for every aspect of the identity system.

For the logo itself, the designers worked through more than a dozen variations of a calligraphic representation of the word *Mauzan* in Arabic. They tilted the characters to the right, giving them the aura of being windswept, much like the flowing fabric of an abaya. A classic yet clean typeface was fashioned to represent both Arabic and English word marks and to balance them, one atop the other, beneath the icon.

The main color scheme was inspired by the shell of a pearl and includes desert rose, cream, and gold. The mark also appears in pearlescent foil on applications such as shopping bags, packaging, stationery, and on the walls of the Mauzan retail spaces.

The Brand Union tilted the Arabic characters of the final logo to appear windswept, much like the flowing fabric of a woman's abaya.

When it launched in early 2011, the identity system helped to give a much-loved and respected UAE luxury brand the confidence to speak to a global audience. As part of a five-year expansion strategy, Mauzan has begun to branch out, with stores in Abu Dhabi, Al Ain, and Dubai. At the same time, Rafia's designs continue to forge ahead with cutting-edge interpretations of the local Arab dress.

The designers played with different configurations of the word mark and name in search of the right abaya-like effect.

Design Firm | Lippincott
Client | Office Depot / Viking
Project | Identity Redesign

Founded in the United States, the global office-supply retailer Office Depot has two brands in Europe: Office Depot, which supplies large corporations and public sector organizations; and Viking, which has a distinctive small- and medium-sized business focus, along with a growing consumer and home-office audience that shops via its website and catalog.

In the wake of the 2008 global recession, which hit the retail industry hard, Office Depot brought in Lippincott's London office to help reposition the Viking brand. A greater emphasis was placed on making it more small-business and consumer focused.

Through market research, coupled with extensive interviews with business leaders, Lippincott discovered that there was little difference between Viking and its office-supply competitors. The team even conducted an exercise in which they removed the logos from the covers of eight different office-supply catalogues and challenged industry professionals to identify the brands. This proved to be a sobering test of how similar the leading brands had become.

Through market research, coupled with extensive interviews with business leaders, Lippincott discovered that there was little difference between Viking and its office-supply competitors.

Lippincott's logo for Viking incorporates doodling as though it is a natural, whimsical addition to the type itself. The identity system centers around the concept of "office life." The previous Viking logo focused on the company's delivery capabilities.

On top of the problem of differentiation was the fact that local competitors were more customer-focused. For example, small businesses in London could better address London small-business owners' needs by offering a more bespoke service. Online competitors were also moving into the market. A new generation of future business leaders and university graduates were going directly online for their products.

In order to customize as well as localize its business, Viking had to understand its customers' needs and reorganize its business to meet those needs. The Viking catalog was noisy and cluttered, with products competing against one another on every page. The opportunity was to simplify through better design and to deliver an experience that was easier and more enjoyable; in short, like shopping should be.

"The role of design," says Lee Coomber, creative director of Lippincott in London, "was to bring the experience of shopping back into the catalog

The doodle concept in its original stage, and how it was carried out in the first doodle logo.

Early logo explorations sought out the right font.

Design trials took the Viking logo in different directions.

pages themselves." It had to steer the aesthetic away from cheap and cheerful, or "market table," as Coomber describes it, toward a more upscale environment that was potentially capable of selling higher-end electronics. It had to achieve all this without coming across as too expensive and turning away home-office buyers. Simplification was the key.

Lippincott put itself in the Viking customer's shoes and created a brand positioning around the concept of "office life." "The office is far more than just a desk with some stuff on it: It's where you take on the big challenges in your life," Coomber states. "Both the efficiency of your home office and its aesthetics are critical to getting the most out of your day."

Reenvisioning the office as a place where you want to be and that supports and inspires you, Lippincott came up with four broad directions to achieve this. The first idea was based upon doodling, a visual language that humanizes office life. As Coomber puts it, "You don't get many people doodling at home; it's a special thing people do in meetings and on the phone." The second idea was to create a style-magazine attitude toward office working spaces. A third route used an existing character within the brand portfolio and reinvigorated him as the office mascot. The fourth direction was to bring the Viking customer to the center of the communication and make him the hero.

When these concepts were presented to Office Depot for feedback, the doodle concept won out. Office Depot liked that it was fresh, and a completely new direction for them, and saw that it connected well to the theme of office life.

Lippincott's concept for the new Viking catalog was based on simplifying the design to deliver an experience that was easier and more enjoyable, more like thumbing through a magazine.

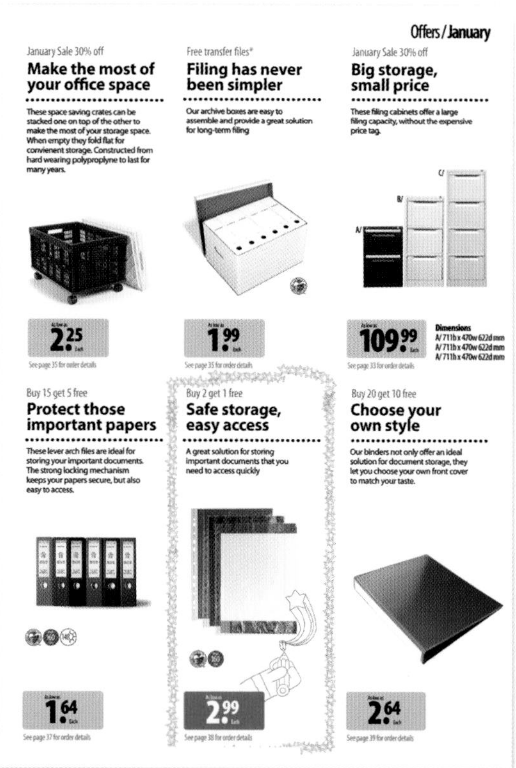

The first doodle imagery participated more as background for the logotype. It didn't have to appear everywhere, but its power would be in guiding shoppers through the catalog pages lightly, keeping them entertained and engaged. The final logo design incorporates doodling as though it is a natural whimsical addition to the type itself. Future applications may ask customers to contribute their own doodles for even further customization.

Lippincott created a typeface especially for the Viking logo. The team knew it had to be a masthead and thus strong, standing out in front of various product images.

"The type needed to do two contradictory things," Coomber explains. "It needed to sit still on the page and occupy its space, but because Viking is also a delivery company, we wanted to give a nod to that aspect of the business. The curve of the *V* and *g* give it a sense of motion without making it look like a delivery company. Lippincott also wanted it to be friendly, and therefore made the *k* cute. Everything is round and geometric and dependable, yet cuddly." The dots on the *i*'s, for instance, are smaller than they normally would be in this type of font.

And, because the name "Viking" is masculine in connotation, it needed to speak more to female customers, who in fact make up the majority of Viking buyers. This was achieved by bringing in lightness and humor. The designers spent countless hours kerning each letter to attain the right balance in the word mark.

The Viking catalog was greatly altered under the new identity with more customer guidance and navigation help, plus advice on office issues such as ergonomics and the environment. Mailed to thirty million customers in the United Kingdom and Ireland in May 2011, followed by other key European markets, the response has been enormously positive. The catalog will eventually have even more outreach from its online position, which in the next ten years will replace the print edition. Lippincott also designed the concept packaging for the majority of Viking applications, which Office Depot is following to great effect.

The design project extended into customer service as well, influencing the phone operators to respond to customer inquiries in a way that was aligned with the new brand strategy.

The packaging concept uses doodling to make boxes look more like presents.

> Lippincott put itself in the Viking customer's shoes and created a brand positioning around the concept of "office life."

Giti Tire
Identity Design

Lippincott, London, England

Lippincott's logo design for Giti puts all the information into one easy-to-understand box. The typeface mirrors the strong, square-like characters in the Chinese alphabet as well as the character of the elephant icon.

Although China's largest tire manufacturer, Giti, was not well known, it saw an opportunity to rise to the ranks of the world's top five by overhauling its brand.

Giti brought on Lippincott London to evaluate its brand and determine a new positioning, which in essence would answer the question, "What does the world need from a tire company that it is not getting?" Lippincott recommended that Giti create a more distinct brand identity to accomplish this.

"The world of cars and tires is noisy and filled with performance jargon that doesn't translate to the ordinary tire shopper," says Lee Coomber, who headed the project. "It's a very male world, when in fact many of those who take cars to get their tires checked are women." The experience of selecting the right "shoes" for one's car needed to be simplified and made more accessible to everyone.

The Lippincott team explored a number of design directions. One idea centered on animal analogies to make the brand language more friendly and easy to understand. For instance, a picture of duck feet would symbolize a wet-weather tire, whereas a lemur's hands wrapped around a tree trunk would say "good grip." The second direction considered the end use of the tire and the type of car the customer drives.

The third direction, which became the chosen route, focused on labeling. This concept aimed to simplify Giti's offering by visually putting all the information into one easy-to-understand "box."

It was critical that the logo feel simultaneously contemporary and as though the company had been around for a long time—that it was a top-five brand. Lippincott simplified the colors to caution-tape yellow, a color associated with safety, and tire black.

For the icon, Lippincott chose the elephant. But, out of so many elephant identities, how would the designers make this a Giti elephant? Lippincott knew it wanted a mascot, and one that was somewhat friendly, since other elements of the system are purposefully technical and hard-edged. The typeface was designed especially for Giti by Lippincott to mirror the strong black, square-like characters in the Chinese alphabet as well as the character of the elephant.

"When using animals in logos, you have to think about what aspect of the animal you want to get across," says Coomber. "If you draw the head of an elephant, you are referring to characteristics of its personality, like intelligence or its great memory. But we wanted it for its strength and durability, so we focused on the side profile."

The final drawing had to be tweaked once more in the end, because the Giti team saw the number *4*—unlucky in Chinese culture—in the line creating the elephant's ear.

The previous Giti logo, which Lippincott transformed.

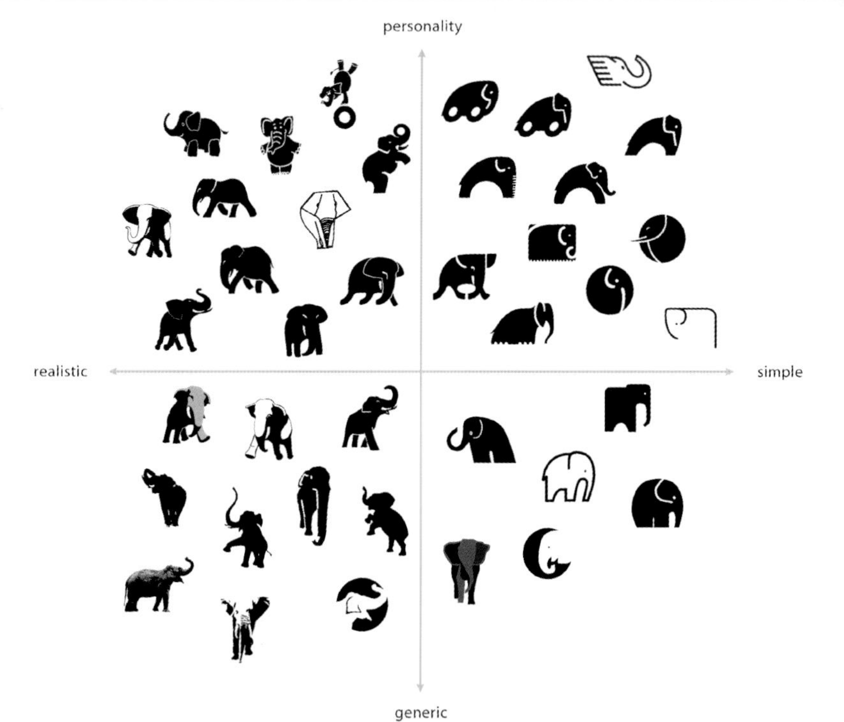

Above Left: Different aspects of the elephant express different characteristics. Lippincott wanted to convey its durability and so drew the body in profile. Above Right: Design trials for the elephant icon first put the animal on wheels. A later trial had to be adjusted because the line of the ear formed the number 4, which is unlucky in Chinese culture.

The elephant icon had to hold up visually on the tire wall.

The logo feels contemporary but also representative of a top-five brand that has been around for a long time.

Lippincott produced a stacked logo as well as a horizontal version that could curve around the tire wall, making the most out of the four-letter name. Most tire brands have longer names, which help in this instance.

The identity launched in early 2010 and appeared on tires by the middle of that year. Giti mailed Lippincott one of the first tires as a thank-you gift, and Coomber keeps it proudly in the studio.

Design Firm	Siegel+Gale
Client	CooperVision
Project	Identity Design

Few things are more important than clear vision, for practical reasons as well as conceptual ones. Our perception shapes the world around us, a fact that is especially meaningful for a global contact lens manufacturer such as CooperVision.

When the company approached Siegel+Gale New York about crafting an identity system, it wanted to correct the *mis*perception that it was still, after all these years, only a niche player in the contact lens universe. In fact, CooperVision had grown to be the third-largest contact lens manufacturer in the world—but no one saw the company that way.

Two big shifts in the industry made the outdated perceptions even more worrisome: Chain stores and big-box retailers had emerged as key customers for lens manufacturers, and contact lens wearers themselves were increasingly involved in the selection of their lenses. All of these potential customers needed to know what CooperVision had to offer.

The manufacturing of CooperVision contact lenses is quite a technological exercise, and yet the act of wearing them is quite intimate.

Siegel+Gale's strategy called for CooperVision to adopt a "Challenger Brand" position, promising customers and potential contact lens wearers an unexpectedly refreshing perspective. Whereas other manufacturers go to great metaphorical lengths to portray the pleasure of wearing their lenses, often implementing the look and feel of a silky splash of water to invoke the concept of moisture, the new CooperVision identity challenged this with a more down-to-earth guarantee: that it will help users experience the everyday in a clearer, brighter, and more colorful way. Vision is the offering, not just more comfortable lenses.

"The manufacturing of CooperVision contact lenses is quite a technological exercise, and yet the act of wearing them is quite intimate," points out Siegel+Gale co-president and CEO Howard Belk. The team wanted to find a new way of conveying the beauty that wearers discover and enjoy when they have better vision. The concept of watercolor paintings—their unique color and texture on paper—was the perfect fit for the identity. It marries the splendor that one experiences through vision with the clarity, comfort, and revitalizing essence of water.

Siegel+Gale's CooperVision logo blends technology and artistry by combining a refreshingly hand-painted icon with a crisp typeface in gray on white.

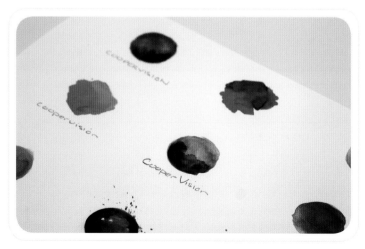

Design trials play with different watercolor applications to shape the CooperVision icon.

COOPER VISION

COOPER VISION

COOPER VISION

The designers chose the font Foundry Sterling for its light crispness to balance the vibrancy of the icon.

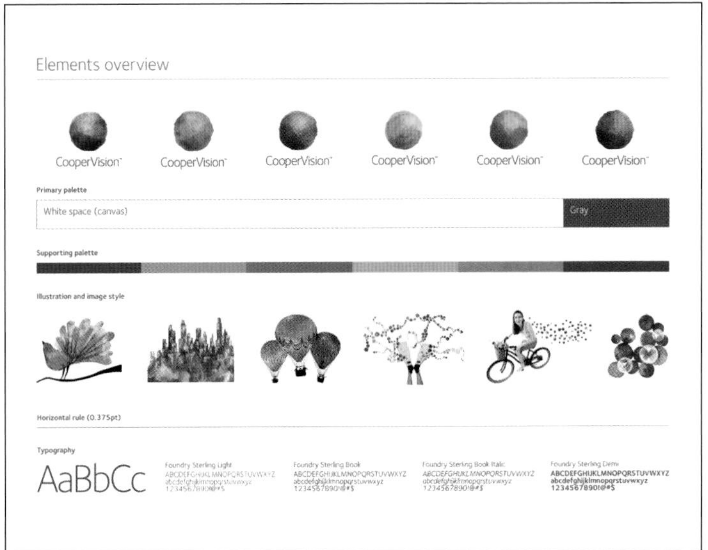

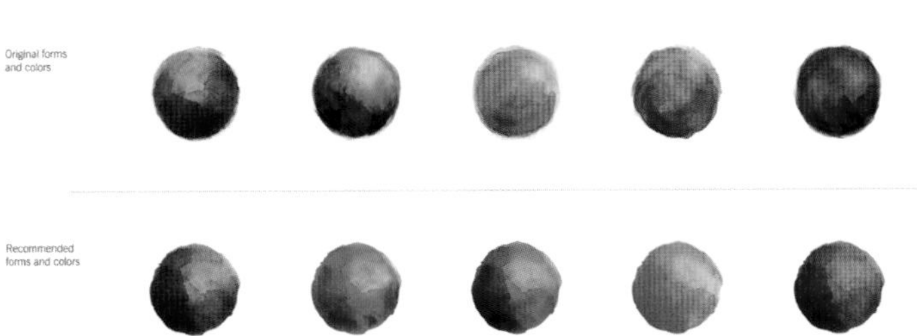

The top row shows original trial forms and colors for the icon; their revisions are shown underneath.

The process board displays color and imagery explorations for illustrations. All of the color elements of the identity system play against a primary palette of white and gray.

In order to capture the duality of technology and tactile experience, Siegel+Gale created spherical watercolor paintings in a spectrum of colors and took them one step further by hand painting them on the computer. Accompanied by a crisp, light typeface (Foundry Sterling), the logo design blends technology with handcrafted artistry, which in a larger sense is precisely what contact lenses do.

The digital imagery itself adds both a practical and a metaphorical layer. Because it is created in RGB color in a primarily digital environment, it can transmit the depth and texture of watercolor without sacrificing its continuous tone, as in four-color printing. Not only is this the wave of the future in logo design, as more and more identities are made to communicate online and through digital media, but the digital creation of these spheres also allows them to be seen in the way they should be seen—with all of the tangibility and color gradation of real life. At the same time, the fact that the logo is hand painted as opposed to assembled by the tap of computer keys, is visually refreshing.

The impact of the logo rises far and above the time-old, two-dimensional, two-color mark. It lives in a realm of high-tech computer art, such as the work posted by world-renowned artist David Hockney, who in 2010 launched an exhibition of six hundred drawings made on iPads. This was right when the Siegel+Gale team was commencing its design work.

"We thought the juxtaposition of handmade art rendered on sophisticated computer technology was a visual direction worth exploring," says Belk. "Time will tell us whether this represents the beginning of a real trend." No matter what, it remains a one-of-a-kind execution. "We simply love the humanity it conveys, the purity of color it makes possible, and how it comes alive in digital, illuminated environments such as PDAs, tablets, and monitors."

The identity system includes a set of logos, each one representing a different hue from the rainbow, which provides audiences with a vitalizing change of color here and there while still maintaining the brand's recognizability. Siegel+Gale also fashioned vivid everyday illustrations for brand communications, from packaging to interface to print advertisements and business cards. The illustrations carry the watercolor concept further, making art, and create an emotive connection and happiness when you see them.

Together with the CooperVision leadership team, Siegel+Gale developed a statement of purpose for the new identity: "We help improve the way people see each day." Simply and powerfully expressing the functional role contact lenses play in people's everyday lives, this theme celebrates the optimism that comes from a lifestyle of enhanced vision.

Business cards rotate through the spectrum.

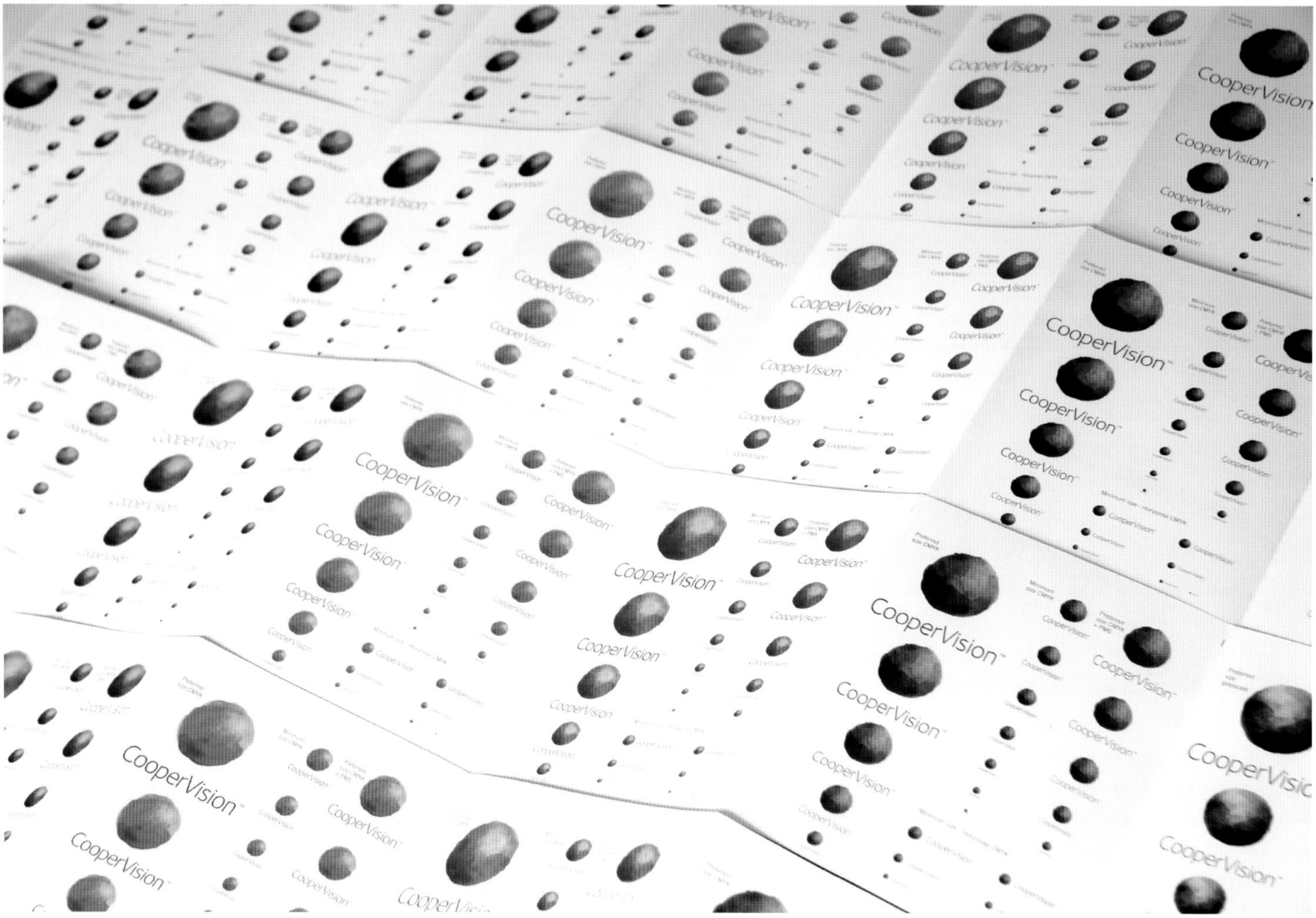

The new CooperVision logo comes in a full spectrum of lush, vibrant colors.

An illustration on a poster advertisement carries the watercolor concept further, making art.

Packaging and print applications display the vivid everyday illustrations Siegel+Gale fashioned for the brand.

Equa bank
Identity Design

Siegel+Gale, London, England

Before launching Equa bank in September 2011, it was important to get the bank's identity right. Siegel+Gale's London office was appointed to create a brand positioning and identity system that worked together seamlessly, producing all aspects of the system eight months in advance so that they could be tested in local communities.

This was especially important for a bank launching first in Poland and the Czech Republic with the aim of spreading across Eastern and Central Europe. This part of the world was not as hard-hit by the 2008 financial crisis farther west, but it did experience a dip in consumer confidence. The client saw this as an opportunity to learn from what worked in banking—and what didn't—to create an entirely new entity.

Direct or "branchless" banking, in which customers perform most tasks online or at the ATM, provided the perfect model for the new bank because of its goal of simplifying the banking process. "The promise of simplicity was to be the role of design," says Creative Director, EMEA, Clive Rohald of Siegel+Gale. "Most of the competition had big, faceless, corporate presences. Our client wanted something fresh that would stand out among these larger entities." Siegel+Gale developed a positioning that revolved around the idea, "simply better banking."

The most important step was to establish a name that could translate easily across a variety of Central European languages. The Siegel+Gale team knew from experience that Western or English-sounding terms worked well in the region and signified progress and modernity. They explored hundreds of options and then managed the trademark process, URL screening, and linguistic "disaster" checks on those shortlisted with the client.

The final name combines *equa*, which taps into the notion of a direct relationship between equals, and *bank*, which the team recommended using to establish an immediate understanding of the business in consumers' minds.

The designers wanted to move completely away from the serif typography found in banking and create something clean and crisp. "We crafted a typeface that replaces the serif with the diagonal slant of a highlighter pen," Rohald explains. "The shapes created in the lettering are symmetrical, and yet we humanized them with rounded, more organic forms."

Equa bank

The final logo for the new Equa bank in Central Europe exudes simplicity and approachability. The bright blue accent on the E *ties back to the symbol of the highlighter pen used throughout the identity system.*

The symbolism of the highlighter pen ties back to the brand strategy of providing "simply better banking" by referencing the way we highlight what is important. The *E* in Equa is accented by a single blue stroke to bring the concept in visually.

The challenge was, as it is for most Eastern European businesses, ease of implementation. "We knew we wanted a black mark for onscreen legibility as well as cost-effectiveness," says Rohald. "The mark had to translate seamlessly across channels, and so we knew it had to be two-dimensional. Three-dimensional or animated would have been too much of a headache, and too expensive."

The design team created all applications well in advance, including signage, posters, collateral materials, artwork on credit cards, and stationery, as well as nontraditional imagery and architecture for the Equa bank website.

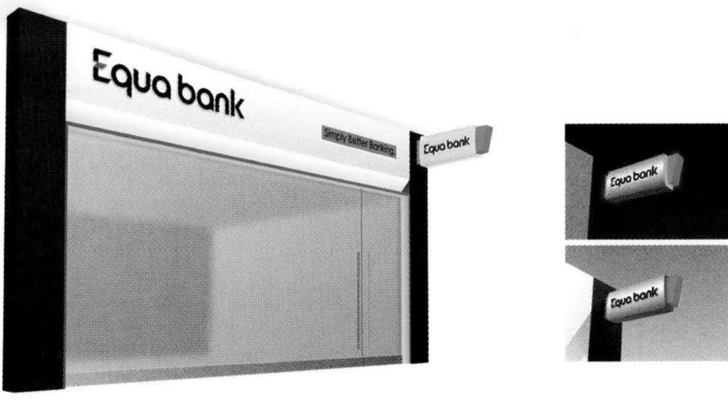

Left: The brand strategy called for smaller retail spaces and more direct, branchless banking.

Center: The design team created looks for basic applications, from corporate stationery to debit cards.

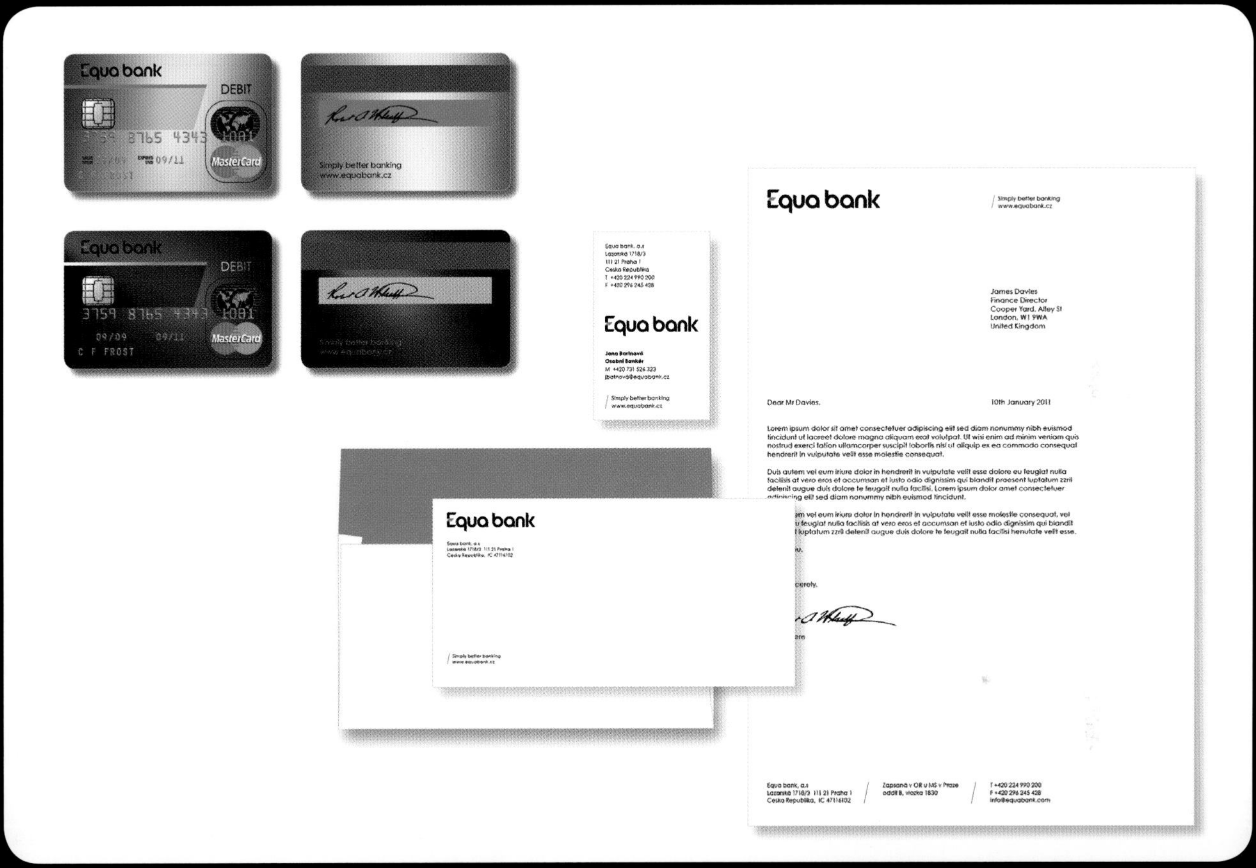

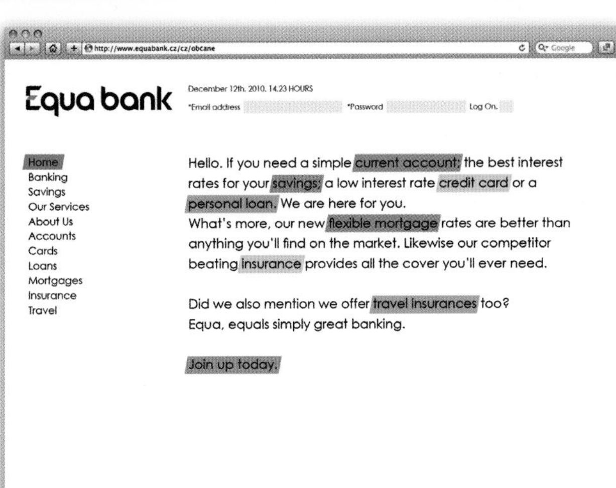

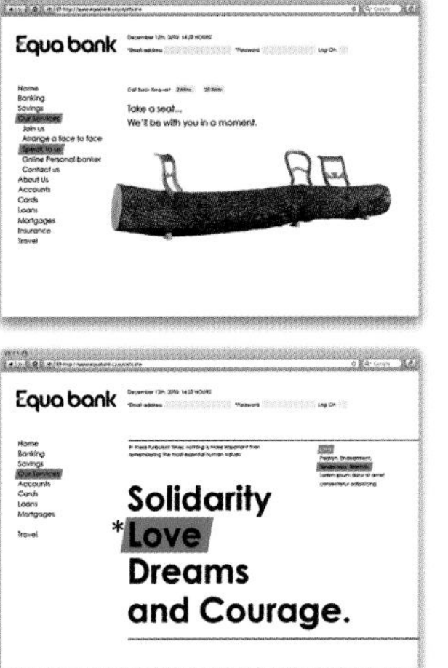

Siegel+Gale designed a unique style of photography for the Equa bank website, incorporating a cut-out approach and image selection in stark contrast to the familiar stock photography used by most banks. The graphic system poses the high-lighter colors of pink, blue, yellow, and green against black, a scheme that is simple yet eye-catching.

Design Firm | **The Brand Agency**

Client | **Perth Zoo / "Nocturnal Concerts at the Zoo"**

Project | **Identity Design**

Very often, a new logo design comes with a new name. Brands seeking a fresh start are advised to first seek a new brand name, and out of this a logo can be born.

This was the case with the Perth Zoo's successful Twilight Concert Series. The park had been offering summer concerts on its grounds for more than one hundred years. When a new promoter was brought in to expand the series with higher-profile acts appealing to an older demographic, it was time for an identity change.

The first step The Brand Agency, based throughout Western Australia, took when designing a logo for the new series was to rethink the name. "Twilight" had grown overused. After wading through many possibilities, the team settled on "Nocturnal Concerts at the Zoo," as it tied in with the concert setting—nighttime at the zoo with all the animal intrigue this implied—as well as a certain level of adult sophistication.

It was quickly established that we were trying to target a demographic who were seeking a safe and comfortable environment to enjoy quality, live entertainment.

The new identity for "Nocturnal Concerts at the Zoo" appears in bus-shelter advertisements and as stage decoration at the concerts themselves.

"It was quickly established that we were trying to target a demographic who were seeking a safe and comfortable environment to enjoy quality, live entertainment," explains Daniel Agostino, head of design at the agency's Perth office. "They would much prefer the relaxed surroundings of the zoo's location to a packed auditorium or crammed pub environment. It also needed to reflect a level of fun one would expect from being at the zoo as well as showcase a feeling of a relaxed West Australian summer's night."

Early on, the team had the idea to create a suite of logos that could be ever-changing and flexible yet still remain part of an overarching "family," as Agostino calls it. "This can add another level of depth and dimension to a brand, keeping the viewer entertained by what it will become next," he says.

The Brand Agency team also knew it wanted a layered identity to represent the event's many characteristics: music, nighttime, summer, and of

A suite of logos can add another level of depth and dimension to a brand, keeping the viewer entertained by what it will become next.

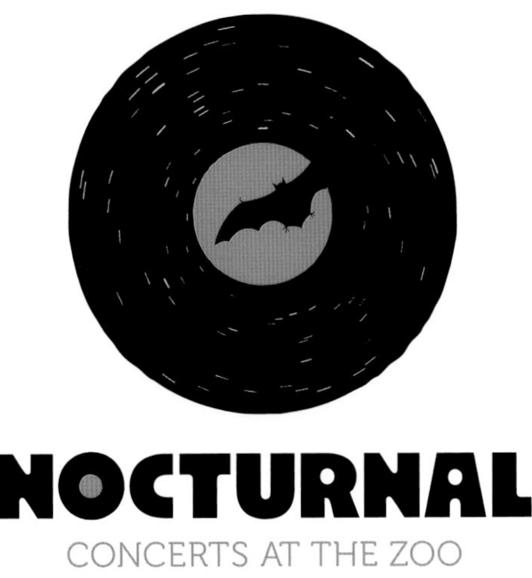

The Brand Agency created a suite of logos for Perth Zoo's "Nocturnal Concerts at the Zoo" series that could be ever-changing and flexible yet still remain part of an overarching family.

course, the animals. It outlined a number of different directions, including constellations in a night sky, nocturnal animal calling signs, and the shapes of musical instruments.

Of the directions, the image of the vinyl record stood out. Not only did it link to the demographic, who would certainly connect with the icon more so than, say, today's iPod generation, but also the team could tie the aesthetic elements of a record to a full summer moon against a backdrop of star trails.

With the basic route determined, the designers played more thematically with color and with animal shapes embedded in the central "moon." They chose Dez Boulder Id for the word type because of its bold, fat characteristics, which link well to the feel of vinyl and recall the lettering of album

The team experimented with different names for the series, which inspired different logo trials, before arriving at "Nocturnal Concerts at the Zoo."

CONCERTS IN THE WILD

Twilight CONCERT SERIES

Nocturnal CONCERT SERIES

Concerts in the WILD

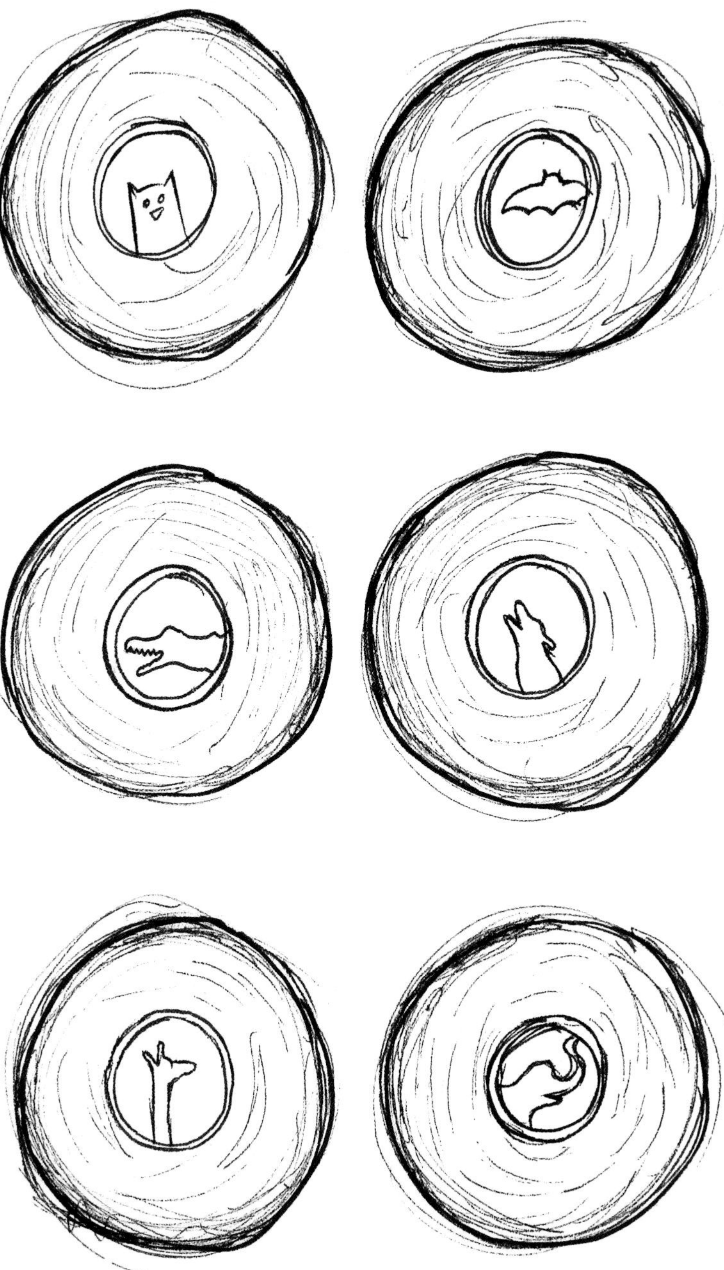

Sketches for the logo mark played with a number of different "characters" at the center of the album image.

covers. The typeface is understated and so does not compete with the icon itself.

Ultimately the font needed to create a solid foundation but really take on a supporting role. The circular forms bring a feeling of repetition that again links to the circular form of the logo shape, and a splash of color added to the inside of the letter *O* gives a small nod to the color of each record label.

"The logo encourages people to discover more," says Agostino. "So many who look at it see only one or two elements. For example, they might only focus on the silhouette of an animal against a bright-colored moon, but later they recognize that it also looks like a vinyl record. On another glance they might see star trails in the night sky, or even a different animal altogether. Over time, they discover more and more, and the reaction is always a positive one."

The variation-on-a-theme approach worked perfectly with the series, so that each concert would have a certain measure of individuality and personality. And, with the ability to add new "albums" to the suite each summer, the system allows for greater longevity. With the accumulation of slightly different album covers, the identity will gradually become quite eclectic, rather than static.

"I love design that challenges, and almost invites, the viewer to keep looking and keep discovering," Agostino continues. "If you can do it at the initial branding level, then it has the potential to add so much more depth to each and every level of application. Why does a logo have to be this one static mark that always appears in the same way, shape, and form? Why can't it come to life and change, yet still represent the same thing?"

The logo launched in the Australian summer of 2010/11, with six concerts held between November and February, and was used across a wide variety of print, press, and online applications.

Why does a logo always have to be this one static mark that appears in the same way, shape, and form? Why can't it come to life and change, yet still represent the same thing?

Telethon Speech & Hearing Centre for Children
Identity Redesign

The Brand Agency, Perth, Western Australia

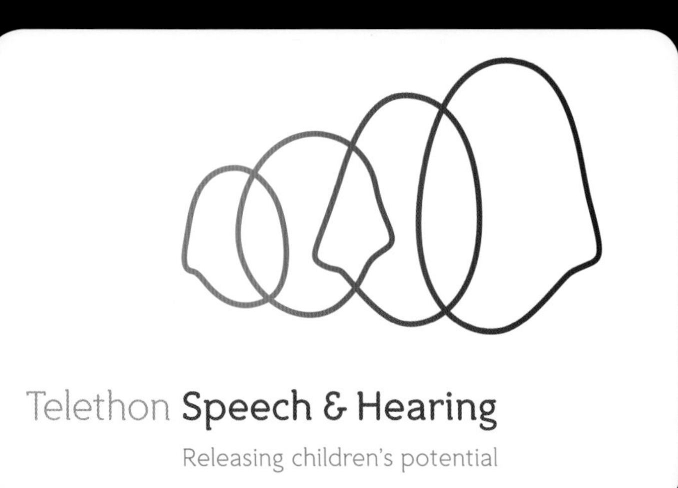

The Brand Agency's final logo for Telethon Speech & Hearing Centre for Children.

Initiated forty-five years ago by a small group of parents, Telethon Speech & Hearing Centre for Children has grown into one of the premier providers of health care and education for children with speech and language and hearing impairments in Western Australia. With plans to expand into larger, state-of-the-art facilities as well as online with a new website, the organization required an identity that communicated its growing capabilities.

The previous logo had been well used by the time The Brand Agency stepped in to revitalize the brand. What's more, its use across a range of applications became more varied over the years, leaving the brand fragmented and inconsistent. At first the team thought it could refresh the design. But after some initial exploration, it decided to completely overhaul the brand and its positioning.

The new system would have to appeal to two different audiences at once: first, to child health professionals, and second, to internal stakeholders such as staff, teachers, and health workers. The Brand Agency worked closely with the leadership team at the Centre to strike the right balance both visually and emotionally.

"The identity had to walk a fine line between a modern and professional design appealing to those in the health care industry, but also reflect the fact that the Centre works alongside families and children," explains Daniel Agostino, who headed the project. "It had to be friendly, caring, and human."

In the first trials, using fluid lines and experimenting with shape was key. As the line work developed, it began to look more like a child's illustration. The circular forms came together and intersected much like sound waves visualized. At the same time, their changing sizes say more about a child's development. Within the shapes profiles appear to represent people coming together to help.

"The logo visually brings the organization out of a tired and static environment," Agostino says about the solution. "It answers the call for professionalism, yet still appears personable to children and families."

The team chose Croog for the typeface because of its sense of personality and round, friendly edges. Its geometric form also allows for broader use in a corporate and professional setting.

The logo was unveiled in July 2011 in advance of the new facilities and refurbished web presence. The new identity now graces a full range of applications, from corporate stationery to exterior signage to video communications. The Centre's staff members have also been given templated collateral to use, manage, and ultimately take ownership of their brand.

The previous logo was well used across a range of applications and had become more varied over the years.

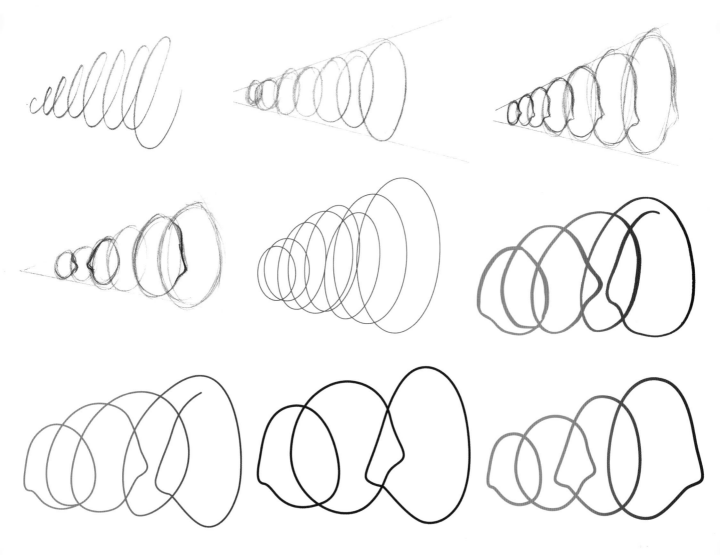

This drafting process reveals the different stages of the logo icon design, from sound waves to "people waves."

The logo appears on print communications such as brochures for the Centre as well as employee business cards.

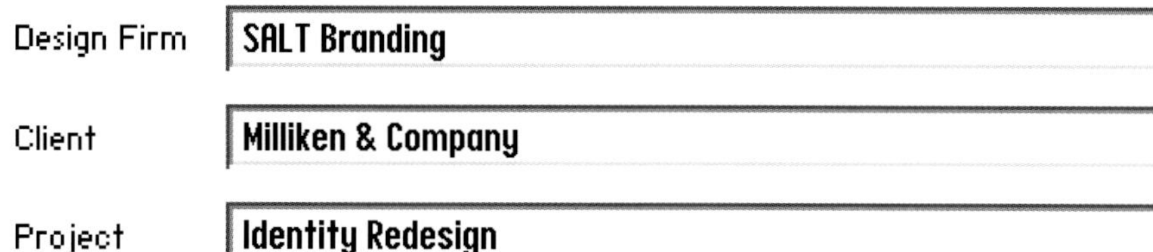

Design Firm
SALT Branding
Client
Milliken & Company
Project
Identity Redesign

The identity system Milliken & Company unveiled in April 2011 was the culmination of an entirely new business strategy. Appearing first at a company-wide launch, the identity centered on a redesigned logo: a blue handwritten mark that broke free from its predecessor of forty years, the stark black-and-white *M* that stood for quality in textile manufacturing. Almost immediately, onlookers realized where they had seen the handwriting before: It belonged to Roger Milliken, the company's beloved CEO of sixty-five years, who had passed away in December 2010.

> The new logo not only looks completely different, it tells a different story about Milliken than the old logo did.

SALT Branding's Milliken logo is a complete departure from its predecessor of forty years. The blue handwritten mark is based on the handwriting of the late Roger Milliken, who was CEO for sixty-five years.

Milliken's president and CEO since 2008, Joe Salley, PhD, had brought San Francisco–based SALT Branding onboard with a very specific goal in mind: to reposition the company. With 2,200 registered patents and more than one hundred PhDs on staff, including Salley himself (in chemical engineering), Milliken has been a leader in industrial fabrics, floor coverings, performance products, and specialty chemicals for decades. But retaining a manufacturing presence on American soil when so many competitors were turning to China required the business to adapt. It was time to reaffirm Milliken's identity as an innovator.

Salley envisioned this as a greater evolution from the inside out: The new identity would be the result of a total restructuring toward innovation within the company itself.

Innovation had been one of Milliken's core values since its inception in 1865. Roger Milliken, whose father handed him the reins in 1947, declared an unwavering commitment to both quality and innovation. When other textile companies were sending their factories overseas in the 1970s, Milliken's Spartanburg, South Carolina, headquarters stayed put. Roger Milliken believed that the minute a company exported its manufacturing was the minute it stopped innovating. The key to quality, then, was innovation.

But over time, the black-and-white mark became synonymous with quality only, leaving the innovation part out. It became common to talk about the superiority of the end product rather than the process that got it there.

Before approaching SALT, the leadership team at Milliken had already begun working with the company to think differently about itself: as an innovation company equally invested in the process as it is in the product.

When it came to getting the message out, however, Milliken needed help. Not only was Milliken less focused on its external presence as a purely business-to-business brand, but it also was cynical about large marketing communications in general. A remarkably tight-knit company, employees were nervous about changing outside perceptions at the risk of giving the wrong impression. SALT Branding stepped in to strategize the best way for it to speak out about innovation.

As it was conducting research, the team repeatedly saw Milliken's signature on documents and suddenly realized what it could achieve as a logo. They culled countless examples of handwritten thank-you notes Milliken wrote to employees and picked one from the 1980s. Most employees today have one of these notes to share.

Milliken's personal attention and approachability was treasured, and so his signature is utterly meaningful. Unlike many CEOs who act as a face to a business but have little substantive stake, Milliken *ran* the company. "I never worked a day in my life," he liked to say. His employees held him in the utmost esteem and saw the company as his legacy.

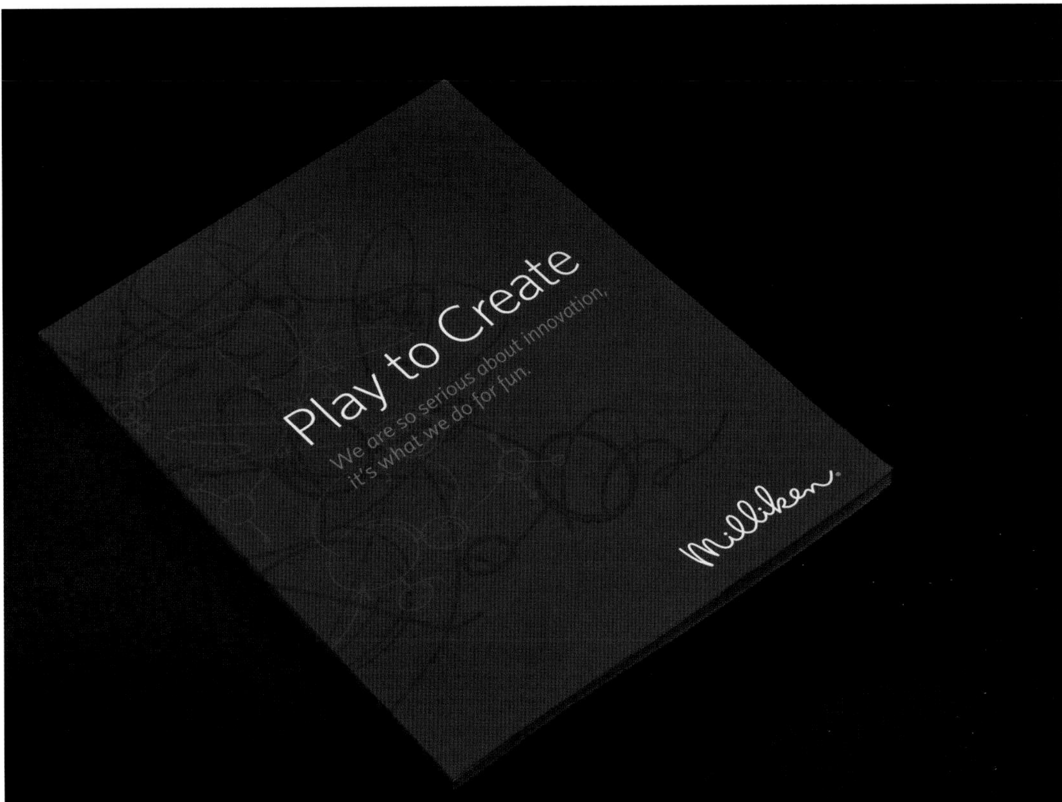

The new identity system is the result of a total restructuring toward innovation within the company itself. This brochure highlights this with fresh visuals evoking a sense of discovery as well as the new logo, which conveys creativity, softness, and play.

Business cards communicate the essence of the visual identity. The color blue refers to the blue ink that signifies authenticity on signed documents.

As it was conducting research, the team repeatedly saw Milliken's signature on documents and suddenly realized what it could achieve as a logo.

The signature makes a statement at industry conventions.

Certain characteristics of his signature lent themselves well to a logo: the balanced loops of the two *l's* and the *k*, for example. The SALT team experimented with many iterations to hit upon just the right mix of the real signature and an overall feeling of creativity, softness, and play. Whereas the old mark stood for quality and was used when quality was what counted, the new logo is approachable and fun, ushering a sense of discovery into the spotlight.

Of course, for legal reasons the logo could not be Roger Milliken's exact signature. And because it would have global usage, the *M* had to be adjusted for legibility and clarity around the world, so that it wouldn't be mistaken for a *W*.

At one point during the design process, Salley hit upon the fact that original signatures are typically blue, not black. The team decided the scheme had to be blue, as blue communicates the authenticity of a document. It also puns on the concept of "identity" design itself at a time when identity design is critical to business survival. In one way, the solution returns to the basics; in another, it is truly groundbreaking.

They are not just putting a new logo on everything they do, they are literally putting Roger Milliken's signature on everything they do.

The shift from quality to innovation will take time. Milliken does not want people to think it is walking away from quality. "They are not just putting a new logo on everything they do, they are literally putting Roger Milliken's signature on everything they do," states Paul Parkin, creative director, Salt. Wisely, they want to proceed cautiously with this new guarantee.

Innovation had always been a core value of Milliken & Company since its inception in 1865. Now it is the theme of the Milliken brand identity.

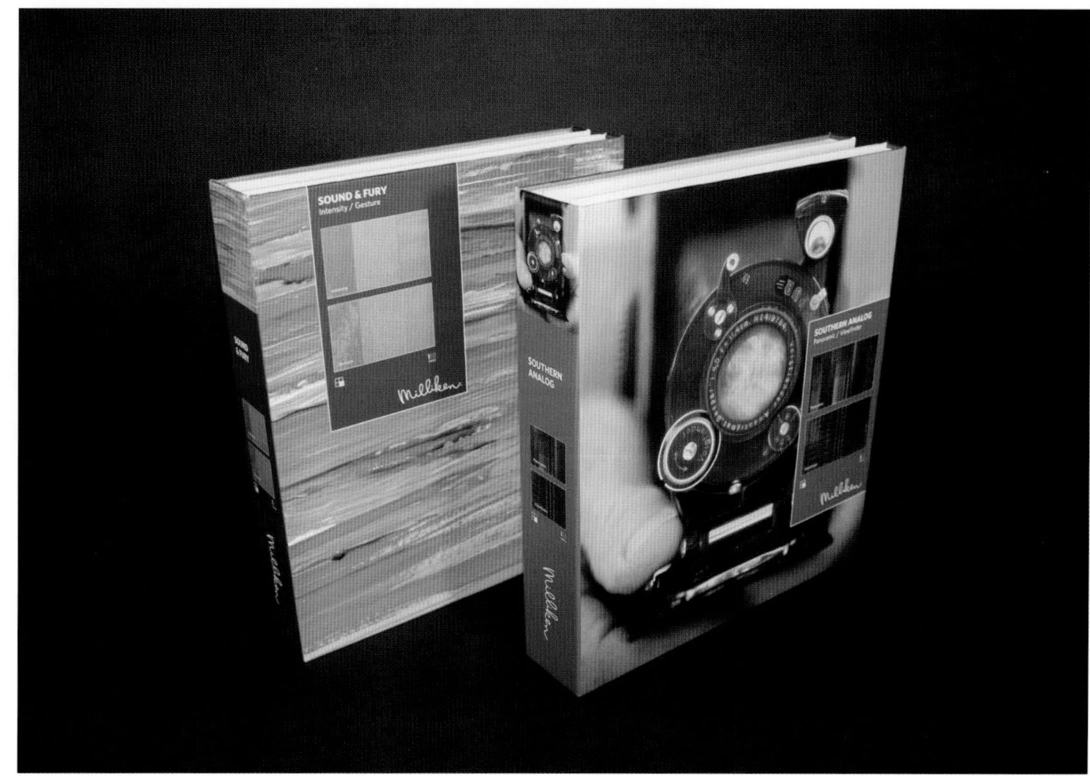

San Francisco Design Week Identity Design

SALT Branding, San Francisco, California

SALT designer César Chin believed the new San Francisco Design Week logo should capture the essence of the city beyond its obvious tourist attractions. The color scheme conveys the mood and atmospheric qualities of the city's foggy climate.

If any event showcases what design can do, certainly a "design week"—of which there are many throughout the world each year—does just that. The San Francisco Design Week, organized by the city's AIGA chapter, is no exception, bringing together twenty thousand design professionals as well as local businesses to explore how design of all disciplines affects the Bay Area.

AIGA San Francisco initially hired SALT to refresh the event website to reach a wider audience, including nonprofits, entrepreneurs, the design public, and even tourists. To this end, SALT principal and creative director César Chin proposed more than a site but an entire identity, complete with a new logo.

The previous mark, a square formed of red scribbled words ("passion," "culture"), framed outlines of a cable car or the Golden Gate Bridge. Chin believed the logo should capture the essence of the city beyond its obvious tourist attractions. And what makes San Francisco unique more than its ever-moving, shape-shifting fog?

"A lot of these design weeks have identities that don't seem to reflect the city they are in," explains Chin. "What makes them special is *where* you are. We wanted to inject more of this into the logo and identity."

Chin worked through many logo variations. An early one streamed the fog through the letters, obscuring them in different places. The final logo uses digital technology to make the fog look as though it is moving around the letters, so that they become more or less readable depending on how long you look. For example, the *F* is almost completely lost at different points. In the still version of the logo, viewers are left to fill in the letterforms with their imaginations.

The typeface is wide and cushiony to allow room for shifting colors, from purple to teal to gray to blue, and to give the effect of light shining through fog. SALT experimented with using the International Orange of the Golden Gate Bridge, but it decided it was too reminiscent of the city's NFL team, the 49ers, and even *too* San Francisco, as the bridge itself has become. The chosen color scheme conveys instead the mood and atmospheric qualities of the city's climate.

Online, design can do anything in terms of color, tonal shift, and movement. "The whole idea of the logo is that it doesn't have to be the same every year," says Chin. "Next year, it could be a different color. The year after, it could be solid, and so on. What we wanted to establish was the base from which the design could develop each year."

The previous SFDW logo relies on red to tie in with the Golden Gate Bridge.

The solution uses digital technology to make the fog look as though it is moving around the letters. The designer also created two-dimensional versions that convey the sense of the letters appearing and disappearing with a simple black-and-white line.

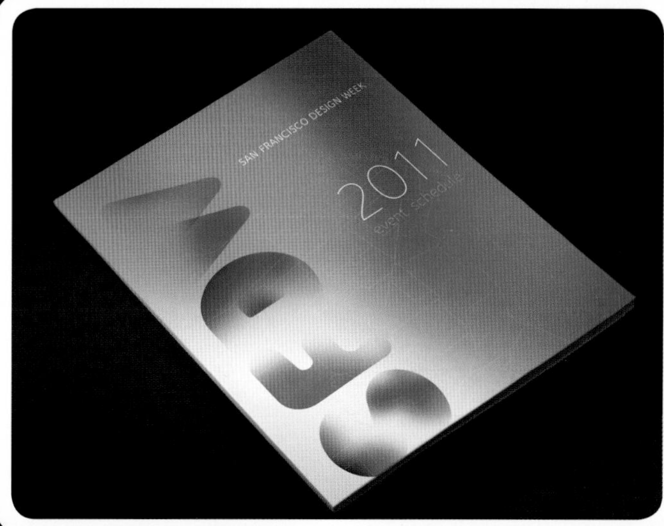

Bus shelter posters as well as Design Week brochures play off the color scheme. The designer wanted to create a base for a dynamic identity that can evolve from year to year.

SALT did make a 2-D version to be used in print and on collateral such as t-shirts. This logo also works well, as it captures the sense of the seen and unseen letterforms that the fog in the final logo created through color and animation.

collections and sketches

A B C D

1

LOGO SEARCH

Keywords: Initials

Type:  Symbol Typographic  Combo All

2

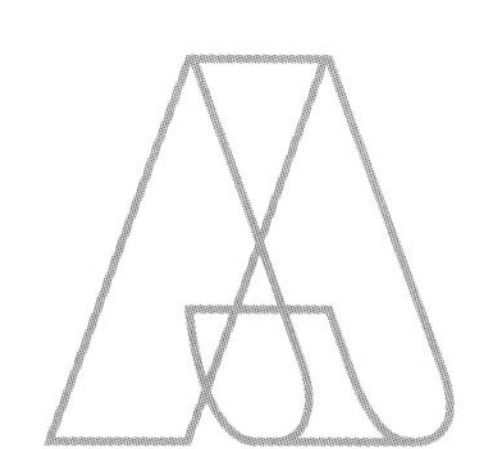

3

4

5

ALL POWER INC

Ⓓ = Design Firm Ⓒ = Client

1C Ⓓ DOXA Ⓒ Assisting Single Parents in Reaching Education 1D Ⓓ Gizwiz Studio Ⓒ AETERNA
2A Ⓓ Face. Ⓒ Agent 2B Ⓓ One Man's Studio Ⓒ Anna Jones Photography 2C Ⓓ Glad Head Ⓒ Advance Inform 2D Ⓓ Gavula Design Associates Ⓒ Ani Villas
3A Ⓓ Studio Absolute Ⓒ Mary F. Anderson, PC 3B Ⓓ vanillashake media Ⓒ Acadia Real Estate Properties 3C Ⓓ Gehring Co. Ⓒ Adaptor 3D Ⓓ petervasvari.com Ⓒ ACTUART
4A Ⓓ Studio French Ⓒ Anchor Publishing 4B Ⓓ Matto Ⓒ Altorius Community of Catholics 4C Ⓓ Chris Trivizas | Design Ⓒ Stellas Philotheos 4D Ⓓ LPA Ⓒ Creative Arts Alliance
5A Ⓓ entz creative Ⓒ Vanessa Williams 5B Ⓓ notamedia Ⓒ Actual Comments 5C Ⓓ J.D. Gordon Advertising Ⓒ All Power, Inc. 5D Ⓓ fallindesign Ⓒ Vladimir Afanasenko

A B C D

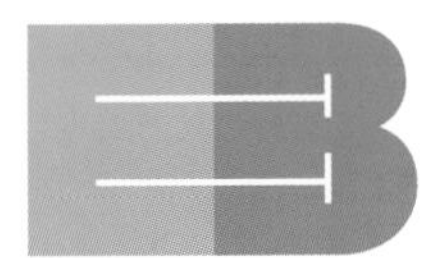

1

2

3

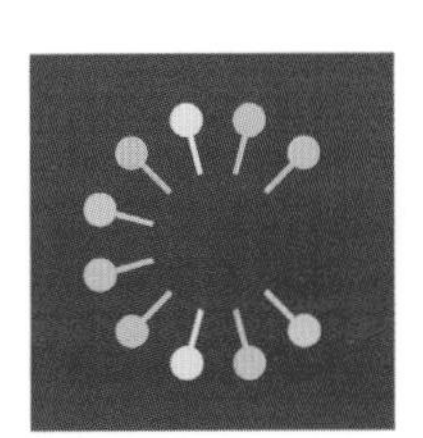

4

5

Ⓓ = Design Firm Ⓒ = Client

1A Ⓓ Gizwiz Studio Ⓒ Beebe Commercial 1B Ⓓ Ninet6 Ltd. 1C Ⓓ Hellofolio s.r.o. Ⓒ Endresz Boldizsar 1D Ⓓ Principals Pty Ltd. Ⓒ The Bionics Institute of Australia
2A Ⓓ Emilio Correa Ⓒ Arteis, Inc. 2B Ⓓ BRAND BROTHERS Ⓒ La Boqueria 2C Ⓓ Worthen Design Ⓒ Bid Boomerang 2D Ⓓ FutureBrand BC&H
3A Ⓓ Poppyseed Creative Ⓒ Jeff Boerboon Aerobatics 3B Ⓓ Lemon Design Pvt Ltd. Ⓒ Brahma Group 3C Ⓓ The Netmen Corp Ⓒ Bounce 3D Ⓓ The Martin Group Ⓒ LH Brubaker Appliances
4A Ⓓ Worthen Design Ⓒ Bennett and Porter 4B Ⓓ Brook Hagler Ⓒ Circle Craft 4C Ⓓ Studio Ink Ⓒ OpenCandy 4D Ⓓ Hayes Image Ⓒ Candysource
5A Ⓓ J Fletcher Design Ⓒ Celadon 5B Ⓓ Steve Biel Design Ⓒ Careers Industries 5C Ⓓ Tandem Design Agency Ⓒ Cone Drive 5D Ⓓ 01d Ⓒ Blue Whale

	A	B	C	D
1				
2				
3				
4			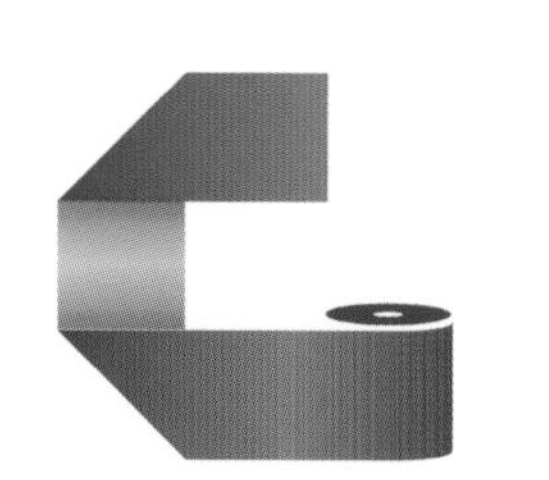	
5				

Ⓓ = Design Firm Ⓒ = Client

1A Ⓓ Glitschka Studios Ⓒ OnWired 1B Ⓓ EAT Advertising and Design, Inc. Ⓒ ColorMark 1C Ⓓ Sabingrafik, Inc. Ⓒ Civita 1D Ⓓ Tielemans Design Ⓒ Courtney Landscape & Pools
2A Ⓓ Jacob Tyler Creative Group Ⓒ Cinnabar Health Collective 2B Ⓓ A.D. Creative Group Ⓒ Chlorophyll 2C Ⓓ The Clear Agency Ⓒ The Clear Agency 2D Ⓓ Karl Design Vienna Ⓒ Bertha Benz Challenge
3A Ⓓ Dara Creative Ⓒ Consulting Ireland 3B Ⓓ Paradigm New Media Group Ⓒ Paradigm New Media Group 3C Ⓓ Vanja Blajic 3D Ⓓ Rene Rutten Design & Digital
4A Ⓓ Fernandez Design Ⓒ Courtney Construction 4B Ⓓ Kuznetsov Evgeniy | KUZNETS Ⓒ Slovo 4C Ⓓ insight design Ⓒ Cast Sheet Metal 4D Ⓓ Gyula Nemeth Ⓒ 6Base
5A Ⓓ Sparkfly Creative Ⓒ Chicken Addiction 5B Ⓓ rizen creative co. Ⓒ CK Rogers Remodeling 5C Ⓓ morninglori Graphic Design Ⓒ Carol Levin 5D Ⓓ the serif design Ⓒ Saer Richards, Founder

	A	B	C	D	
			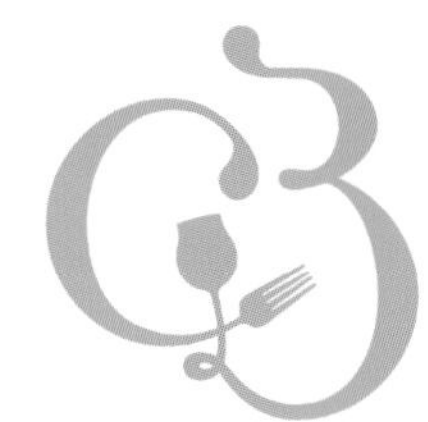		1
	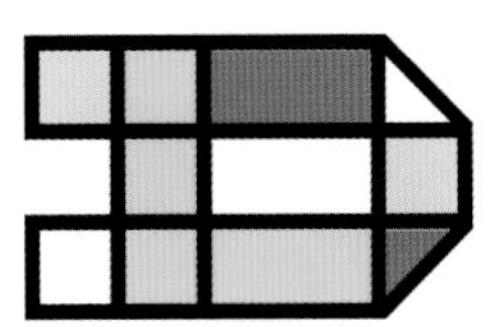				2
					3
					4
				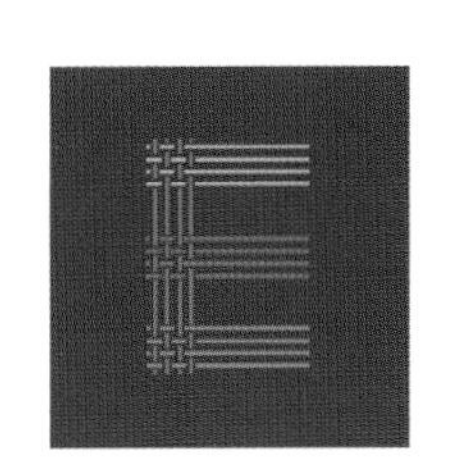	5

Ⓓ = Design Firm Ⓒ = Client

1A Ⓓ QUIQUE OLLERVIDES Ⓒ Oliver Castro 1B Ⓓ THINKMULE Ⓒ Black Book Gallery 1C Ⓓ Vlad Boerean Ⓒ Cristian Boerean 1D Ⓓ hellozacharnold Ⓒ The Koman Group
2A Ⓓ Traction Ⓒ Downtown Lansing, Inc. 2B Ⓓ Tran Creative Ⓒ DE 2C Ⓓ petervasvari.com Ⓒ Andrzej Bielski 2D Ⓓ Rise Design Branding, Inc. Ⓒ KD Transport
3A Ⓓ Dana Rocha Ⓒ Dana Rocha 3B Ⓓ Gizwiz Studio Ⓒ Dunn Vending 3C Ⓓ Logo Design Works Ⓒ EvigDin 3D Ⓓ Karl Design Vienna Ⓒ Braunhofer Visions
4A Ⓓ Baris Atiker Ⓒ Euroclean 4B Ⓓ redeemstrategic Ⓒ PT. Lithinai Hudriai 4C Ⓓ Whole Brain Design Ⓒ Efinity Networks 4D Ⓓ BalazsCreative Ⓒ Maternity Health
5A Ⓓ QUIQUE OLLERVIDES Ⓒ Casa Cuervo 5B Ⓓ TAPHOUSE GRAPHICS Ⓒ eConsortium 5C Ⓓ Z&G 5D Ⓓ Paul Black Design Ⓒ Polly Ellerman

A B C D

1

2

3

4

5

Ⓓ = Design Firm Ⓒ = Client

1A Ⓓ Candor Advertising Ⓒ Edwin Dudley Antiques 1B Ⓓ Sullivan Higdon & Sink Ⓒ Westar Energy 1C Ⓓ Communication Agency Ⓒ Maja Bozovic 1D Ⓓ Gabe Re Ⓒ Go Fit
2A Ⓓ Odney Ⓒ True Faith 2B Ⓓ Nikita Lebedev 2C Ⓓ HELOHOLO Ⓒ Octava Capital 2D Ⓓ Karl Design Vienna Ⓒ Inarea / Massimo Ferrero
3A Ⓓ Field Branding & Design Ⓒ Formby Vintners 3B Ⓓ Device Ⓒ Fiell 3C Ⓓ Motiv Design Ⓒ Orlando Wines 3D Ⓓ ohTwentyone Ⓒ Forecast Dynamics
4A Ⓓ Murillo Design, Inc. Ⓒ redGizmo Interactive 4B Ⓓ ilogo.pl Ⓒ Activ sp z o.o. 4C Ⓓ b2 kreativ Ⓒ Gallo Construction 4D Ⓓ Davina Chatkeon Design Ⓒ Global Knives
5A Ⓓ Double A Creative Ⓒ Gretna Wine & Spirits 5B Ⓓ Gröters Design Ⓒ Gröters Design 5C Ⓓ Riordon Design Ⓒ Gary Gerovac 5D Ⓓ Brandburg Ⓒ Grambud

A	B	C	D	
				1
				2
				3
	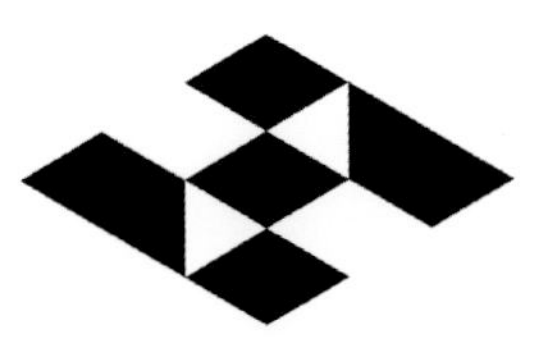			4
			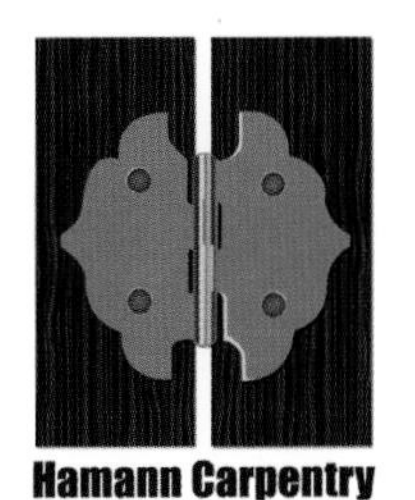	5

Ⓓ = Design Firm Ⓒ = Client

1A Ⓓ SANDIA, Inc. Ⓒ Green Gold Lubricants 1B Ⓓ Kahn Design Ⓒ greenTouch 1C Ⓓ Tactix Creative Ⓒ Landmark Landscaping 1D Ⓓ TBWA\Chiat\Day Ⓒ Gatorade
2A Ⓓ Helius Creative Advertising Ⓒ GearSwap.com 2B Ⓓ BRIGGS Ⓒ Green Can Composting 2C Ⓓ Almosh82 2D Ⓓ Traina Design Ⓒ Give Glasses
3A Ⓓ The Creative Underground Ⓒ Greater Good Alliance 3B Ⓓ Identivos Ⓒ Personal Monogram for PG 3C Ⓓ GDNSS Ⓒ HeyRoomee.com 3D Ⓓ Focus Lab, LLC Ⓒ Fitz Haile
4A Ⓓ The Key Ⓒ Helsinki Agency 4B Ⓓ The Key Ⓒ Helsinki Agency 4C Ⓓ The Key Ⓒ Helsinki Agency 4D Ⓓ Gardner Design
5A Ⓓ Double A Creative Ⓒ The Hub Gym 5B Ⓓ Justin Ardrey Ⓒ Hiding the Word Ministries 5C Ⓓ Jeremy Honea Ⓒ Harvest Food Pantry 5D Ⓓ Tone Graphic Design Ⓒ Hamann Carpentry

	A	B	C	D
1				
2			HENRY JAMES SALON	
3				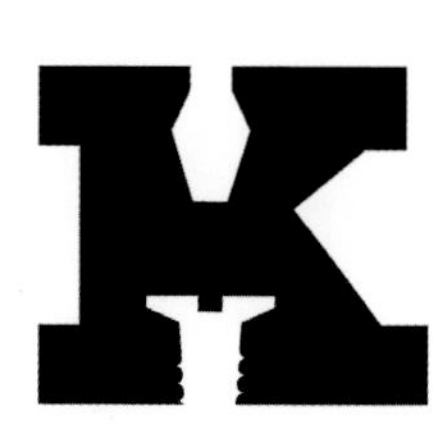
4			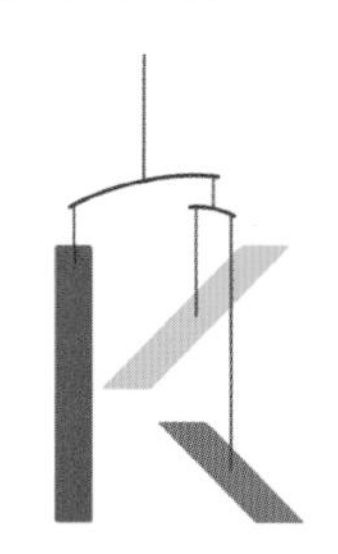	
5		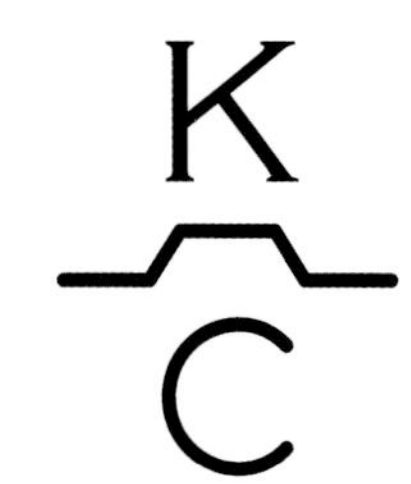		

Ⓓ = Design Firm Ⓒ = Client

1A Ⓓ Jerron Ames Ⓒ Arteis 1B Ⓓ kaimere Ⓒ Cutting Here 1C Ⓓ Larkef Ⓒ Home Adverts 1D Ⓓ Siah Design Ⓒ HotFusion, Inc.
2A Ⓓ Matt Lehman Studio Ⓒ Warner Brothers 2B Ⓓ Imaginaria Ⓒ Hotel New Yorker 2C Ⓓ Jerron Ames Ⓒ Arteis 2D Ⓓ Tomasz Politanski Design Ⓒ Market Intelligence
3A Ⓓ Chris Gorney Design Ⓒ Jeanne Beatrice 3B Ⓓ J Fletcher Design Ⓒ J Fletcher Design 3C Ⓓ Q Ⓒ Jochen Koehler 3D Ⓓ Matias Fiori & Juan Pablo Sabini Ⓒ kromo
4A Ⓓ Rule29 Ⓒ Konjo 4B Ⓓ Kongshavn Design Ⓒ Kongshavn Design 4C Ⓓ jo Ⓒ Kinetic Art International 4D Ⓓ Shawn Wideman Ⓒ KiniKinRawMa
5A Ⓓ Roy Smith Design Ⓒ Kallaway 5B Ⓓ Thoburn Design & Illustration, LLC Ⓒ Karla Collegeman 5C Ⓓ Sebastiany Branding & Design Ⓒ Lirquen 5D Ⓓ Logo By Design Ⓒ Loan Library

	A	B	C	D	
					1
					2
					3
				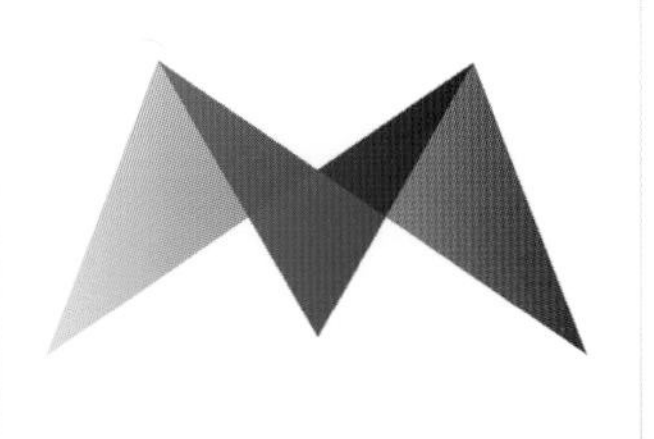	4
				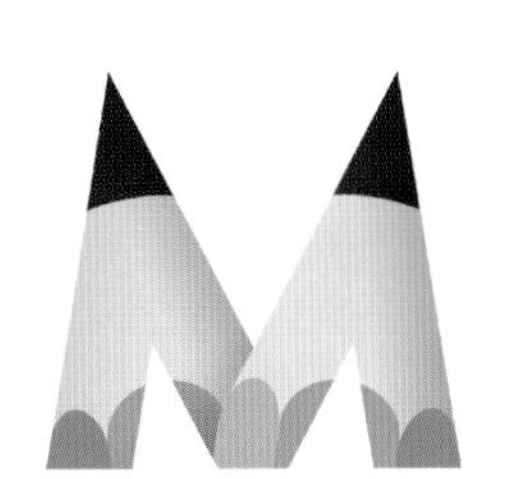	5

Ⓓ = Design Firm Ⓒ = Client

1A Ⓓ ffsako Ⓒ Larry Jay 1B Ⓓ Gizwiz Studio Ⓒ Left + Right Consulting 1C Ⓓ Nikita Lebedev 1D Ⓓ J Fletcher Design Ⓒ Michael Mitchell
2A Ⓓ The Joe Bosack Graphic Design Co. Ⓒ Muskegon Lumberjacks 2B Ⓓ Disciple Design 2C Ⓓ Oxide Design Co. Ⓒ Metro Transit 2D Ⓓ Art Machine
3A Ⓓ Milou Ⓒ Milou 3B Ⓓ mitchel design, inc. Ⓒ Gallery M 3C Ⓓ Murillo Design, Inc. Ⓒ Modern Design + Build 3D Ⓓ Higher Ⓒ One Interactive
4A Ⓓ Larkef Ⓒ Patrick Mandia 4B Ⓓ CREACTIS Ⓒ Moto Marketing 4C Ⓓ elina frumerman design Ⓒ MasterImage 3D 4D Ⓓ Burocratik Design Ⓒ Morigami
5A Ⓓ Device Ⓒ MATHENGINE 5B Ⓓ Akhmatov Studio Ⓒ Almaty Metropolitan 5C Ⓓ ffsako Ⓒ Mayara Rubino 5D Ⓓ Richards Brock Miller Mitchell & Associates Ⓒ Michelle Martinez

	A	B	C	D
1	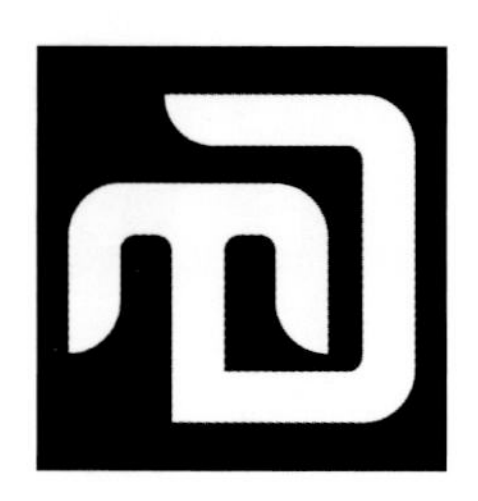		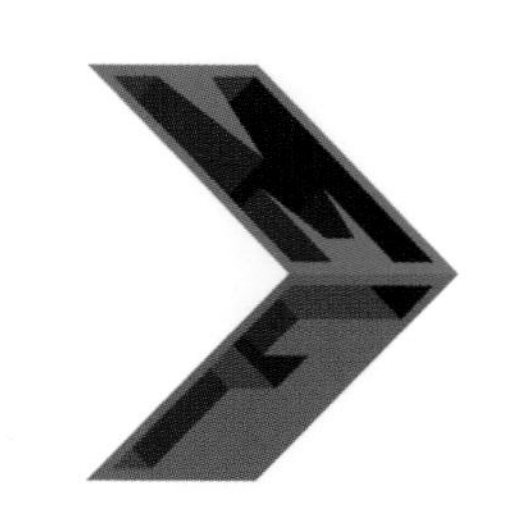	
2				
3				
4				
5				

Ⓓ = Design Firm Ⓒ = Client

1A Ⓓ Causality Ⓒ Mark Dacascos 1B Ⓓ Logoworks by HP Ⓒ Media Forum 1C Ⓓ addicted2be Ⓒ Pavlina Boneva 1D Ⓓ Enter98 Ⓒ Hungarian Graphic Designers Association
2A Ⓓ Jacob Tyler Creative Group Ⓒ Nulogx 2B Ⓓ Banowetz + Company, Inc. Ⓒ The Hilton Anatole Hotel 2C Ⓓ Gardner Design Ⓒ Natalie Moyer 2D Ⓓ Travis Quam Ⓒ Noteworthy Books
3A Ⓓ J Fletcher Design Ⓒ North Charleston Magazine 3B Ⓓ Surface 51 Ⓒ new chapter 3C Ⓓ Infinite Scale Design Group Ⓒ Natural History Museum of Utah 3D Ⓓ Brian Buirge Design Ⓒ NoiseFirm via Paul Shearer
4A Ⓓ Surface 51 Ⓒ next kitchen 4B Ⓓ 1310 Studios Ⓒ Orange Product Design 4C Ⓓ Today Ⓒ Quantumize 4D Ⓓ Shay Isdale Design Ⓒ AXON
5A Ⓓ Marcos Calamato Ⓒ Olive Bar 5B Ⓓ Vanja Blajic 5C Ⓓ mmplus creative Ⓒ Ollino Garden Hotel 5D Ⓓ Identivos Ⓒ Ovune.com

A B C D

1

2

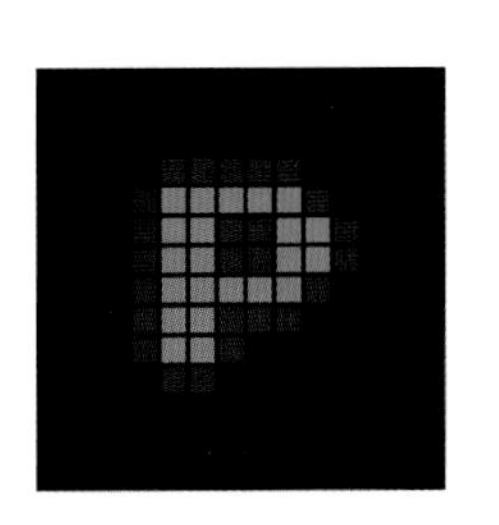

3

4

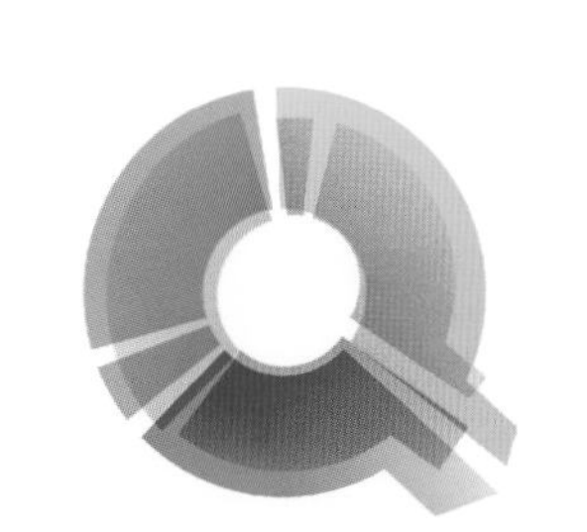

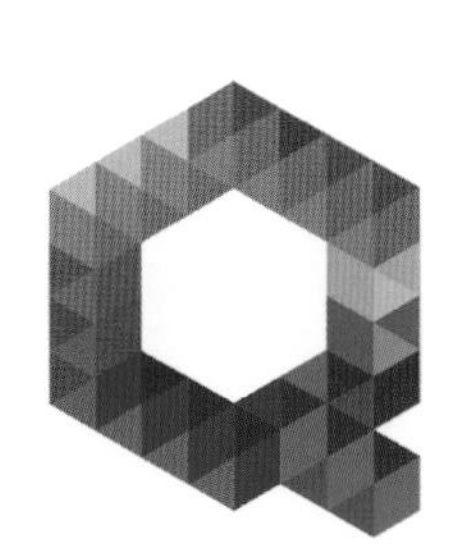

5

Ⓓ = Design Firm Ⓒ = Client

1A Ⓓ QUIQUE OLLERVIDES Ⓒ HQTR 1B Ⓓ Fezlab Ⓒ The Peacock 1C Ⓓ Extension Ⓒ Salvo Property Group 1D Ⓓ Ninet6 Ltd. Ⓒ Plush
2A Ⓓ Eric Mower & Associates Ⓒ Patient Portal 2B Ⓓ Sunshinegun Ⓒ Proconics 2C Ⓓ Bitencourt 2D Ⓓ Karl Design Vienna Ⓒ Prosoniq GmbH
3A Ⓓ Morillas Ⓒ Premo 3B Ⓓ Nikita Lebedev 3C Ⓓ mmplus creative Ⓒ pundi cafe and bistro 3D Ⓓ 01d Ⓒ Pivburg
4A Ⓓ Gizwiz Studio Ⓒ Wong Photonics 4B Ⓓ stanovov 4C Ⓓ 01d Ⓒ QXSolutions 4D Ⓓ Hand dizajn studio Ⓒ Quantum Virtus
5A Ⓓ Joanna Malik Ⓒ Quality Fish 5B Ⓓ Paraphernalia Design Ⓒ Relish Sydney 5C Ⓓ HALFNOT indesign Ⓒ Wahgo International / Cushman Wakefield Indonesia 5D Ⓓ Murillo Design, Inc. Ⓒ redGizmo Interactive

	A	B	C	D
1			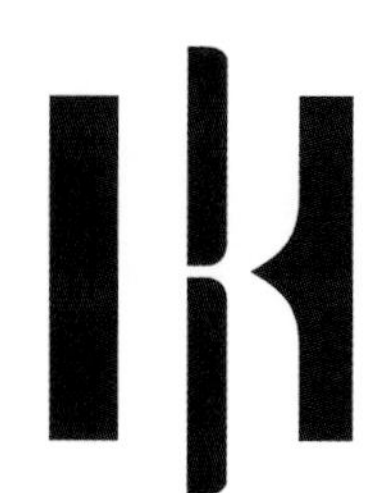	
2	ROTTMANN | COLLIER ARCHITECTS			
3				
4				
5				

Ⓓ = Design Firm Ⓒ = Client

1A Ⓓ Odney Ⓒ 5R Construction 1B Ⓓ Nikita Lebedev 1C Ⓓ Enter98 Ⓒ BK Management 1D Ⓓ Plenty Creative Ⓒ Grand Rapids Community Media Center
2A Ⓓ Timber Design Company Ⓒ Rottmann Collier Architects 2B Ⓓ Funnel Design Group Ⓒ Randy Floyd Architects 2C Ⓓ FLOVEY Ⓒ Robert Filcsik 2D Ⓓ A.D. Creative Group Ⓒ Ripley Hunting Reserve
3A Ⓓ Kuznetsov Evgeniy | KUZNETS Ⓒ wpr 3B Ⓓ Thrillustrate Ⓒ Angela Arnold 3C Ⓓ J Fletcher Design Ⓒ Brent Sweatman 3D Ⓓ Brook Hagler Ⓒ Sazerac
4A Ⓓ Matto 4B Ⓓ FLOVEY Ⓒ Surgent Networks 4C Ⓓ Hulsbosch Ⓒ SCEC 4D Ⓓ Richards Brock Miller Mitchell & Associates Ⓒ Stewart Organization
5A Ⓓ Lance LeBlanc Design Ⓒ Servco 5B Ⓓ SANDIA, Inc. Ⓒ Spectware 5C Ⓓ Colin Saito Ⓒ onespine 5D Ⓓ Visual Lure, LLC Ⓒ Salvatore Cincotta Films

sea sentinel

1

2

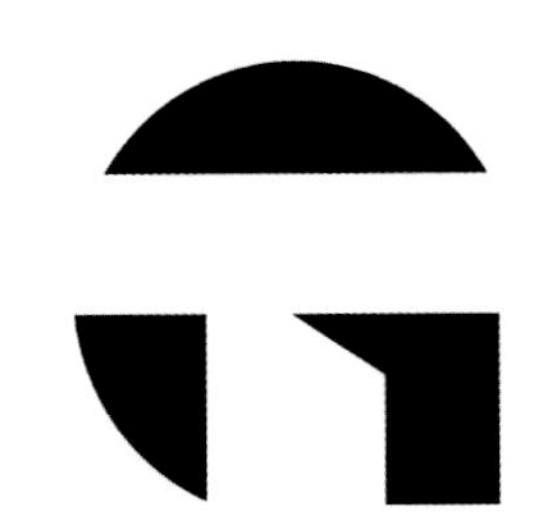

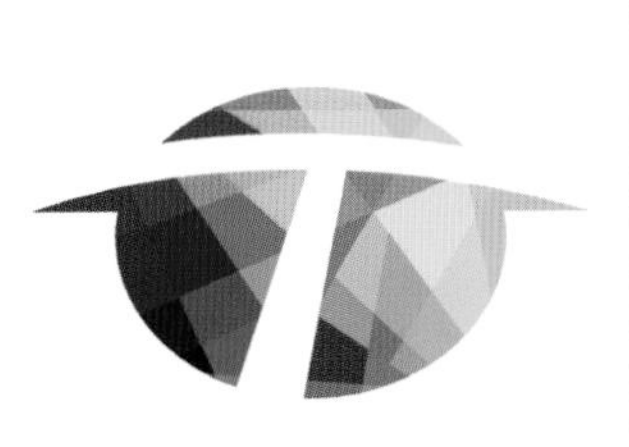

3

4

ПЯТЫЙ
ЭЛЕМЕНТ

5

Ⓓ = Design Firm Ⓒ = Client

1A Ⓓ petervasvari.com Ⓒ Sea Sentinel Organization 1B Ⓓ Glitschka Studios Ⓒ D Studios 1C Ⓓ Gabe Re Ⓒ Strikeforce MMA 1D Ⓓ Fezlab Ⓒ Systech
2A Ⓓ 20nine Ⓒ Synergis Egineering Design Solutions 2B Ⓓ Type08 Ⓒ Shock Studios 2C Ⓓ Sean Heisler Ⓒ Sean Heisler 2D Ⓓ Hand dizajn studio Ⓒ SiP d.o.o
3A Ⓓ Chapa Design Ⓒ Treasury of Great Children's Books 3B Ⓓ entz creative Ⓒ Talmont Group 3C Ⓓ Almosh82 Ⓒ Telos Geoservices 3D Ⓓ Morillas
4A Ⓓ Neutra Design Ⓒ AgencyPort 4B Ⓓ 3906 Design 4C Ⓓ Impact Media Design Ⓒ Unfold Consulting 4D Ⓓ 20nine Ⓒ Urban Blazers
5A Ⓓ Cricket Design Works 5B Ⓓ Ingenia Creative Ⓒ Competition Logo 5C Ⓓ Grabelnikov Ⓒ Fifth Element trade center 5D Ⓓ BASIS Ⓒ Estes Valley Library

A B C D

1

2

3

4

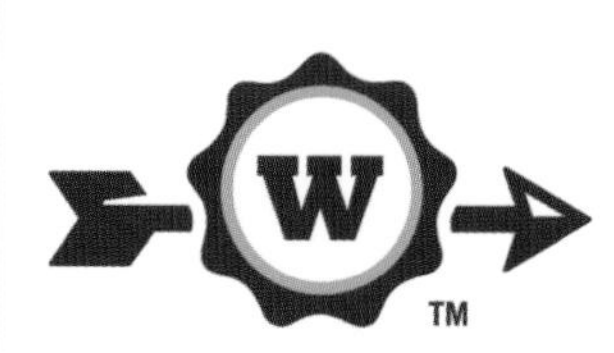

5

Ⓓ = Design Firm Ⓒ = Client

1A Ⓓ TunnelBravo Ⓒ Valkyrie Advanced Development Systems 1B Ⓓ Made By Thomas 1C Ⓓ BrandBerry Ⓒ Vidix 1D Ⓓ Mrs Smith Ⓒ Vertopia
2A Ⓓ petervasvari.com Ⓒ ACTUART 2B Ⓓ Chris Rooney Illustration/Design Ⓒ HereWeClick 2C Ⓓ GregScottDesign Ⓒ Wiggle Learning Design 2D Ⓓ BrandBerry Ⓒ Wecanomy
3A Ⓓ Winnow Creative Ⓒ Winnow Creative 3B Ⓓ Faduchi Group 3C Ⓓ Corporate Image Design & Marketing Ⓒ Western Health 3D Ⓓ Corporate Movement Ⓒ Waterfunk, LLC
4A Ⓓ Melissa Ott Design Ⓒ Wilkinsburg Community Ministry 4B Ⓓ Carol Gravelle Graphic Design Ⓒ Los Padres ForestWatch 4C Ⓓ Sunday Lounge Ⓒ Weathervane Farm 4D Ⓓ Boost Marketing Ⓒ West Willow Family Dental
5A Ⓓ Odney Ⓒ Ward Electric 5B Ⓓ Face. Ⓒ Artwork 5C Ⓓ Emilio Correa Ⓒ emiliographics 5D Ⓓ rjd creative Ⓒ Velo Van

A B C D

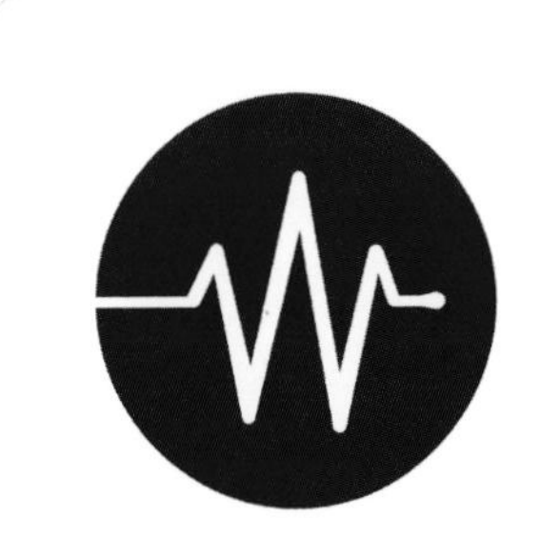

1

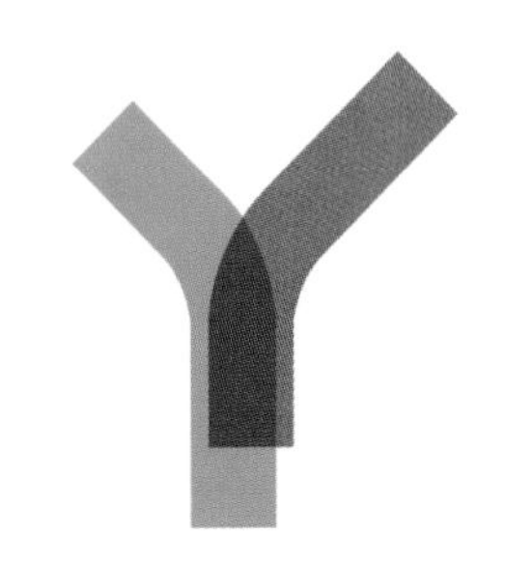

2

3

4

5

Ⓓ = Design Firm Ⓒ = Client

1A Ⓓ DOXA Ⓒ Washington Regional Medical Center 1B Ⓓ petervasvari.com Ⓒ Digital Solutions, Inc. 1C Ⓓ BrandBerry Ⓒ UW store 1D Ⓓ McDill Associates
2A Ⓓ Talal Obeid 2B Ⓓ Vlad Boerean Ⓒ The Extra Hour Collective 2C Ⓓ jsDesignCo. 2D Ⓓ RONODESIGN Ⓒ Yontrakit
3A Ⓓ Karl Design Vienna Ⓒ Braunhofer Visions 3B Ⓓ Imaginaria Ⓒ Zukali Mexican Gourmet 3C Ⓓ MKJ Creative Ⓒ Zanshin Lair 3D Ⓓ 36creative Ⓒ Z Travel Board
4A Ⓓ TD2 Ⓒ Liverpool Inmobiliaria 4B Ⓓ Anthony Lane Studios Ⓒ Aldo Zarza 4C Ⓓ DOXA Ⓒ Fayetteville Public Library 4D Ⓓ Lowercase a: Design Studio Ⓒ Alert
5A Ⓓ Savacool Secviar Brand Communications Ⓒ Ocean Beach Elementary 5B Ⓓ Che Woo Design 5C Ⓓ Jan Vranovsky Ⓒ CG Aid 5D Ⓓ Eytan Schiowitz Design Ⓒ Eytan Schiowitz Design

OCAD University Identity Design

Bruce Mau Design, Toronto, Canada

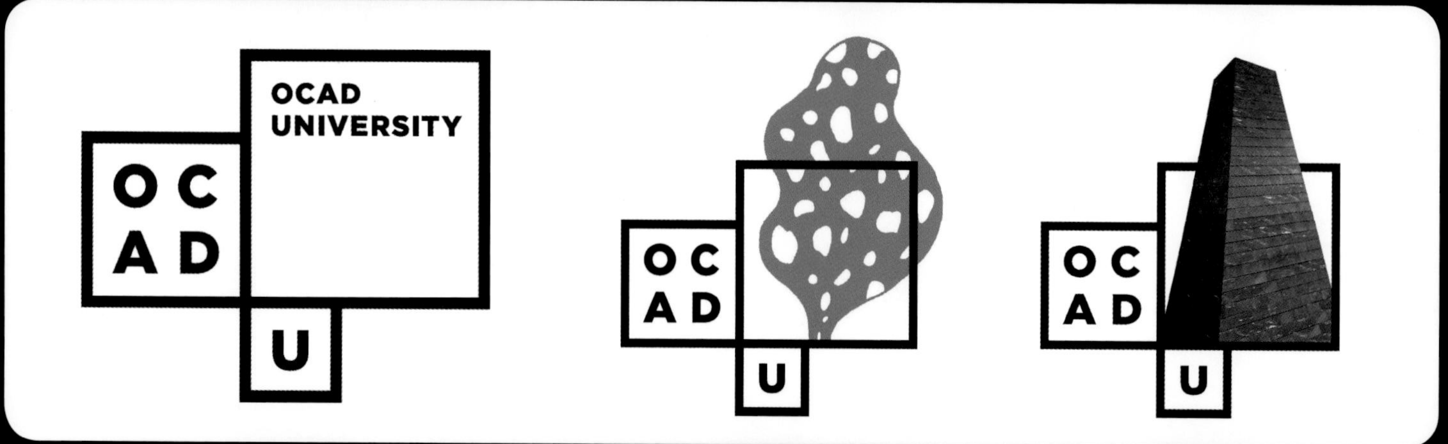

Bruce Mau Design's solution for OCAD University's logo asks students of all disciplines to submit images to be incorporated into a base design.

The Ontario College of Art and Design in Toronto recently became OCAD University, with the ability to grant full-fledged degrees to its graduating students. The university needed a new visual identity to signal this momentous shift.

Bruce Mau Design was a strong fit for the project. Based in Toronto, the studio not only has worked with higher-education institutions before, but its design team also includes two proud alumni of the college. This intimate knowledge of OCAD University's unique teaching philosophy and the talent that it breeds motivated the designers to think outside of the box.

By engaging faculty, students, and university leaders in its research, BMD developed five key insights about the university from which it could draw design guidelines for the project. They posted these guidelines in their work space and checked every exploration against them. For example: "Insight: We are built on risk. Guideline: Be fearless and future-facing."

The designers explored a number of concepts and presented a range of three very different directions to the steering committee, composed of art and design educators, students, and staff members. After some debate the chosen direction, a student body-generated logo, was unanimously agreed upon.

"What we found in the research phase among faculty and the student body was an extraordinary creative energy," says creative director Laura Stein. "We asked ourselves how this logo could reveal that energy. And focusing on student work felt like the right way to do it."

Each year, graduating students from all disciplines submit images to be incorporated into a base of black-and-white pixel "windows," which act like modular frames to hold student work. Those selected see their art turned into the university's logo for the coming year.

"We could imagine that after ten years of using this identity, OCAD U would have created an incredible archive of logos and a snapshot of thinking and making from year to year," adds Stein.

The base of the design was inspired by the campus's world-renowned Alsop building. The team chose a Gotham typeface for its square proportions and because it wouldn't compete with the student artwork.

The design won the inaugural 2011 Core77 Design Award in the Graphics/Branding/Identity category.

A B C D

LOGO SEARCH

Keywords 

Type: ◯ Symbol ◯ Typographic ◯ Combo ◉ All

Inc.

Make™
MakeFab.com

1

Ellis

1911 & Co.

2

Typo Doctor

inspired by love,
CREATED TOGETHER

the
Hype Writer

3

O
so
ya
THAÏ

BITS
THIRTY ONE BITS

CITRUS
CONSULTANTS

4

JERDE

VISION

5

Ⓓ = Design Firm Ⓒ = Client

1C Ⓓ Tactix Creative Ⓒ Incentec 1D Ⓓ Hollis Brand Culture Ⓒ Make Fabrication
2A Ⓓ C-moll Design Ⓒ ELLIS software 2B Ⓓ Elixir Design Ⓒ The Coffee Bean & Tea Leaf 2C Ⓓ Sebastiany Branding & Design Ⓒ Instituto 5 elementos 2D Ⓓ bethvansistine Ⓒ 1911 & Co.
3A Ⓓ Joanna Malik Ⓒ TypoDoctor website 3B Ⓓ Type08 Ⓒ End Movie Piracy 3C Ⓓ Woods Creative Ⓒ Inspired by love 3D Ⓓ Tribe Design, LLC Ⓒ The Hype Writer
4A Ⓓ Absolu communication marketing Ⓒ Osoya 4B Ⓓ Type08 Ⓒ Type08 4C Ⓓ Collaboration Reverberation Ⓒ 31 Bits 4D Ⓓ The Design Farm Ⓒ Charles Kizer
5A Ⓓ Elixir Design Ⓒ The Jerde Partnership 5B Ⓓ bethvansistine Ⓒ Vision Brand Consultancy 5C Ⓓ Eric Mower & Associates Ⓒ Southern Comfort 5D Ⓓ Worthen Design Ⓒ Eternal Perspective

A B C D

1

HERITAGE ON THE YELLOWSTONE

2

%c CADINHA&CO

3

4

scooling

everytime

matchbook

5

smartgrain

cause

Ⓓ = Design Firm Ⓒ = Client

1A Ⓓ Anagraphic Ⓒ farkas-bori.hu 1B Ⓓ rjd creative Ⓒ Heritage on the Yellowstone 1C Ⓓ Craft Creation and Design, LLC Ⓒ Empire State South 1D Ⓓ Kiku Obata & Company Ⓒ Shakespeare Festival St. Louis
2A Ⓓ Nikosey Design, Inc. 2B Ⓓ Arsenal Design, Inc. Ⓒ Earl's Antiques 2C Ⓓ TheNames Ⓒ Stenser 2D Ⓓ Wall-to-Wall Studios Ⓒ Cadinha & Co
3A Ⓓ Worthen Design Ⓒ Eternal Perspective 3B Ⓓ Just Creative Design Ⓒ Eton Financial 3C Ⓓ mardi.be Ⓒ Benevista 3D Ⓓ Mircea Constantinescu Ⓒ Bolster Defense
4A Ⓓ bailey brand consulting Ⓒ Triboro Quilt 4B Ⓓ Tomasz Politanski Design Ⓒ Scooling 4C Ⓓ Jerron Ames Ⓒ Arteis 4D Ⓓ Austin Logo Designs Ⓒ Matchbook
5A Ⓓ Honey Design Ⓒ Smartgrain 5B Ⓓ Oscar Morris Ⓒ FixedUp 5C Ⓓ Logoworks by HP Ⓒ Cause 5D Ⓓ Firefly Branding Boutique Ⓒ Go Trip

A B C D

1

island

tulips

glaad glaad glaad glaad

2

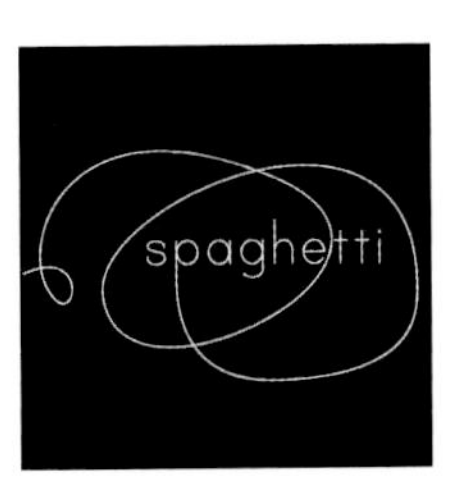

★ PRIME STEAK ★
insignia
SUSHI

3

4

yogg

coco

coco

5

FOREVER
YOUNG

Brooksville Florida
BLUEBERRY
Festival

DESIGN UNION

(D) = Design Firm (C) = Client

1A (D) Doug Beatty (C) Zaha Hadid 1B (D) Paraphernalia Design (C) Living Style 1C (D) Logoworks by HP (C) Tulips 1D (D) Lippincott (C) GLAAD - Gay and Lesbian Alliance Against Defamation
2A (D) Mrs Smith (C) Mrs Smith 2B (D) Gavula Design Associates (C) Ani Villas 2C (D) Logoidentity.com (C) Insignia 2D (D) R&R Partners
3A (D) DAIS (C) Adentica 3B (D) Nikita Lebedev 3C (D) AtelierLKS (C) The Toy Shop, Bristol RI 3D (D) Made By Thomas
4A (D) jsDesignCo. (C) inServ 4B (D) yogg (C) yogg 4C (D) Kelley Nixon (C) Coco Bliss 4D (D) MDG (C) Cindy Ozmun Company Pet Products
5A (D) SivierolNahas (C) TV Land 5B (D) H2 Design of Texas (C) www.floridablueberryfestival.org 5C (D) DesignUnion (C) DesignUnion 5D (D) Smyers Design (C) Chapel Hill Printing & Graphics

A B C D

1

WALLS

CALENDART

2

PARKS

3

MILLEON

BOOKTIQ

4

KIDNEY
FOUNDATION

SHOES

5

HIDE

TODAY

Ⓓ = Design Firm Ⓒ = Client

1A Ⓓ Studio Absolute Ⓒ Volcano Wine & Spirits 1B Ⓓ Design Hovie Studios, Inc. Ⓒ Great Walls 1C Ⓓ Hellofolio s.r.o. Ⓒ CalendArt 1D Ⓓ Michael Patrick Partners Ⓒ Bohannon
2A Ⓓ A.D. Creative Group Ⓒ Brunton Outdoor Group 2B Ⓓ cresk design Ⓒ Twyst 2C Ⓓ Gardner Design Ⓒ Parks Motors 2D Ⓓ Florin Negrut Ⓒ Pârvu
3A Ⓓ Oronoz Brandesign 3B Ⓓ Art Machine Ⓒ milleon 3C Ⓓ reaves design Ⓒ inkd 3D Ⓓ notamedia Ⓒ ria
4A Ⓓ Eric Rob & Isaac 4B Ⓓ Karl Design Vienna Ⓒ Braunhofer Visions 4C Ⓓ Hulsbosch Ⓒ Kidney Foundation Australia 4D Ⓓ Communication Agency Ⓒ Shoes
5A Ⓓ Ninet6 Ltd. 5B Ⓓ genarodesign Ⓒ Greenpeace (stop fin whale shortage) 5C Ⓓ Shawn Meek Ⓒ HIDE ID 5D Ⓓ Today Ⓒ Today bvba

A	B	C	D	
			ANGULAR	1
		DCDCDC	VIDIO™	2
			Boiabá	3
			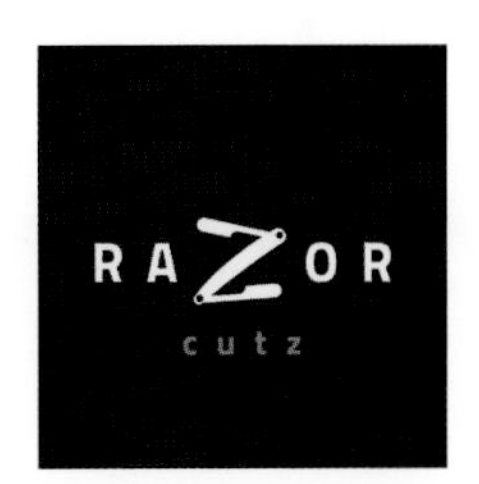	4
I'M GONNA GET ME SOME BACON® DESIGN & DIGITAL				5

Ⓓ = Design Firm Ⓒ = Client

1A Ⓓ Doug Beatty Ⓒ Zaha Hadid 1B Ⓓ Leo Burnett Ⓒ Rites 1C Ⓓ Collaboration Reverberation Ⓒ Architxture 1D Ⓓ Face. Ⓒ Angular
2A Ⓓ PUSH Branding and Design Ⓒ MODUS 2B Ⓓ 3 Advertising, LLC Ⓒ New Day 2C Ⓓ Art Machine 2D Ⓓ Seth Cable Design Ⓒ Smith Micro Software
3A Ⓓ Just Creative Design Ⓒ Radar 3B Ⓓ Overhaul Ⓒ L5 INTERIORS 3C Ⓓ Brandmor Ⓒ Minimal 3D Ⓓ Sebastiany Branding & Design Ⓒ Boiaba
4A Ⓓ Yury Akulin | Logodiver Ⓒ Bella Pelle 4B Ⓓ Magnetic Creative Ⓒ Gen-Probe 4C Ⓓ Clark & Co. Ⓒ French Press Coffee & Crepes 4D Ⓓ Anna Kovecses Ⓒ Razor Cutz
5A Ⓓ Rene Rutten Design & Digital Ⓒ Bacon 5B Ⓓ Shay Isdale Design Ⓒ Texas Motion Picture Alliance 5C Ⓓ Device Ⓒ DC Comics 5D Ⓓ Device Ⓒ Device

Before settling on the concept of cultural contradictions for its client Wines of Argentina, FutureBrand explored myriad directions for this preeminent wine promoter. Passion, diversity, heritage, vastness, old but at the same time new, authenticity, exotic, nature, and the Argentine value of sharing were all considered. FutureBrand finally decided to leverage a different facet of Argentine culture: its unique ability to encompass two extremes.

What could break more rules in wine branding than hot, magenta pink? The bold color scheme of magenta, black, and white was a direct result of a positioning based on personality. As was the use of two opposite-personality fonts in the logo mark: Baskerville, a serif font created in the mid-eighteenth century, and Gotham, a geometric font developed in 2000. Elements of the *W* are positioned to complete the *A*, but the two are not blended together, however, and this is on purpose. The line created by the brand name, also in Gotham, visually cuts through the scene.

"Our contradictions are what make us who we are," says Laura Alfano, director of brand strategy and verbal branding in FutureBrand's Buenos Aires office. "Ultimately, through contradictions we could represent multiple aspects of our country, our people, our wines, in one identity."

When Argentina first started exporting its wines in 2003, it needed to introduce its wine-producing capabilities to the world market. Communications initially focused on Malbec, later pairing it with other Argentine assets such as tango and soccer. However, after seven years it was time to express the sophistication and complex varieties in Argentinian wines for an even larger global audience.

Wines of Argentina—which represents more than two hundred wineries from each of the country's wine regions, accounting for 95 percent of its wine exports—entrusted FutureBrand with the development process beginning to end. This hands-off approach allowed FutureBrand to work speedily and to go from sign-on to launch in less than eight months.

It also allowed the team to break some unwritten rules in the category. By playing with oxymorons in Argentine culture—"informal elegance," "thoughtful passion," "sociable individualism"—FutureBrand developed a brand positioning completely focused on personality, when most winemakers tend to speak about infrastructure such as technology, land quality, production volume, and the diversity of their markets.

"The coexistence of organic and geometric shapes, curves and straight lines, define a space where opposites exist side by side but do not merge," says Design Director Guillermo Altube about the design.

Alfano adds, "The black and white colors represent the unquestionable sophistication of our wines, while magenta brings differentiation, irreverence, and freshness, and connects us to the world of wine through the intensity, warmth, and passion it denotes."

The identity premiered internationally in June 2011 at Vinexpo in Bordeaux, France, where the radicalness of the system made a big splash with a redesigned stand, graphics, merchandising, and promotional brochures. FutureBrand continues to work with Wines of Argentina's leadership team to create applications that play off the logo, which they say is meant to respond to today's ever-evolving marketing environment.

Above: A Baskerville W *meets a Gotham* A *in FutureBrand's Wines of Argentina logo. The black, white, and magenta color scheme combines sophistication with a certain irreverence for wine-category rules.*

A B C D

LOGO SEARCH

Keywords: **Enclosures**

Type: Symbol   Typographic Combo All

1

2

3

4

5

Ⓓ = Design Firm Ⓒ = Client

1C Ⓓ Chris Rooney Illustration/Design Ⓒ Stuff 1D Ⓓ Dessein Ⓒ Soapbox PR
2A Ⓓ Moller Creative Group 2B Ⓓ HELOHOLO Ⓒ Yeah 2C Ⓓ Sculpt Communications Ⓒ Diagonal Clothing 2D Ⓓ Funnel Design Group Ⓒ Beer Distributors of Oklahoma
3A Ⓓ Traction Ⓒ Capital City Film Festival 3B Ⓓ THINKMULE Ⓒ Iliterate Gallery 3C Ⓓ Di Vision Creative Group Ⓒ Edible Assets 3D Ⓓ Dell Ⓒ Dell
4A Ⓓ Proof Advertising Ⓒ High Street Partners 4B Ⓓ Infinit Ⓒ Polished Pearl 4C Ⓓ iQ, inc. Ⓒ Parachute 4D Ⓓ Seth Cable Design Ⓒ Smith Micro Software
5A Ⓓ BRANDiT Ⓒ Little Cake 5B Ⓓ born Ⓒ Eggland 5C Ⓓ brand renew design 5D Ⓓ RONODESIGN Ⓒ Hi! Tea

A B C D

1

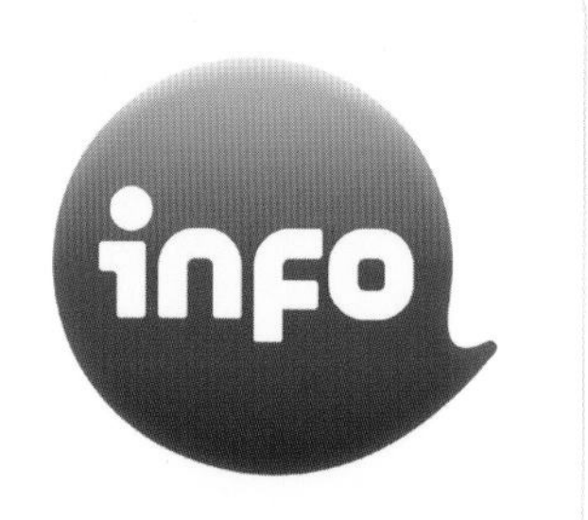

2

3

4

5

Ⓓ = Design Firm Ⓒ = Client

1A Ⓓ born Ⓒ Sonae 1B Ⓓ HELOHOLO Ⓒ Hub Kyiv 1C Ⓓ Kantorwassink Ⓒ The Winchester 1D Ⓓ Voov Ltd. Ⓒ Info Város

2A Ⓓ Denbo Design Ⓒ FireFlurry 2B Ⓓ Leo Burnett Ⓒ Alpha 245 2C Ⓓ ex nihilo Ⓒ Ideas on board 2D Ⓓ DTM_INC Ⓒ Moku

3A Ⓓ Sequence Ⓒ Chipotle 3B Ⓓ Csordi Ⓒ Hungarian Design Council (Magyar Formatervezesi Tanacs) 3C Ⓓ rizen creative co. Ⓒ 5 Slide Speaking Series 3D Ⓓ Gabe Re Ⓒ 34 SPORT

4A Ⓓ Today Ⓒ City of Leuven 4B Ⓓ Rikky Moller Design Ⓒ Mattera 4C Ⓓ H2 Design of Texas 4D Ⓓ Cassandra Smolcic Ⓒ Ono Loa Sweets

5A Ⓓ inferno Ⓒ Self Tucker Architects 5B Ⓓ Chris Rooney Illustration/Design Ⓒ Stuff 5C Ⓓ Carrmichael Design Ⓒ Chow Down Town 5D Ⓓ Cricket Design Works Ⓒ Summer Skronk

A B C D

1

2

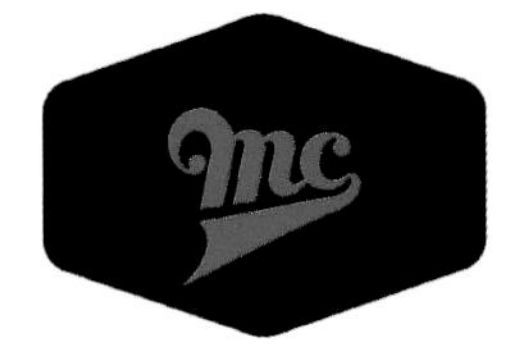

3

4

5

Ⓓ = Design Firm Ⓒ = Client

1A Ⓓ Glitschka Studios Ⓒ Motto Agency 1B Ⓓ Big Communications Ⓒ Alabama Construction Recruitment 1C Ⓓ Morillas 1D Ⓓ Gabe Re Ⓒ 34 SPORT
2A Ⓓ Signifly Ⓒ Plesso 2B Ⓓ Marcos Calamato Ⓒ Marcos Calamato 2C Ⓓ Johnson & Sekin Ⓒ bees knees 2D Ⓓ Caliber Creative, LLC Ⓒ Deep Ellum Brewing Company
3A Ⓓ Arsenal Design, Inc. Ⓒ Metric 3B Ⓓ Just Creative Design Ⓒ BCM 3C Ⓓ TypeOrange Ⓒ Rockford Development Partners 3D Ⓓ A.D. Creative Group Ⓒ Fat Jacks Tap Room
4A Ⓓ Oxide Design Co. Ⓒ Passenger Productions 4B Ⓓ Hand dizajn studio Ⓒ Niva Inzenjering d.d. 4C Ⓓ Dragon Rouge China Limited Ⓒ Kimberly 4D Ⓓ Meir Billet Ltd. Ⓒ Breezy
5A Ⓓ Almosh82 5B Ⓓ Noriu Menulio Ⓒ Musu Reikalas 5C Ⓓ creativefire Ⓒ All Good 5D Ⓓ FMedia Studios Ⓒ BOBO

	A	B	C	D
1				
2				
3				
4				
5				

Ⓓ = Design Firm Ⓒ = Client

1A Ⓓ VIVA Creative Group Ⓒ Forward Society 1B Ⓓ WestmorelandFlint Ⓒ Education Minnesota 1C Ⓓ re:play Ⓒ FORGE 1D Ⓓ TBWA\Chiat\Day Ⓒ Novel Cafe
2A Ⓓ Ewert Design Ⓒ Abilities at Work 2B Ⓓ Glitschka Studios Ⓒ Landor Associates 2C Ⓓ Mattel, Inc. Ⓒ Mattel, Inc. 2D Ⓓ Diseño Porfavor
3A Ⓓ Motif Creative Design Ⓒ Luceo 3B Ⓓ Kruhu Ⓒ GRIT Foundation & Shoppe 3C Ⓓ Riordon Design Ⓒ Fussy Gardener 3D Ⓓ Alphabet Arm Design Ⓒ Ollie Childs
4A Ⓓ FBA (Foxtrot Bravo Alpha) Ⓒ Texas Folklife 4B Ⓓ Principals Pty Ltd. Ⓒ Principals 4C Ⓓ QUIQUE OLLERVIDES Ⓒ Televisa / Verano de Amor 4D Ⓓ Hollis Brand Culture Ⓒ Eat. Drink. Sleep.
5A Ⓓ Werger Design Ⓒ theMrs. 5B Ⓓ graham yelton creative, llc Ⓒ Yazee Crepes & Yogurt 5C Ⓓ Chris Rooney Illustration/Design Ⓒ Thinkbox 5D Ⓓ Banowetz + Company, Inc. Ⓒ The Hockaday School

A | B | C | D

LOGO SEARCH

Keywords: Display

Type: Symbol Typographic Combo All

1

2

3

4

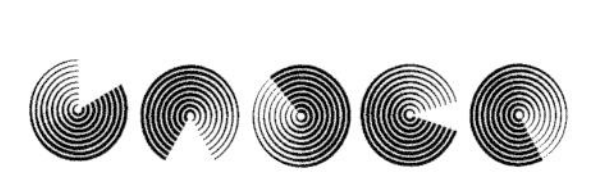

5

Ⓓ = Design Firm Ⓒ = Client

1C Ⓓ S3design studio graficzne Ⓒ AFRYKA Reggae Festival 1D Ⓓ Faduchi Group Ⓒ Army Of Us
2A Ⓓ origo branding company Ⓒ Columbus Metropolitan Library 2B Ⓓ 36creative Ⓒ Who's Playing Boston 2C Ⓓ wray ward Ⓒ Birmingham Museum of Art - Unused 2D Ⓓ INFECCION VISUAL Ⓒ Jägermeister
3A Ⓓ Green Olive Media Ⓒ 55 South 3B Ⓓ angryporcupine*design Ⓒ Park City Productions 3C Ⓓ Boss Creative Ⓒ HCRM 3D Ⓓ Lodge Design Ⓒ Shine on Shano
4A Ⓓ Red Design Consultants Ⓒ Red Design Consultants 4B Ⓓ Device Ⓒ Marvel Comics 4C Ⓓ Creative Squall Ⓒ Cityview 4D Ⓓ Wox Ⓒ Zum Rio
5A Ⓓ TOKY Branding+Design Ⓒ Spaces 5B Ⓓ QUIQUE OLLERVIDES Ⓒ Coca-Cola 5C Ⓓ Roy Smith Design Ⓒ RSD 5D Ⓓ Kuznetsov Evgeniy | KUZNETS

A B C D

1

2

HEL SIN KI

3

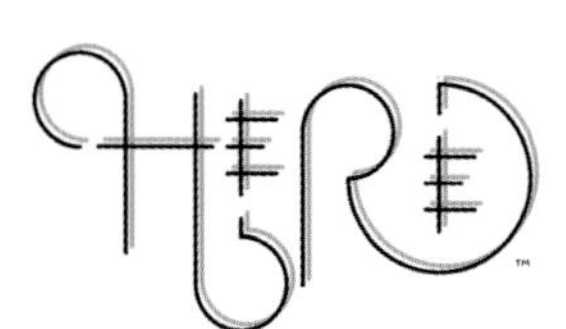

VISUAL CRIMINALS

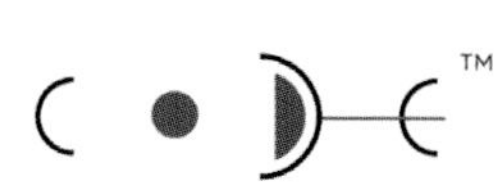

4

5

Ⓓ = Design Firm Ⓒ = Client

1A Ⓓ Shubho Roy Ⓒ Sandesh Magazine 1B Ⓓ Oleg Peters Ⓒ Red Keds Creative Agency 1C Ⓓ Paradox Box Ⓒ Building trust #3 1D Ⓓ Laboratorium Ⓒ Dubrovnik Tourist Board
2A Ⓓ The Key Ⓒ Helsinki Agency 2B Ⓓ dee duncan 2C Ⓓ EDC Studio Ⓒ Eric D. Carver 2D Ⓓ Face. Ⓒ Traveo
3A Ⓓ Steve DeCusatis Design Ⓒ Here Snowboards 3B Ⓓ Voov Ltd. Ⓒ Visual Criminals Ltd. 3C Ⓓ Hellofolio s.r.o. 3D Ⓓ Acute Cluster Ltd. Ⓒ Flip
4A Ⓓ QUIQUE OLLERVIDES Ⓒ Televisa / Verano de Amor 4B Ⓓ Glitschka Studios Ⓒ Reign 4C Ⓓ Glitschka Studios Ⓒ Timbuk Teas 4D Ⓓ QUIQUE OLLERVIDES Ⓒ Kut Culture
5A Ⓓ QUIQUE OLLERVIDES Ⓒ Televisa / Verano de Amor 5B Ⓓ QUIQUE OLLERVIDES Ⓒ Televisa / Verano de Amor 5C Ⓓ QUIQUE OLLERVIDES Ⓒ Sony BMG / La Quinta Estacion 5D Ⓓ Glitschka Studios Ⓒ Jada

	A	B	C	D	
					1
	LEMON				2
					3
					4
	KABAH	WOLVERINE	Tappe		5

Ⓓ = Design Firm Ⓒ = Client

1A Ⓓ Glitschka Studios Ⓒ Street 2 Street 1B Ⓓ Rudy Hurtado Global Branding Ⓒ Tail Wags 1C Ⓓ SivierolNahas Ⓒ Nathalie Nahas 1D Ⓓ Koodoz Design Ⓒ Vala Developments
2A Ⓓ born Ⓒ Lemon 2B Ⓓ QUIQUE OLLERVIDES Ⓒ YOGOOD 2C Ⓓ Floris Design Ⓒ Skyfire 2D Ⓓ Maks Shvahin [Polar]
3A Ⓓ Type08 Ⓒ Fox Flare 3B Ⓓ Momentum Worldwide Ⓒ Momentum Worldwide 3C Ⓓ Cubic Ⓒ Tulsa Chamber of Commerce/Tulsa Young Professionals 3D Ⓓ Delikatessen Ⓒ ING Bank
4A Ⓓ Rise Design Branding, Inc. Ⓒ Youvita Beverages 4B Ⓓ BRAND BROTHERS Ⓒ Numerissimo 4C Ⓓ addicted2be 4D Ⓓ Akhmatov Studio Ⓒ Alexey Arkhangelsky
5A Ⓓ QUIQUE OLLERVIDES Ⓒ EMI / Kabah 5B Ⓓ Device Ⓒ Marvel Comics 5C Ⓓ Karl Design Vienna Ⓒ Tappe / Umdasch 5D Ⓓ Jon Kay Design Ⓒ Fangamer

	A	B	C	D
1				
2				
3				
4				
5				

Ⓓ = Design Firm Ⓒ = Client

1A Ⓓ Airtype Studio Ⓒ Giador Management 1B Ⓓ Thrillustrate Ⓒ Mikee Bridges 1C Ⓓ Joy Renee Design Ⓒ Colton Pingel 1D Ⓓ Thrillustrate Ⓒ Mikee Bridges
2A Ⓓ Filip Komorowski Ⓒ Motto Agency 2B Ⓓ addicted2be Ⓒ 5_ urban clothing 2C Ⓓ Filip Komorowski Ⓒ Brand New Intention 2D Ⓓ Oscar Morris Ⓒ South Austin Brewing Co.
3A Ⓓ Javier Garcia Design Ⓒ Javier Garcia 3B Ⓓ Kastelov Ⓒ Dancing Swingers 3C Ⓓ Faduchi Group Ⓒ Army Of Us 3D Ⓓ HABERDASHERY Ⓒ inServ Worldwide
4A Ⓓ One Man's Studio Ⓒ Gifts of Giving 4B Ⓓ Limeshot Design 4C Ⓓ Dez Propaganda Ⓒ Massey Ferguson 4D Ⓓ Savacool Secviar Brand Communications Ⓒ Kaya Salon
5A Ⓓ Art Machine Ⓒ Wavestar 5B Ⓓ BenKandoraDESIGN Ⓒ BenKandoraDESIGN 5C Ⓓ serrano design Ⓒ US Painting Company 5D Ⓓ Device Ⓒ Illustration Art Gallery

A B C D

LOGO SEARCH

Keywords: Calligraphy

Type: Symbol Typographic Combo All

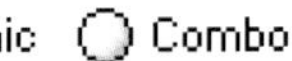

1

Roast Reunion

2

Glacier's Cupboard

3

Way to Go! the ECUMEN way

4

Parsons Wildlife

5

Ⓓ = Design Firm Ⓒ = Client

1C Ⓓ Piotr Ciesielski Ⓒ DSG Studio 1D Ⓓ Piotr Ciesielski Ⓒ Fantomachine
2A Ⓓ Gardner Design Ⓒ American Diabetes Association 2B Ⓓ Inky Lips Letterpress Ⓒ Ric Anderson 2C Ⓓ Karl Design Vienna Ⓒ Braunhofer Visions 2D Ⓓ Mrs Smith Ⓒ Mrs Smith
3A Ⓓ A.D. Creative Group Ⓒ Glacier Park, Inc. 3B Ⓓ Sergey Shapiro Ⓒ E-buro 3C Ⓓ Sergey Shapiro Ⓒ Ascus 3D Ⓓ Sergey Shapiro Ⓒ Zubaba creative group
4A Ⓓ WestmorelandFlint Ⓒ Ecumen 4B Ⓓ Roskelly, Inc. Ⓒ Allie's Tack 4C Ⓓ Essex Two Ⓒ BSA LifeStructures 4D Ⓓ oakley design studios Ⓒ Patrick Lamb
5A Ⓓ bob neace graphic design, inc. Ⓒ Parsons Wildlife 5B Ⓓ Starlight Studio Ⓒ Grace Colón 5C Ⓓ Design im Barockhaus Ⓒ Tenia Wohnen 5D Ⓓ Bad Feather Ⓒ The Poetry Project

A B C D

1

langa

recess

2

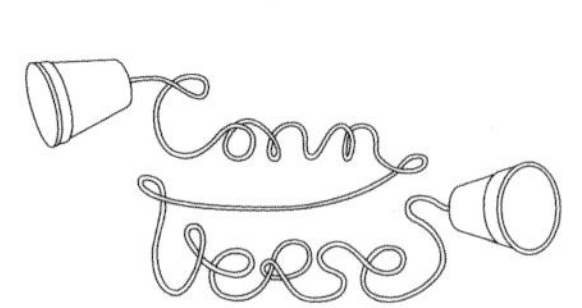

3

Jigoolē

launchpad

4

gemingle

5

Violeto

Ⓓ = Design Firm Ⓒ = Client

1A Ⓓ Mrs Smith Ⓒ Langa Brand Consultancy 1B Ⓓ ex nihilo Ⓒ EEZEE I.T. 1C Ⓓ cresk design Ⓒ Recess Records 1D Ⓓ Gilah Press + Design Ⓒ Matthew Bright
2A Ⓓ fusecollective Ⓒ error clothing 2B Ⓓ co:lab Ⓒ AIGA CT 2C Ⓓ Bittersweet Design Boutique Ⓒ Bittersweet Design Boutique 2D Ⓓ Anoroc Agency, Inc. Ⓒ Stonebridge
3A Ⓓ Hole in the Roof Ⓒ Jigoole 3B Ⓓ The Brand Agency Ⓒ LandCorp 3C Ⓓ co:lab Ⓒ Bated Breath Theatre Company 3D Ⓓ The Loomis Agency Ⓒ Confection Perfection
4A Ⓓ La Roche College Ⓒ Fostercat, Inc. 4B Ⓓ Pinkerton Design Ⓒ Robin Willingham 4C Ⓓ Studio Absolute Ⓒ Gemingle 4D Ⓓ DeGraf Design Ⓒ Sweet Pea Designs
5A Ⓓ bigoodis Ⓒ Violeto 5B Ⓓ Filip Komorowski Ⓒ Spontan Wear 5C Ⓓ Odney Ⓒ Real Fruit Vitamins 5D Ⓓ Sunday Lounge Ⓒ Guadalupe Brewing Co.

L'Arte del Gelato
Identity Redesign

Louise Fili, New York City, New York

Louise Fili's logo design for L'Arte del Gelato takes its inspiration from vintage Italian pasticceria *papers and 1930s typefaces to bring old-world Italy into the gelateria's identity.*

The story behind the very small and very gourmet L'Arte del Gelato is fittingly romantic: Two diamond cutters meet working in New York and leave it all behind to discover the secrets behind the best gelato recipes in Italy. They find them and whisk them home to New York, where they open their own artisanal gelateria. Since then, their creations have been heralded as some of the best gelato in the city, which, given the number of gelato shops these days, says a great deal.

But at first, no one would take them seriously. Although they used only the freshest ingredients and were founded on the serious craft of gelato making, they did not yet have a logo that did justice to the finesse and expertise of their output.

The job was perfect for Louise Fili, who specializes in identity and packaging design for food purveyors. She also collects vintage Italian ephemera—an aesthetic that has influenced her work over and over again. The look and feel of old-world Italy was exactly what the L'Arte del Gelato identity needed.

Fili's collection includes patterned *pasticceria* papers from the 1930s. "They have been a constant inspiration for me," says Fili. "I also love designing with triangles and use any excuse to taper type to a point."

Given the shape the type was to fit into, Fili hand lettered it based on 1930s typefaces. The juxtaposition of an upright script and a chunky Deco font created a good balance. "I wanted the logo to have a timeless yet slightly nostalgic mood," Fili explains.

Because her client had a limited budget, she presented only one direction, which was the clear winner among three options she designed at her studio. Fili showed them a number of color schemes and let them choose the pink-and-orange combination, which was the most relevant in terms of gelato hues.

The logo has graced cups, take-out packaging, aprons, signage, the L'Arte del Gelato website, and special pushcarts that appear throughout New York City, including on the High Line and at Lincoln Center. Customers are finally taking L'Arte del Gelato seriously.

The L'Arte del Gelato cart enhances a coveted spot on the High Line in New York.

A B C D

1

LOGO SEARCH

Keywords: Crests

Type: ◯ Symbol ◯ Typographic ◯ Combo ◉ All

2

3

4

5

Ⓓ = Design Firm Ⓒ = Client

1C Ⓓ Rubber Design Ⓒ Roam Artisan Burgers 1D Ⓓ Tim Frame Design Ⓒ REDCAST
2A Ⓓ Copilot Creative Ⓒ Colorado Farm and Art Market 2B Ⓓ H2 Design of Texas Ⓒ www.floridablueberryfestival.org 2C Ⓓ SGNL Studio Ⓒ Morgan's BBQ 2D Ⓓ Odney Ⓒ Lone Star Olive Oil Ranch
3A Ⓓ Tim Frame Design Ⓒ Touristees.com 3B Ⓓ Big Communications Ⓒ GULF Seafood 3C Ⓓ Red Rooster Group Ⓒ Monmouth Custom Builders 3D Ⓓ Wox
4A Ⓓ Tallgrass Studios Ⓒ Bauer Farm 4B Ⓓ hellozacharnold Ⓒ The Koman Group 4C Ⓓ The Potting Shed Ⓒ Albens 4D Ⓓ Sudduth Design Co. Ⓒ Stopsky's Jewish Deli
5A Ⓓ Second Street Creative Ⓒ Gunner's Glass Recycling 5B Ⓓ Green Olive Media Ⓒ The Boxcar Grocer 5C Ⓓ Visual Lure, LLC Ⓒ Salvatore Cincotta 5D Ⓓ Tim Frame Design Ⓒ TOWNE BAKERY

	A	B	C	D	
					1
					2
					3
					4
					5

Ⓓ = Design Firm Ⓒ = Client

1A Ⓓ Green Olive Media Ⓒ Dan Latham 1B Ⓓ Square Feet Design Ⓒ Crescent Pie & Sausage Co 1C Ⓓ Hole in the Roof Ⓒ warrior society 1D Ⓓ RONODESIGN Ⓒ Tokyo Bakery
2A Ⓓ RONODESIGN Ⓒ Tokyo Bakery 2B Ⓓ tuttle design Ⓒ Caribou Coffee 2C Ⓓ A.D. Creative Group Ⓒ DNC 2D Ⓓ Jeremy Slagle Design Ⓒ PinchFlat Bicycle Poster Show
3A Ⓓ hellozacharnold Ⓒ The Koman Group 3B Ⓓ Sunday Lounge Ⓒ Weathervane Farm 3C Ⓓ Gardner Design Ⓒ College Hill Neighborhood Association 3D Ⓓ Gardner Design Ⓒ College Hill Neighborhood Association
4A Ⓓ Stiles Design Ⓒ Kholer, GSD&M 4B Ⓓ Sunday Lounge Ⓒ Saint Francis Organics 4C Ⓓ A.D. Creative Group Ⓒ DNC 4D Ⓓ Brook Hagler Ⓒ The Laughing Seed
5A Ⓓ Jon Kay Design Ⓒ Fangamer 5B Ⓓ 903 Creative, LLC Ⓒ Poor Valley Bee Farm 5C Ⓓ Gardner Design 5D Ⓓ THINKMULE

A B C D

1

2

3

4

5

Ⓓ = Design Firm Ⓒ = Client

1A Ⓓ Scott Pridgen Design Co Ⓒ Polaris Industries 1B Ⓓ A.D. Creative Group Ⓒ DNC 1C Ⓓ 3906 Design 1D Ⓓ dee duncan
2A Ⓓ Kruhu Ⓒ Creative Pharmacist 2B Ⓓ Rickabaugh Graphics Ⓒ ICLA 2C Ⓓ Itchy Illustration Ⓒ Daytona Beach Chamber of Commerce 2D Ⓓ Braue: Brand Design Experts Ⓒ Apr1l Magazine
3A Ⓓ Jerron Ames Ⓒ Willow Haven Outdoor 3B Ⓓ Scott Oeschger Ⓒ The Star Group 3C Ⓓ Theory Associates Ⓒ nocountryfornewnashville.com 3D Ⓓ Jon Kay Design Ⓒ 2 Player Productions
4A Ⓓ Tim Frame Design Ⓒ TOWNE BAKERY 4B Ⓓ Sudduth Design Co. Ⓒ Jetburger 4C Ⓓ Arsenal Design, Inc. Ⓒ Atlas Health Club 4D Ⓓ The Robin Shepherd Group Ⓒ Saltwater Marsh BBQ
5A Ⓓ Redhead Design Studio Ⓒ A Piece o' Cake Bakery / Le Bon Macaron 5B Ⓓ Dotzero Design Ⓒ Lucia 5C Ⓓ Dotzero Design Ⓒ Lucia 5D Ⓓ Jerron Ames Ⓒ Arteis

A B C D

1

2

3

4

5

Ⓓ = Design Firm Ⓒ = Client

1A Ⓓ jamjardesign Ⓒ DARTFOOD 1B Ⓓ Device Ⓒ Vital 1C Ⓓ Sebastiany Branding & Design Ⓒ Dona Doceira 1D Ⓓ Fleishman Hillard Ⓒ Peabody Opera House
2A Ⓓ Sharisse Steber Design Ⓒ Sweet Bella Cookie Company 2B Ⓓ Jerron Ames Ⓒ Arteis 2C Ⓓ Sudduth Design Co. Ⓒ Great Northern Pasta Co. 2D Ⓓ Webcore Design Ⓒ Anchor Marine
3A Ⓓ designproject Ⓒ Marriott 3B Ⓓ DOXA Ⓒ The Roan Group 3C Ⓓ Smart! Grupo Creativo Ⓒ Mario Reynoso 3D Ⓓ Headshot brand development Ⓒ Foodmarket LLC, Velyka Kishenya
4A Ⓓ Marlin Ⓒ Castaway Outfitters 4B Ⓓ Jerron Ames Ⓒ Arteis 4C Ⓓ Steve DeCusatis Design Ⓒ JEG 4D Ⓓ Jerron Ames Ⓒ Arteis
5A Ⓓ Heisel Design Ⓒ Kenny's Que 5B Ⓓ Denis Aristov Ⓒ Museum of Samovar 5C Ⓓ Second Street Creative Ⓒ Tara Mauldin 5D Ⓓ Char Davidson Design Ⓒ Udders Mozzarella Company

Evo
Logo Design

almosh82, Kolkata, India

The logo for the Mumbai fashion label Evo, designed by almosh82, balances a tightly woven cohesiveness with a sense of the erratic and chaotic.

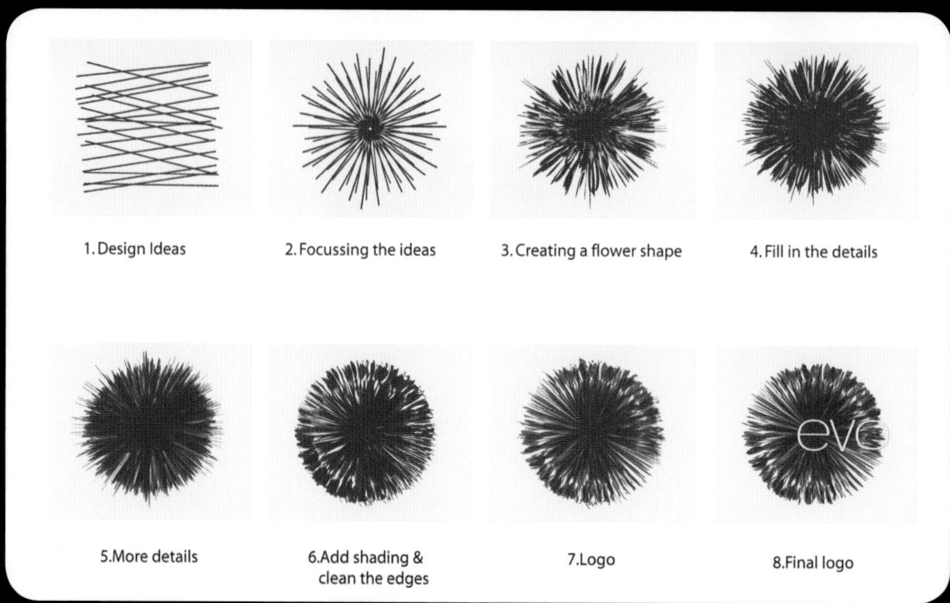

Designer Shyam B worked from singular strands to reach a fully layered flower image.

When approached to craft the logo for a new Mumbai-based fashion label called Evo, designer Shyam B—who operates the independent graphic design studio almosh82 in Kolkata, India—immediately envisioned a flower. His client's aesthetic stemmed from nature, inspiring clothing dominated by asymmetrical silhouettes, bold patterns, and colorful motifs all made of layered, organic fabrics.

As a new fashion presence catering to style-conscious women ages twenty to forty-five, Evo needed to carve its own niche in the Mumbai couture scene. The logo would have to be fresh and distinctive but also effective as a stand-alone icon on shopping bags, garment labels, and hangtags, as well as on catalogs and business cards.

Shyam believed a flower fit both structurally and thematically with this vision. "I love the way different elements come together to form a whole flower," he explains. "My client describes her designs as 'effortless' in spite of being rich in layering and different textures, and so I was keen on keeping these elements intact. Because of this you can see a certain easiness and 'erraticness' of form in the logo."

He began his work with a group of haphazardly crossed strands or threads that evoke fabric seen through a microscope. He then spun the threads to create a circular form resembling a flower's center. The final image has traces of the way a photogram illuminates flower petals, balancing nature with a touch of the artificial. The flower shines with vibrant, almost electric color. Shyam paired the icon with a thin, light font to balance the denser areas and overall vibrancy of the mark.

With the black-and-white base of the flower icon, Shyam could create versions in a variety of colors to keep the mark fresh throughout different applications.

"The hardest part was perfecting the art of imperfection, as is evident in the random shapes of the individual strands," the designer adds.

The label launched in late August 2011.

A | B | C | D

LOGO SEARCH

Keywords: Sports

Type: ◯ Symbol ◯ Typographic ◯ Combo ◉ All

1

2

EARTHBOUND fanfest 15 YRS

3

4

5

Ⓓ = Design Firm Ⓒ = Client

1C Ⓓ Murillo Design, Inc. Ⓒ toquigny 1D Ⓓ Sunday Lounge Ⓒ Salida High School
2A Ⓓ Threds Ⓒ Arby's 2B Ⓓ GeniusLogo 2C Ⓓ JSCameron Design Ⓒ The Beaver League 2D Ⓓ Nikosey Design, Inc. Ⓒ NBA Properties
3A Ⓓ Jon Kay Design Ⓒ Fangamer 3B Ⓓ hellozacharnold Ⓒ STL Blues 3C Ⓓ Nikosey Design, Inc. Ⓒ Jeff Suppan 3D Ⓓ The Joe Bosack Graphic Design Co. Ⓒ Southeastern Conference
4A Ⓓ Worthen Design Ⓒ Wisconsin Rapids Rafters 4B Ⓓ Ten26 Design Group, Inc. Ⓒ Go Hardball 4C Ⓓ Patten ID 4D Ⓓ Helius Creative Advertising Ⓒ Wasatch Rugby Club
5A Ⓓ 343 RLP sports marketing Ⓒ Traffic Sports USA/Fort Lauderdale Strikers 5B Ⓓ Imaginaria Ⓒ Univision Radio 5C Ⓓ Flight Deck Creative Ⓒ Janice Brammer 5D Ⓓ Gyula Nemeth Ⓒ Denes Pocsik Foundation

	A	B	C	D
1				
2	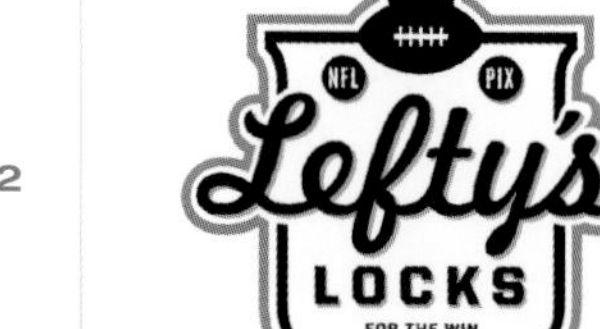			
3				
4				
5				

Ⓓ = Design Firm Ⓒ = Client

1A Ⓓ Hollis Brand Culture Ⓒ Tavern Bowl, TVRN Bowl 1B Ⓓ RJ Thompson Ⓒ Route 19 Bowl & Lounge 1C Ⓓ Limelight Advertising & Design Ⓒ The Help Centre 1D Ⓓ Wox
2A Ⓓ Big Communications Ⓒ Lefty's Locks 2B Ⓓ Artsmith Communications Ⓒ Edmonton Eskimos 2C Ⓓ Diann Cage Design Ⓒ Farmegeddon 2D Ⓓ Diann Cage Design Ⓒ Farmegeddon
3A Ⓓ Fierce Competitors 3B Ⓓ Artsmith Communications Ⓒ Edmonton Eskimos 3C Ⓓ Matt Lehman Studio 3D Ⓓ Jon Flaming Design Ⓒ Brett Johnston
4A Ⓓ High Bandwidth Ⓒ Shawn Humphries 4B Ⓓ Akhmatov Studio Ⓒ Sary Agash golf club 4C Ⓓ lumo 4D Ⓓ Haller Design
5A Ⓓ 144design Ⓒ Minot Minotauros 5B Ⓓ Yellow House Design, LLC 5C Ⓓ Type08 Ⓒ PPS 5D Ⓓ Enter98 Ⓒ Promo Sport

A	B	C	D	

LOGO SEARCH

Keywords: **Heads**

Type: ◯ Symbol ◯ Typographic ◯ Combo ◉ All

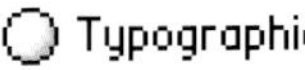
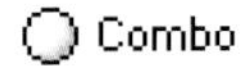

1

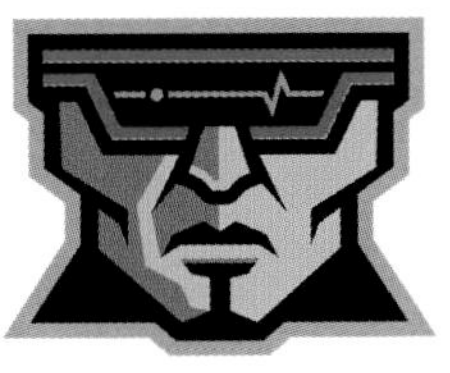

2

GALLWITZ
1880

3

4

5

Ⓓ = Design Firm Ⓒ = Client

1C Ⓓ BrandBerry Ⓒ Jin Media 1D Ⓓ XY ARTS Ⓒ Corporate Events
2A Ⓓ Piotr Ciesielski Ⓒ Piotr Ciesielski 2B Ⓓ The Joe Bosack Graphic Design Co. Ⓒ Greenville Road Warriors Hockey 2C Ⓓ Damian Dominguez 2D Ⓓ Gyula Nemeth Ⓒ Hong Kong Mercs
3A Ⓓ Csordi Ⓒ Gallwitz Pipes 3B Ⓓ Traction Ⓒ Ultimate Indoor Football League 3C Ⓓ yogg Ⓒ Henrico Citizen 3D Ⓓ Worthen Design Ⓒ Rebel Politics
4A Ⓓ Forthright Strategic Design Ⓒ SKYY Spirits, LLC 4B Ⓓ deili Minsk Ⓒ Man's beauty salon 4C Ⓓ Koodoz Design Ⓒ Keith Home Made Cakes 4D Ⓓ ZEBRA design branding Ⓒ Papa Pekar
5A Ⓓ concussion, llc Ⓒ Choctaw Casino 5B Ⓓ dmDesign Ⓒ Hot Sauce Festival 5C Ⓓ Tomasz Politanski Design Ⓒ Stones World 5D Ⓓ Disciple Design Ⓒ Shepherd King Publishing

A B C D

1

2

3

4

5

Ⓓ = Design Firm Ⓒ = Client

1A Ⓓ Jerron Ames Ⓒ Arteis 1B Ⓓ Oronoz Brandesign 1C Ⓓ Unreal Ⓒ Baton Rouge Blues Foundation 1D Ⓓ Johnson & Sekin Ⓒ fresh beard
2A Ⓓ Lifeblue Media Ⓒ Get Grok 2B Ⓓ Webcore Design 2C Ⓓ Anemone Design Ⓒ 9:30 Club 2D Ⓓ Alama Marketing & Design Ⓒ Ushi Nail Spa
3A Ⓓ Hue Studio Ⓒ Nanna Rich 3B Ⓓ BrandBerry Ⓒ MyApple 3C Ⓓ Powell Allen Ⓒ I Like Music Ltd. 3D Ⓓ Heins Creative, Inc. Ⓒ Northwest Stroke Solutions
4A Ⓓ FBA (Foxtrot Bravo Alpha) Ⓒ South by Southwest 4B Ⓓ Fierce Competitors Ⓒ PrivacyGuard.com 4C Ⓓ 13thirtyone Design Ⓒ Charlene Cervenka 4D Ⓓ Bitencourt Ⓒ Alessio Mosca
5A Ⓓ Gardner Design Ⓒ Grumpy Old Men 5B Ⓓ Travers Collins & Company Ⓒ Park Lane 5C Ⓓ R3M1X3D Ⓒ OpenMinds Foundation 5D Ⓓ Strange Ideas

A B C D

1

2

3

4

5

Ⓓ = Design Firm Ⓒ = Client

1A Ⓓ Diseño Porfavor Ⓒ Fundacion Carisma 1B Ⓓ Modern Species Ⓒ Milk For Thought 1C Ⓓ Grabelnikov Ⓒ Motto 1D Ⓓ Deney Ⓒ Union of Actors
2A Ⓓ Nikita Lebedev 2B Ⓓ Gyula Nemeth Ⓒ Ironhead 2C Ⓓ Ninet6 Ltd. 2D Ⓓ petervasvari.com Ⓒ ACTUART
3A Ⓓ Nikita Lebedev 3B Ⓓ Nikita Lebedev 3C Ⓓ Zapunk Ⓒ concept 3D Ⓓ Type08 Ⓒ Pampo
4A Ⓓ reaves design Ⓒ inkd 4B Ⓓ RONODESIGN Ⓒ Hokkaido Milk 4C Ⓓ Gizwiz Studio Ⓒ Babe Organic 4D Ⓓ Sean Heisler Ⓒ Sharebaby
5A Ⓓ bailey brand consulting Ⓒ Triboro Quilt 5B Ⓓ Hirschmann Design Ⓒ OwnersLike.Me 5C Ⓓ instudio 5D Ⓓ ARTENTIKO Ⓒ MONOMAN

A B C D

1

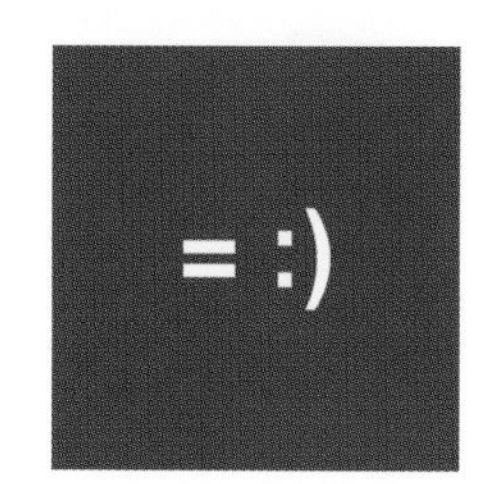

2

Le
Le

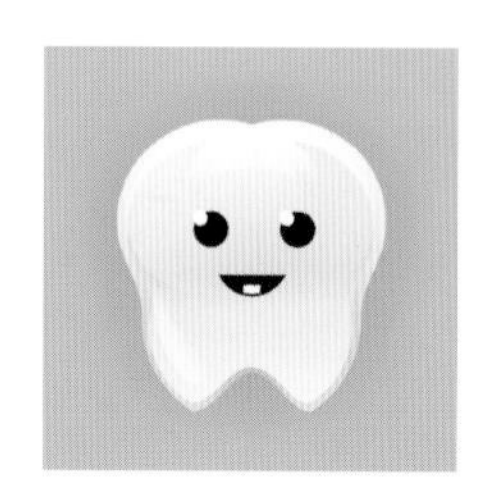

3

4

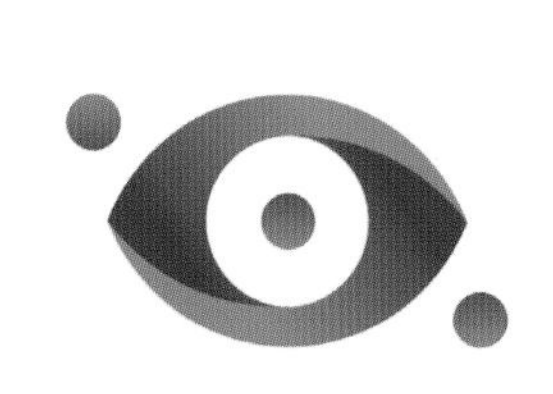

5

Ⓓ = Design Firm Ⓒ = Client

1A Ⓓ Hollis Brand Culture Ⓒ Tootle U 1B Ⓓ Kuznetsov Evgeniy | KUZNETS 1C Ⓓ Lockheed Martin Ⓒ Employee Engagement 1D Ⓓ Glitschka Studios Ⓒ The Great Debate
2A Ⓓ Stanislav Topolsky Ⓒ Musical duet Le Le 2B Ⓓ Karl Design Vienna Ⓒ Prosoniq GmbH 2C Ⓓ Totem Ⓒ The White House 2D Ⓓ 3x4 Design Studio
3A Ⓓ Brand Agent Ⓒ Frito-Lay 3B Ⓓ Worthen Design Ⓒ Rebel Politics 3C Ⓓ Dunham Design, Inc. Ⓒ Exchange Club of Lake Highlands 3D Ⓓ Laura Bardin Design Ⓒ Bad Manners
4A Ⓓ Talal Obeid Ⓒ Visual Therapy 4B Ⓓ Erwin Bindeman Ⓒ Bare Creative 4C Ⓓ Fierce Competitors Ⓒ PrivacyGuard.com 4D Ⓓ Strange Ideas
5A Ⓓ Design im Barockhaus Ⓒ oculus Mundi 5B Ⓓ Hirschmann Design Ⓒ Hank Pantier 5C Ⓓ Webcore Design Ⓒ Tytology 5D Ⓓ Diseño Porfavor Ⓒ Estudios Cuatro Ojos

The Pool
Identity Design

Carbone Smolan Agency, New York City, New York

THE POOL

Based on the typeface Subway Ticker with some adjustments, the Carbone Smolan Agency's logo for The Pool gives the effect of being half-submerged under water.

The Pool is what it says it is: a new brand consultancy composed of marketers from all backgrounds who pool their resources and talents to help drive their clients' business growth. Founded by three seasoned advertising executives, The Pool provides a cross-discipline approach to strategic business development, offering services in brand vision and strategy, product development, cultural and market research, public relations, and capital raising.

As a new consultancy with an imaginative idea, the company needed an equally imaginative visual identity. The leadership team invited New York design and branding firm Carbone Smolan Agency into "the pool" to fashion an innovative look for the startup.

The group agreed that the logo should be simple, clear, memorable, and have a sense of wit to it, all of which would appeal to the company's elite clientele. The initial scope of application was modest, including a suite of stationery items, a pocket folder, email signature, and website. Acknowledging that the logo was not for a large corporation, the designers realized that they could take some liberties in the development and give it a certain playfulness.

"Right from the start, we knew that with a name as short and sweet as 'The Pool,' we wouldn't need to include a mark in the logo," says founding partner Ken Carbone. "Some directions depicting a literal pool were abandoned toward the beginning of the sketching process."

The team derived the ultimate solution from the typographic language typically used at swimming pools, with the letters formed out of a common pool-tile design. The two distinct blues, dark above light, imply the water line, creating the illusion that the bottom half of the name has been submerged under water.

The final logo establishes the startup as a professional consultancy while not coming across as too corporate.

"You know not to expect the next giant agency when you see the identity," Carbone adds. "It's approachable and authentic. It's not trying to be more than the new consultancy can deliver."

Designer Ken Carbone played with ideas of reflection and pools of water in his initial sketches. The solution emerged from the tiled letters.

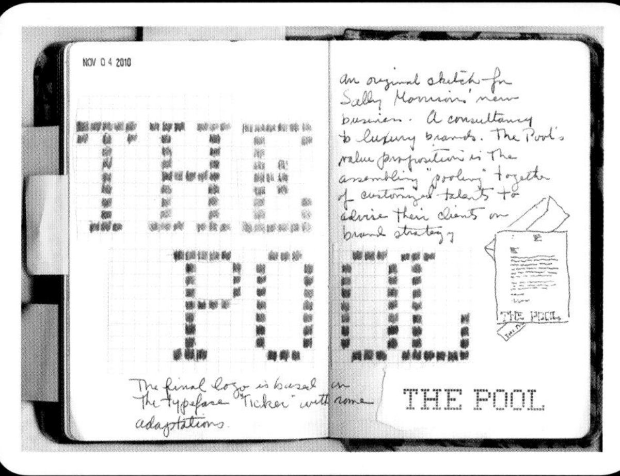

A B C D

1

LOGO SEARCH

Keywords: People

Type: ◯ Symbol ◯ Typographic ◯ Combo ◉ All

2

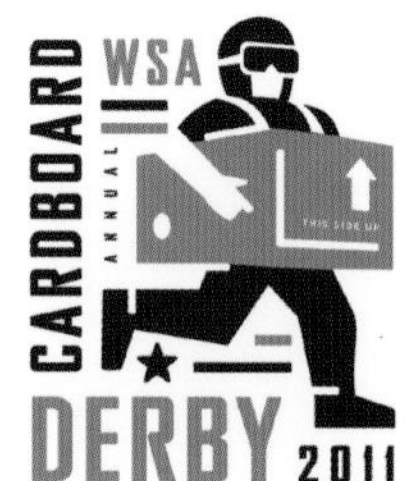

3

4

5

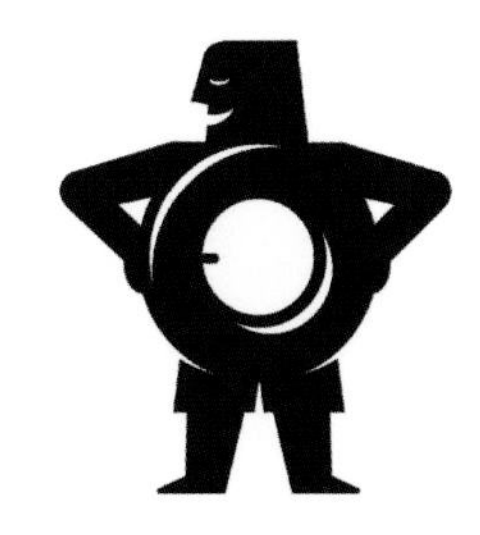

Ⓓ = Design Firm Ⓒ = Client

1C Ⓓ Double A Creative Ⓒ Tango de Tightrope 1D Ⓓ Sunday Lounge Ⓒ Gypsy Journeys
2A Ⓓ 01d Ⓒ Admin2010.ru 2B Ⓓ Marlin Ⓒ Castaway Outfitters 2C Ⓓ Strange Ideas 2D Ⓓ Hue Studio Ⓒ Express Sushi
3A Ⓓ Double A Creative Ⓒ Cowboy Cheer 3B Ⓓ Double A Creative Ⓒ Double A Creative 3C Ⓓ Jodi Bearden Ⓒ Tuttrup Music Company 3D Ⓓ Diseño Porfavor Ⓒ Estudios Cuatro Ojos
4A Ⓓ Tactix Creative Ⓒ Warrior Parents 4B Ⓓ dark horse productions Ⓒ Firewagon 4C Ⓓ Copilot Creative Ⓒ Mobile Auto Detailing 4D Ⓓ A3 Design Ⓒ International Business Council
5A Ⓓ Dotzero Design Ⓒ The Big Float 5B Ⓓ Dotzero Design Ⓒ The Big Float 5C Ⓓ Glitschka Studios Ⓒ Street Level 5D Ⓓ Sharisse Steber Design Ⓒ TN Roads to Relief

A B  C  D

1

2

3

4

5

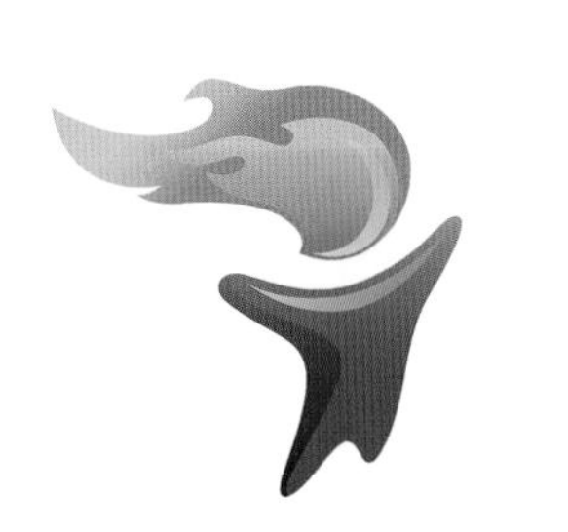

Ⓓ = Design Firm Ⓒ = Client

1A Ⓓ Yatta Yatta Yatta Ⓒ Methow Valley Sport Trails Assn 1B Ⓓ jsDesignCo. 1C Ⓓ Dickerson 1D Ⓓ Javier Garcia Design Ⓒ Javier Garcia
2A Ⓓ Asgard Ⓒ St.Petersburg Idoor Trial 2B Ⓓ Double A Creative Ⓒ Double A Creative 2C Ⓓ Fernandez Design Ⓒ Lost Cowboys 2D Ⓓ Wissam Shawkat Design Ⓒ Rashid Al Habtoor Group
3A Ⓓ Jane Kelley Ⓒ Lakeland Regional Cancer Center 3B Ⓓ deili Minsk Ⓒ The trade mark of bags for women 3C Ⓓ Bitencourt Ⓒ Alessio Mosca 3D Ⓓ FutureBrand Ⓒ International Cricket Council
4A Ⓓ Roy Smith Design Ⓒ Kallaway 4B Ⓓ R&R Partners Ⓒ Envision EMI 4C Ⓓ Carol Gravelle Graphic Design Ⓒ The Body Education Alignment Center for Health 4D Ⓓ Jerron Ames Ⓒ Arteis
5A Ⓓ Murillo Design, Inc. Ⓒ ROCK Apparel and Products 5B Ⓓ Insight Design Ⓒ Wichita Art Museum 5C Ⓓ Murillo Design, Inc. Ⓒ BookFresh 5D Ⓓ Kuznetsov Evgeniy | KUZNETS Ⓒ saofi aventis

A B C D

1

2

3

4

5

Ⓓ = Design Firm Ⓒ = Client

1A Ⓓ Fernandez Design Ⓒ Heschel Day School 1B Ⓓ Strange Ideas 1C Ⓓ TD2 Ⓒ Grupo Natura Mexico 1D Ⓓ Just Creative Design Ⓒ Yoga Tripper
2A Ⓓ Sean Heisler Ⓒ Dawn Attebery 2B Ⓓ atom 2C Ⓓ Ryan Cooper 2D Ⓓ Infinit Ⓒ Polished Pearl
3A Ⓓ Matto 3B Ⓓ Brandburg Ⓒ Double Brand 3C Ⓓ Karl Design Vienna Ⓒ Braunhofer Visions 3D Ⓓ Milou
4A Ⓓ Magic Identity Ⓒ Punch Quotes 4B Ⓓ SGNL Studio Ⓒ Creative Land Strategies 4C Ⓓ Strange Ideas 4D Ⓓ moko creative Ⓒ Our Food
5A Ⓓ Nikita Lebedev 5B Ⓓ Delikatessen Ⓒ baby guru 5C Ⓓ Murillo Design, Inc. Ⓒ the Art shack 5D Ⓓ Michael Lashford Design Ⓒ Heart Your Body

A	B	C	D

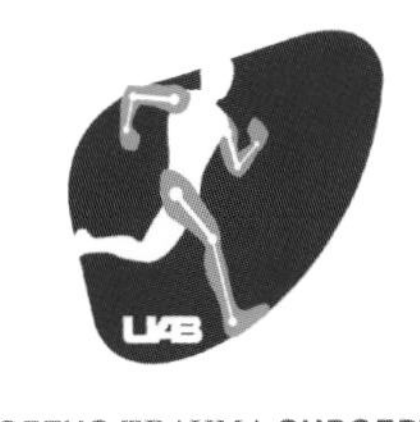

3

4

5

(D) = Design Firm (C) = Client

1A (D) Brandburg (C) Suniberia Travel 1B (D) Double A Creative (C) Double A Creative 1C (D) Kendall Creative Shop, Inc. (C) Beardski 1D (D) Denis Aristov
2A (D) DOXA (C) The Breast Center 2B (D) petervasvari.com (C) ACTUART 2C (D) Glitschka Studios (C) Barbara Vick Design 2D (D) Glitschka Studios (C) Barbara Vick Design
3A (D) Gyula Nemeth (C) Ironhead 3B (D) Schwartzrock Graphic Arts (C) Target 3C (D) Doug Barrett Design (C) UAB Ortho Trauma Surgery 3D (D) Murillo Design, Inc. (C) redGizmo Interactive
4A (D) Oronoz Brandesign (C) Go Green 4B (D) Oronoz Brandesign 4C (D) XCLV / Superheroes (C) Dobriana 4D (D) encompus (C) San Diego Fire-Rescue Department
5A (D) Velocity Design Group (C) Lehi Valley Caskets 5B (D) Insight Design (C) CP 5C (D) Insight Design (C) Lost Art Development Co. 5D (D) Sunday Lounge (C) Guadalupe Brewing Co.

	A	B	C	D
1				
2				
3				
4				
5				

Ⓓ = Design Firm Ⓒ = Client

1A Ⓓ 01d Ⓒ Komputarschik 1B Ⓓ Eric Rob & Isaac 1C Ⓓ Motiv Design Ⓒ Hutt Street Centre 1D Ⓓ Shay Isdale Design Ⓒ IMAX Films
2A Ⓓ Steele Design Ⓒ Questa 2B Ⓓ Brandburg Ⓒ Suniberia Travel 2C Ⓓ Disciple Design 2D Ⓓ Fernandez Design Ⓒ Cedar Creek
3A Ⓓ Logoworks by HP Ⓒ Hanzel & Pretzel 3B Ⓓ MDG Ⓒ Second Nature Social Skills 3C Ⓓ mmplus creative Ⓒ Millenia Furniture Industries, PT. 3D Ⓓ mmplus creative Ⓒ Millenia Furniture Industries, PT.
4A Ⓓ Schwartzrock Graphic Arts Ⓒ Frederick & Froberg Design Office 4B Ⓓ Matto 4C Ⓓ Deksia Ⓒ Camp Henry 4D Ⓓ Demographic Inc.
5A Ⓓ Logo Design Works Ⓒ Dylanic 5B Ⓓ Brook Hagler Ⓒ The Kings Ranch 5C Ⓓ Schwartzrock Graphic Arts Ⓒ BI 5D Ⓓ Black Box Studio Ⓒ Bunyan Brothers

	A	B	C	D	
					1
					2
					3
					4
	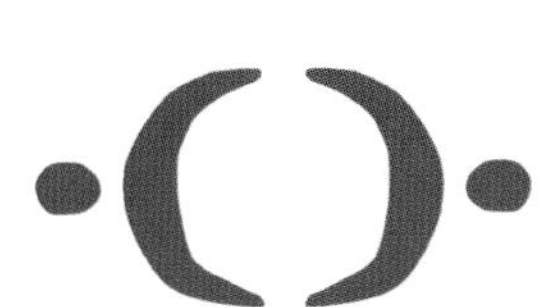				5

(D) = Design Firm (C) = Client

1A (D) Alf Design (C) Vitalis 1B (D) Double A Creative (C) The Hub Gym 1C (D) Communication Agency (C) Kumoamae 1D (D) Today (C) Telegentis
2A (D) instudio 2B (D) Brandcentral (C) Cots.ie 2C (D) Rocketman Creative 2D (D) High Bandwidth (C) Fertility Center of Dallas
3A (D) Sunday Lounge (C) Moonstone Ventures, LLC 3B (D) VOLTAGE, LLC (C) Me Simple 3C (D) S Design, Inc. (C) Absolute Balance Pilates 3D (D) p11creative (C) Kisco Senior Living
4A (D) BANG 4B (D) Sibley Peteet (C) Texas Long-term Care Partnership 4C (D) Tactical Magic (C) PetSmart Charities 4D (D) Murillo Design, Inc. (C) Toquigny
5A (D) Caliente Creative (C) Courage to Connect, LLC 5B (D) Bitencourt (C) Alessio Mosca 5C (D) Hosanna Yau 5D (D) instudio (C) Al Tamasuk

A B C D

1

2

3

4

5

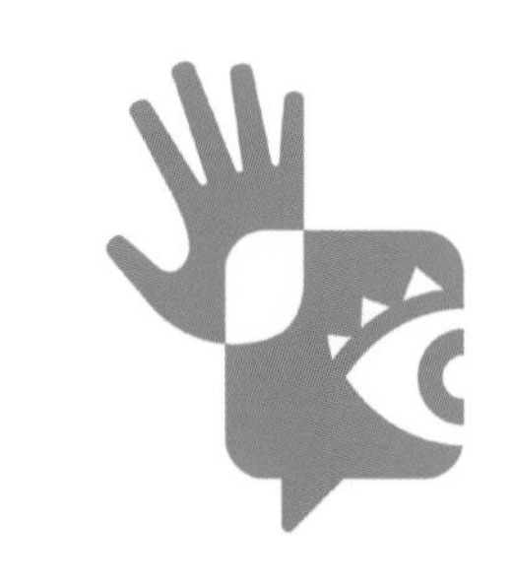

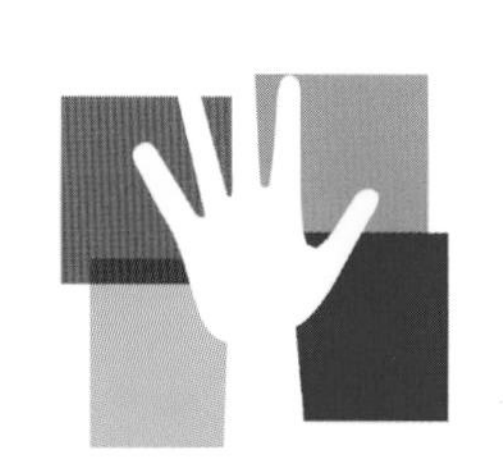

Ⓓ = Design Firm Ⓒ = Client

1A Ⓓ LIOBmedia Ⓒ Motherless Welfare 1B Ⓓ p11creative Ⓒ Cranbrook Senior Living 1C Ⓓ Green Ink Studio Ⓒ Green Ink Studio 1D Ⓓ BlueBossa Design e Comunicação Ⓒ Aguas Claras do Rio Pinheiros
2A Ⓓ Yury Akulin | Logodiver Ⓒ Agelong Tree 2B Ⓓ Murillo Design, Inc. Ⓒ Toquigny 2C Ⓓ Motif Creative Design Ⓒ Melbourne Mammas 2D Ⓓ RONODESIGN Ⓒ Red Cross
3A Ⓓ Elevation Ⓒ CARITAS 3B Ⓓ Burst! Creative Group Ⓒ Vancouver Inner City Community Foundation 3C Ⓓ Jerron Ames Ⓒ Arteis 3D Ⓓ Duffy & Partners Ⓒ Water For People
4A Ⓓ Rudy Hurtado Global Branding Ⓒ Manufacturer 4B Ⓓ Fezlab Ⓒ Southern Arizona Aids Foundation 4C Ⓓ Yury Akulin | Logodiver Ⓒ Golden Cezve 4D Ⓓ Higher Ⓒ Big Richard
5A Ⓓ Lefty Lexington Ⓒ Creative Community Access Stoughton 5B Ⓓ Fixation Marketing Ⓒ Widmeyer Communications/Corporation for Public Broadcasting 5C Ⓓ Doug Barrett Design Ⓒ Gold Standard 5D Ⓓ Larkef

A B C D

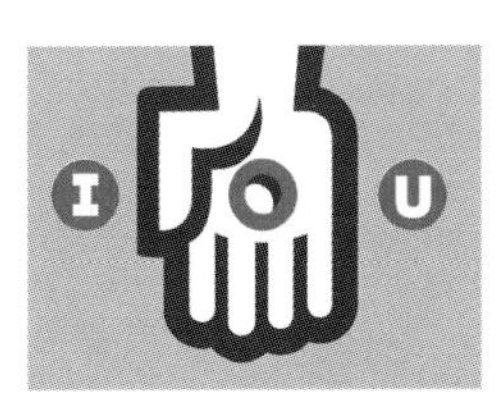

1

2

3

4

5

Ⓓ = Design Firm Ⓒ = Client

1A Ⓓ Brandon Winckler Design, Inc. Ⓒ 6IX Marketing 1B Ⓓ Banowetz + Company, Inc. Ⓒ ProSoap 1C Ⓓ Tactix Creative Ⓒ IOU Ministries 1D Ⓓ Traina Design Ⓒ Drive for Charity
2A Ⓓ Greteman Group Ⓒ Volunteer Kansas 2B Ⓓ Doug Barrett Design Ⓒ Fragility Fracture at UAB 2C Ⓓ Inky Lips Letterpress Ⓒ Inky Lips Press 2D Ⓓ bigoodis Ⓒ Chernika
3A Ⓓ WinshipPhillips Ⓒ International Society for Heart and Lung Transplantation 3B Ⓓ Padilla Speer Beardsley Ⓒ EOS International 3C Ⓓ Howerton+White Ⓒ Howerton+White 3D Ⓓ LOWE Ⓒ Fundacion Luker
4A Ⓓ Joseph Blalock Ⓒ Texas Long-Term Care Partnership 4B Ⓓ VOLTAGE, LLC 4C Ⓓ PUSH Creative Ⓒ Hoyt Archery 4D Ⓓ Karl Design Vienna Ⓒ Braunhofer Visions
5A Ⓓ Emilio Correa Ⓒ A Logo for Human Rights 5B Ⓓ Siah Design Ⓒ Siah Design 5C Ⓓ Hexanine Ⓒ BevReview 5D Ⓓ maria guarracino Ⓒ GSW Worldwide

A B C D

1

2

3

4

5

Ⓓ = Design Firm Ⓒ = Client

1A Ⓓ Made By Thomas Ⓒ Young Scum 1B Ⓓ Strange Ideas 1C Ⓓ Boss Creative Ⓒ Peoples Street Fitness 1D Ⓓ Traina Design Ⓒ Twentyone Volleyball Club
2A Ⓓ Kevin Archie Design Ⓒ Columbia Crossroads Church 2B Ⓓ Gardner Design Ⓒ Lisa Mayhugh 2C Ⓓ Junebug Design Ⓒ Veteran's Legacy 2D Ⓓ Gardner Design Ⓒ Lisa Mayhugh
3A Ⓓ Logoworks by HP Ⓒ Charity Games 3B Ⓓ Kuznetsov Evgeniy | KUZNETS Ⓒ independance 3C Ⓓ Ruth Ⓒ The Hope Effect 3D Ⓓ Sullivan Higdon & Sink Ⓒ Diversity Kansas
4A Ⓓ Kuznetsov Evgeniy | KUZNETS Ⓒ saofi aventis 4B Ⓓ Kuznetsov Evgeniy | KUZNETS Ⓒ saofi aventis 4C Ⓓ inServ Worldwide Ⓒ GSW Worldwide 4D Ⓓ Yury Akulin | Logodiver Ⓒ Flowers & People
5A Ⓓ OrangeRoc Ⓒ Kamaa Ole 5B Ⓓ ecVisualMedia Ⓒ Sojourn Cafe 5C Ⓓ Limelight Advertising & Design 5D Ⓓ giographix Ⓒ Foot Candles Photography

A | B | C | D

LOGO SEARCH

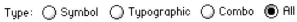

Keywords: Mythology

Type:   

1

2

3

4

5

Ⓓ = Design Firm Ⓒ = Client

1C Ⓓ Gyula Nemeth Ⓒ SDW 1D Ⓓ Glitschka Studios Ⓒ Zombie Stars

2A Ⓓ Thrillustrate Ⓒ Bare Bones Cycles 2B Ⓓ Thrillustrate Ⓒ Jon Broyles 2C Ⓓ Glitschka Studios Ⓒ Vonster Brand Tees 2D Ⓓ 13THFLOOR Ⓒ Harley-Davdson

3A Ⓓ Damian Dominguez Ⓒ El Pirata Fast Food 3B Ⓓ RDQLUS Creative Ⓒ TieDie 3C Ⓓ Steve DeCusatis Design Ⓒ Easy Friend Records 3D Ⓓ THE GENERAL DESIGN CO. Ⓒ Oyamel Cocian Mexicana

4A Ⓓ Traction Ⓒ Ultimate Indoor Football League 4B Ⓓ josh higgins design Ⓒ Love Like Beer 4C Ⓓ Mattel, Inc. Ⓒ Mattel, Inc. 4D Ⓓ 13THFLOOR Ⓒ Harley-Davdson

5A Ⓓ HebelerGraphics Ⓒ Pegasus Art Publishing 5B Ⓓ Alexander Wende Ⓒ Menitiz 5C Ⓓ 01d Ⓒ Giraffeco 5D Ⓓ Type08 Ⓒ Family Media Angels

	A	B	C	D
1				
2				
3				
4				
5	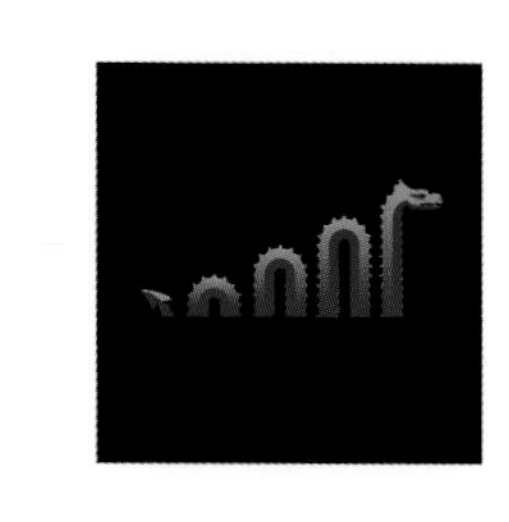			

Ⓓ = Design Firm Ⓒ = Client

1A Ⓓ Fernandez Design Ⓒ LAF 1B Ⓓ Mediascope Ⓒ Mercury Development 1C Ⓓ CPR + Partners Ⓒ Automotive Touchup 1D Ⓓ Brandient Ⓒ Vase Emailate Sighisoara
2A Ⓓ 01d Ⓒ French Florist 2B Ⓓ Westwerk DSGN Ⓒ Letter5 2C Ⓓ Worthen Design Ⓒ Worthen Design 2D Ⓓ Double A Creative Ⓒ Double A Creative
3A Ⓓ Murillo Design, Inc. Ⓒ redGizmo Interactive 3B Ⓓ Alphabet Arm Design Ⓒ Josh McFadden 3C Ⓓ McGuire Design Ⓒ Claudia & Robert McGuire 3D Ⓓ Balazs Vekes Ⓒ Seahorse Trading Co.
4A Ⓓ Worthen Design Ⓒ Wizard Card 4B Ⓓ Swanson Russell Ⓒ FMC 4C Ⓓ Beganik Strategy + Design Ⓒ Orion Airmotive Management 4D Ⓓ origo branding company Ⓒ Columbus Metropolitan Library
5A Ⓓ Jerron Ames Ⓒ Arteis 5B Ⓓ Glitschka Studios Ⓒ Motto Agency 5C Ⓓ 01d Ⓒ Yetti 5D Ⓓ Gyula Nemeth Ⓒ TeeFury

A B C D

1

2

3

4

5

Ⓓ = Design Firm Ⓒ = Client

1A Ⓓ Chapa Design Ⓒ Treasury of Great Children's Books 1B Ⓓ Smart! Grupo Creativo Ⓒ Colon Suites 1C Ⓓ alekchmura.com Ⓒ Team Chimera 1D Ⓓ Florin Negrut Ⓒ Lowe Lawyers
2A Ⓓ Fernandez Design Ⓒ Sima 2B Ⓓ Hollis Brand Culture Ⓒ Haven Gastropub 2C Ⓓ dee duncan Ⓒ dekke 2D Ⓓ instudio Ⓒ Grifey
3A Ⓓ Wissam Shawkat Design Ⓒ Fal Arabian Holdings 3B Ⓓ Logoworks by HP Ⓒ Pegasus 3C Ⓓ BluesCue Designs Ⓒ Pegasus Builders 3D Ⓓ ORFIK DESIGN Ⓒ OCMG Volos 2013
4A Ⓓ instudio 4B Ⓓ Michael Patrick Partners Ⓒ Big Bear Run 4C Ⓓ Field Branding & Design Ⓒ Free Range Cattle Company 4D Ⓓ Odney Ⓒ MBT's
5A Ⓓ Glitschka Studios Ⓒ Reign 5B Ⓓ Worthen Design Ⓒ Grendall Greiner 5C Ⓓ Zapunk Ⓒ Concept 5D Ⓓ Wise Design CG Ⓒ Hop Sqwatch

A B C D

1

2

3

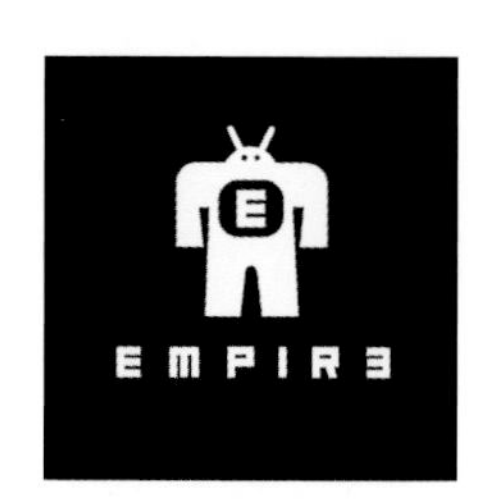

4

5

D = Design Firm C = Client

1A D Scott Oeschger C The Star Group 1B D Blue Sky Design C Freaky Tiki Jewelry 1C D Range C Bitterroot Valley Rugby Football Club 1D D Gyula Nemeth C The Clink Room
2A D Bailey Lauerman C Bailey Lauerman 2B D Strange Ideas 2C D Ty Wilkins C Prediction Appliance 2D D Strange Ideas
3A D Double A Creative 3B D COLOSSAL C Attack of the App 3C D POLLARDdesign C Monkey Fist 3D D Jon Flaming Design C Empire Band
4A D Benjamin Della Rosa Graphic Design C Takeover Tokyo 4B D Mootto Studio C Gebox 4C D Denis Aristov C Gizmo 4D D Double A Creative C Angelic Astronaut
5A D Strange Ideas 5B D 13THFLOOR C Fox Sports 5C D Logorado 5D D Type08 C Dotmonster

Chapada Chophouse and Churrascaria Identity Design

Gardner Design, Wichita, Kansas

In the fall of 2011, Fugate Enterprises, a franchisee of fast-food chains such as Taco Bell and Pizza Hut, broke into new territory with the opening of Chapada Chophouse and Churrascaria, an upscale, small-chain venture in Wichita. Chapada means "tableland" in Portuguese and refers to a region in Brazil known for raising cattle. Throughout Brazil, open-grill restaurants, or churrascaria, serve meat cut from long skewers in the style of the chapada gauchos.

The team at Gardner Design, brought onboard by Fugate, know that the churrascaria could differentiate the identity among the city's many restaurants. Fugate handed them the reins to mastermind and execute fresh visuals for the space: from the logo, signage, and interior detailing to menus, business cards, and gift certificates.

Bill Gardner, principal of the firm, suggested to designers Brian Miller and Luke Bott that they play with imagery he had found on some old Brazilian wallpaper. The print featured pictures from the rainforest, including a monkey, which he thought could bring charm, playfulness, as well as a memorable element to the design.

On first glance, Miller and Bott were skeptical about using the monkey, as they didn't want customers to get the impression that the restaurant served the animal. But this possibility disappeared as they got to work. "We realized the monkey image was unique and could symbolize churrascaria, not just steakhouse," says

Decoration from Brazilian silverware was incorporated into the fork as well as the typeface in Gardner Design's Chapada logo to give it an upscale feel. By cutting pieces of ornamentation and giving them a degenerated look, designer Brian Miller found he could collage and implement them throughout the identity.

Gardner Design presented a range of directions, with and without a mark.

Miller. "It strongly signifies the Brazilian connection, and at the same time its anamorphic qualities allow us to project human feelings and emotions onto the mark. The curious, clever, and fun nature of monkeys is what makes it so compelling as a logo element."

Miller sketched up a number of different monkey images. He wanted to show him in motion, with an active tail, and realized that if the monkey appeared stretched in profile, the form could afford more design opportunities once the designers got into physical manifestations of the logo. He involved the spit to get the monkey climbing and then stepping along it, and added a fork to represent its curiosity and intention to participate in what Chapada had to offer.

To create the punched-through tracery that appears in the logo as well as throughout the detailing of the applications, Miller imagined what gauchos would have carved into everyday utensils while out on the chapada. He gathered pieces of antique decoration from his personal collection and chopped and collaged them to give the system a homemade, folksy quality.

Gardner Design presented seven versions to the client, with and without the monkey. Fugate returned the next day sure the icon was just right.

A B C D

1

LOGO SEARCH

Keywords: Birds

Type: Symbol Typographic Combo All

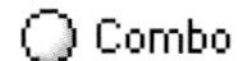

2

3

4

5

Ⓓ = Design Firm Ⓒ = Client

1C Ⓓ THINKMULE Ⓒ Indy Ink 1D Ⓓ THINKMULE Ⓒ THINKMULE™

2A Ⓓ Elixir Design Ⓒ The City of San Francisco 2B Ⓓ Webster Design Associates, Inc. Ⓒ Quality Living, Inc. 2C Ⓓ Sebastiany Branding & Design Ⓒ Powerhawke 2D Ⓓ Strange Ideas

3A Ⓓ Gardner Design Ⓒ EmberHope 3B Ⓓ Synsation Graphic Design Ⓒ Intercamp 3C Ⓓ invectra, inc. 3D Ⓓ Schwartzrock Graphic Arts Ⓒ Community Christian School

4A Ⓓ McGuire Design Ⓒ McGuire Design 4B Ⓓ The Netmen Corp Ⓒ Swiss Eagle 4C Ⓓ Refinery Design Company Ⓒ Wahlert Catholic High School 4D Ⓓ Worthen Design Ⓒ Worthen Design

5A Ⓓ Gardner Design Ⓒ TowerHawk 5B Ⓓ Karl Design Vienna Ⓒ Inarea / M. Ferrero 5C Ⓓ Torch Creative Ⓒ University of The Incarnate Word 5D Ⓓ The Joe Bosack Graphic Design Co. Ⓒ Iowa State

A B C D

1

2

3

4

5

Ⓓ = Design Firm Ⓒ = Client

1A Ⓓ Verve Design Ⓒ Susan Head 1B Ⓓ QUIQUE OLLERVIDES Ⓒ Televisa / Verano de Amor 1C Ⓓ THINKMULE Ⓒ Michael Trenhaile 1D Ⓓ Fugasi Creative Ⓒ Yata for Luda
2A Ⓓ Brook Hagler Ⓒ Rivercane Village 2B Ⓓ design ranch Ⓒ Blue Bird Cafe 2C Ⓓ McGuire Design Ⓒ City Voice 2D Ⓓ 1310 Studios Ⓒ Small Hands Big Art
3A Ⓓ Misign Visual Communication Ⓒ Stefan Wieser 3B Ⓓ Green Jays Communications Ⓒ Green Jays Communications 3C Ⓓ Fernandez Design Ⓒ Briar Chapel 3D Ⓓ Joseph Blalock Ⓒ Raven Styling
4A Ⓓ Green Ink Studio Ⓒ The Sparrow Fund 4B Ⓓ Studio Rayolux Ⓒ Postcardly 4C Ⓓ Gardner Design 4D Ⓓ Down With Design Ⓒ Cath Watson
5A Ⓓ Down With Design Ⓒ Jungpark 5B Ⓓ Blue Orange Ⓒ Stonecraft Memorials 5C Ⓓ Milou Ⓒ Syncrovise 5D Ⓓ Alexander Wende Ⓒ Leafy Sparrow

A B C D

1

2

3

4

5

Ⓓ = Design Firm Ⓒ = Client

1A Ⓓ redeemstrategic Ⓒ Lutroo Clothing Co. 1B Ⓓ Marcos Calamato Ⓒ Mirror Neuron 1C Ⓓ Kuznetsov Evgeniy | KUZNETS 1D Ⓓ QUIQUE OLLERVIDES Ⓒ QUIQUI OLLERVIDES
2A Ⓓ Brandburg Ⓒ Brandburg 2B Ⓓ Webcore Design Ⓒ Dove Financial 2C Ⓓ RP Public Relations Ⓒ Serenity HospiceCare 2D Ⓓ Double A Creative Ⓒ Word of Hope Lutheran
3A Ⓓ Thrillustrate Ⓒ Nike 3B Ⓓ Double A Creative Ⓒ Dangerous Delivery 3C Ⓓ TAPHOUSE GRAPHICS Ⓒ Williams-Sonoma, Inc. 3D Ⓓ Black Box Studio Ⓒ Special Delivery
4A Ⓓ Type08 Ⓒ WorQ 4B Ⓓ Nikita Lebedev 4C Ⓓ BrandExtract Ⓒ Flite Banking Centers 4D Ⓓ Fuelhaus Brand Strategy + Design Ⓒ Causeways
5A Ⓓ Richards & Swensen Ⓒ Tiny Ducky 5B Ⓓ Shine Advertising Ⓒ Madison Mallards 5C Ⓓ Newhouse Design Ⓒ Kate Fisher 5D Ⓓ Sommese Design Ⓒ Dante's Restaurants, Inc.

A B C D

1

2

3

4

5

Ⓓ = Design Firm Ⓒ = Client

1A Ⓓ Oronoz Brandesign Ⓒ Yusuf Mahmood 1B Ⓓ Sunday Lounge Ⓒ Weathervane Farm 1C Ⓓ Joseph Blalock Ⓒ Red Hen Travel 1D Ⓓ Odney Ⓒ MBT's
2A Ⓓ Kuznetsov Evgeniy I KUZNETS Ⓒ AFK 2B Ⓓ One up 2C Ⓓ Veneta Rangelova Ⓒ Gallus Engineering 2D Ⓓ RONODESIGN Ⓒ Chicken Brand
3A Ⓓ Wissam Shawkat Design Ⓒ Fikra Design Studio 3B Ⓓ Nikita Lebedev 3C Ⓓ Roy Smith Design Ⓒ Roadrunner 3D Ⓓ Thoburn Design & Illustration, LLC Ⓒ John Hancock Committee for the States
4A Ⓓ Ninet6 Ltd. 4B Ⓓ Verve Design Ⓒ Modernity Rare Books 4C Ⓓ Gerren Lamson Ⓒ fellow creatives 4D Ⓓ Gardner Design Ⓒ Open Window Learning Systems
5A Ⓓ Jerron Ames Ⓒ Agami Creative 5B Ⓓ Communication Agency Ⓒ Penguin Restaurant 5C Ⓓ Hirschmann Design Ⓒ Robin Murray 5D Ⓓ Tad Carpenter Ⓒ Yummo Yogurt + Smoothies

A B C D

1

LOGO SEARCH

Keywords: Fish, Bugs, Reptiles

Type: ◯ Symbol ◯ Typographic ◯ Combo ◉ All

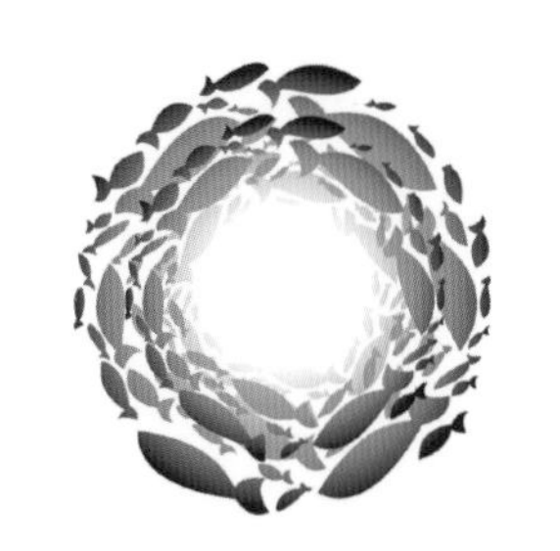

2

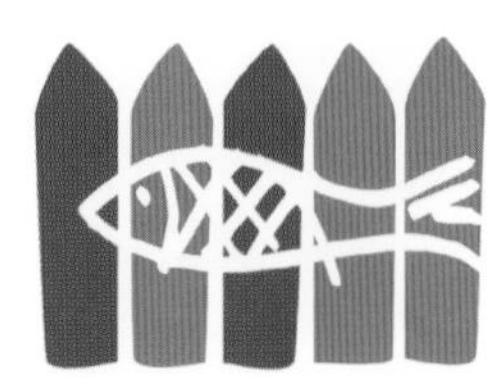

3

4

5

Ⓓ = Design Firm Ⓒ = Client

1C Ⓓ Momentum Worldwide Ⓒ Momentum Worldwide 1D Ⓓ T E D D Y S H I P L E Y Ⓒ Outer Banks Catch
2A Ⓓ Chris Rooney Illustration/Design Ⓒ WETA 2B Ⓓ Andrei Bilan 2C Ⓓ Strange Ideas 2D Ⓓ Asgard Ⓒ The Fish at the Country House restaurant
3A Ⓓ Brook Hagler Ⓒ Poissard Restaurant 3B Ⓓ Denis Aristov Ⓒ Karpof Cafe 3C Ⓓ Denis Aristov Ⓒ Forshmak 3D Ⓓ Logoworks by HP Ⓒ Adaptive Intelligence, Inc.
4A Ⓓ Liquid Agency Ⓒ Tunerfish 4B Ⓓ Marlin Ⓒ Castaway Outfitters 4C Ⓓ Richard Baird Ltd. Ⓒ PD Fish Company 4D Ⓓ Worthen Design Ⓒ USA Swim Club
5A Ⓓ Traction Ⓒ UIFL 5B Ⓓ Skye Design Studios 5C Ⓓ petervasvari.com Ⓒ ACTUART 5D Ⓓ akapustin Ⓒ KITT

A B C D

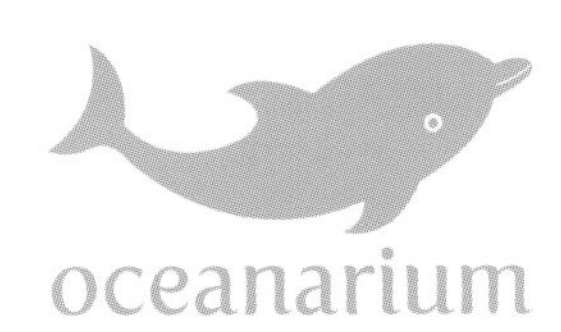

1

2

3

MARGARET RIVER
•PRESS•

4

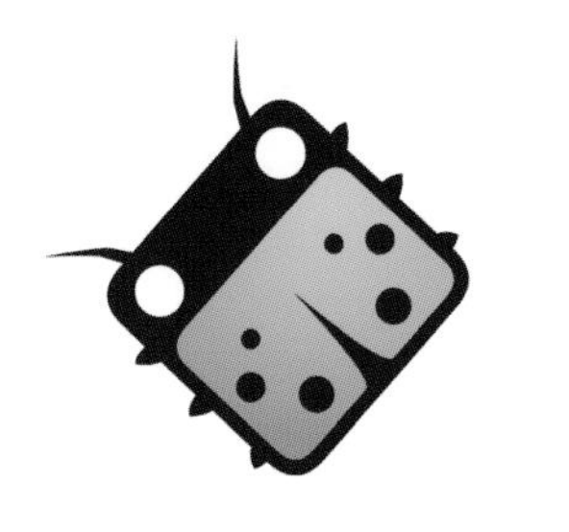
5

Ⓓ = Design Firm Ⓒ = Client

1A Ⓓ Yury Akulin | Logodiver Ⓒ DeelRu 1B Ⓓ Gizwiz Studio Ⓒ Chatr.com 1C Ⓓ Klik 1D Ⓓ Hulsbosch Ⓒ Carnival Cruises
2A Ⓓ Double A Creative 2B Ⓓ Shubho Roy Ⓒ Narwhal, Inc. 2C Ⓓ creative space Ⓒ Alaska Crabby Sisters 2D Ⓓ Yury Akulin | Logodiver Ⓒ FishMarket
3A Ⓓ Allegro Design Ⓒ GoodBookery, LLC 3B Ⓓ Murillo Design, Inc. Ⓒ redGizmo Interactive 3C Ⓓ Lumino Ⓒ Midell 3D Ⓓ Sabingrafik, Inc. Ⓒ Islands of Loreto
4A Ⓓ Fernandez Design Ⓒ Diamond Reef 4B Ⓓ Dessein Ⓒ Margaret River Press 4C Ⓓ Double A Creative 4D Ⓓ Chris Rooney Illustration/Design Ⓒ MOG
5A Ⓓ stanovov 5B Ⓓ Steve Cantrell Ⓒ Raptor Brands 5C Ⓓ Doc4 Ⓒ Doc4 5D Ⓓ pandabanda Ⓒ fun-box.ru

A B C D

1

2

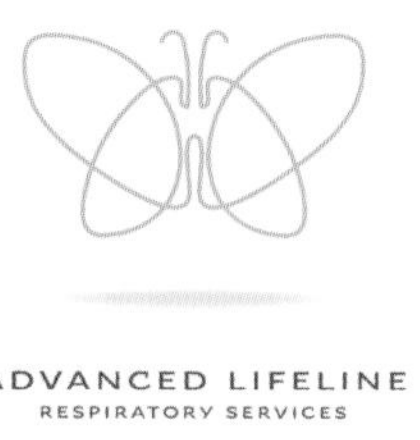

3

4

5

Ⓓ = Design Firm Ⓒ = Client

1A Ⓓ Qualita Design Ⓒ Suco Salad 1B Ⓓ Worthen Design Ⓒ Battle Creek Bombers 1C Ⓓ Mootto Studio Ⓒ Formiko Media 1D Ⓓ Second Street Creative Ⓒ Moonbugs
2A Ⓓ Allegra_East Ⓒ Advanced Lifeline 2B Ⓓ Movement, Inc. 2C Ⓓ Logo By Design Ⓒ Elevate Women 2D Ⓓ Dickerson
3A Ⓓ Gardner Design Ⓒ Lisa Mayhugh 3B Ⓓ Gardner Design Ⓒ Lisa Mayhugh 3C Ⓓ Yury Akulin | Logodiver Ⓒ Valery Live 3D Ⓓ Pretty Pollution Ⓒ Duha Group
4A Ⓓ R&R Partners 4B Ⓓ Denis Aristov Ⓒ Tentorium 4C Ⓓ Messenger Ⓒ Gradale Academy 4D Ⓓ Messenger Ⓒ Gradale Academy
5A Ⓓ The Design Farm Ⓒ Bee Construction, Inc. 5B Ⓓ Oscar Morris Ⓒ The Be Hive 5C Ⓓ Denis Aristov Ⓒ Tentorium 5D Ⓓ Oscar Morris Ⓒ The Be Hive

Star TV Network Identity Redesign

venturethree, London, England

India's most popular TV network, Star, broadcasts to more than four hundred million people, a number larger than the populations of most countries. So well known is the brand, in fact, that it is recognized by a billion people across India. And yet its visual identity conveyed nothing of the excitement, creativity, even electricity of so many minds united.

Star turned to venturethree to reinvigorate its logo and identity system. The first thing the designers did was to drop the word *Star* from the logo to give the symbol itself more power.

"We wanted to share the heat and energy of the content, to capture the excitement of the brand and of India itself," explains Stuart Jane, creative director at venturethree. "Our goal was to create an identity that could live up to a new brand vision: 'Inspiring a billion imaginations.'"

Veering completely away from the flat, cold blue of the previous logo, venturethree tested out images of a "hot star" on both light and dark backgrounds. Keeping the recognizable swoosh within the star, the designers photographed the silhouette in environments of bright light, heat, and illuminated in the dark. After many trials, the team narrowed in on an image of a star that appears to glow from within, a mix of the sun with the unmistakable quality of nighttime electricity.

The team rendered what is called the "White Star" with a yellow swoosh as the main logo, which appears before both black and white backgrounds throughout the identity system. What's remarkable about it is that in both environments it appears to "light up" whatever it is near, like a light that appears out of nowhere, just when you need it.

"The new logo is a hot star, burning bright," says Jason Lowings, design director at venturethree. "It sits alongside customer and product imagery to show how Star TV lights up people's lives with great content, products, and the best technology."

The new identity launched in April 2011, on the same day that the network introduced four new high-definition channels to India and the world, including Star Plus, the first Hindi entertainment channel to provide high-definition content. Uday Shankar, CEO of Star India, was enormously pleased with the new logo design and revitalized identity system. "We see it as a source of energy for the entire company to continue to fire up for the opportunities and challenges in serving and inspiring our viewers," he says.

Above: The final Star TV logo created by venturethree lights up both white and black backgrounds, while the previous logo portrayed a much cooler blue.

Right: The designers experimented with various "hot star" qualities against different backgrounds.

A B C D

1

LOGO SEARCH

Keywords **Animals**

Type: Symbol Typographic Combo   All

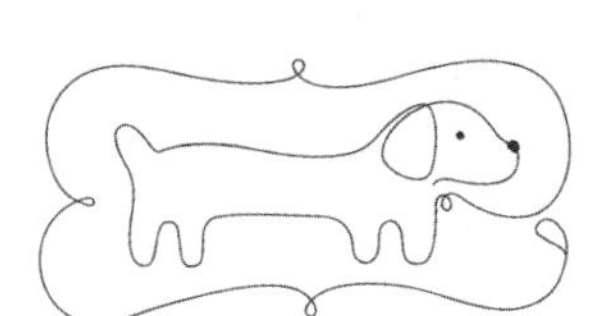

2

LA PERRA MEDIÁTICA
A UN PASO DE SER TACO

3

4

5

Ⓓ = Design Firm Ⓒ = Client

1C Ⓓ Vistaprint 1D Ⓓ Logo Design Works Ⓒ Holistic Hound
2A Ⓓ TheNames Ⓒ otraslevoy.ru 2B Ⓓ HAPI Ⓒ Arizona Humane Society 2C Ⓓ Raul Plancarte Ⓒ La perra mediatica 2D Ⓓ Clay Wiese Ⓒ Sarah Zemunski - Pet Photography
3A Ⓓ bigoodis 3B Ⓓ Impact Media Design Ⓒ Jackalfunk Ltd. 3C Ⓓ Mindgruve Ⓒ A Dog's Life Pet Resort 3D Ⓓ Nikita Lebedev
4A Ⓓ Nikita Lebedev 4B Ⓓ Handoko Tjung Design Ⓒ Singpet.com 4C Ⓓ Device Ⓒ Hepcat Events 4D Ⓓ Handoko Tjung Design Ⓒ White Cat Photography
5A Ⓓ 01d Ⓒ Rukodelnitsa 5B Ⓓ Lunar Cow Ⓒ IMATA 5C Ⓓ R&R Partners Ⓒ Airwave 5D Ⓓ Fernandez Design Ⓒ Briar Chapel

	A	B	C	D	
					1
		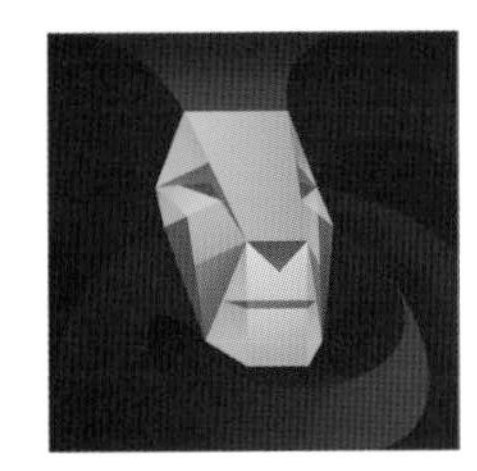			2
					3
					4
					5

Ⓓ = Design Firm Ⓒ = Client

1A Ⓓ 343 Creative Ⓒ International Fight League 1B Ⓓ Thrillustrate Ⓒ Leslie Middle School 1C Ⓓ tugboat branding Ⓒ Doha Drugstore WLL 1D Ⓓ Glitschka Studios Ⓒ Green Jungle
2A Ⓓ Sean Heisler Ⓒ Terex Environmental Group 2B Ⓓ Elua 2C Ⓓ Fierce Competitors 2D Ⓓ Fernandez Design Ⓒ Sima
3A Ⓓ Florin Negrut Ⓒ Lowe Lawyers 3B Ⓓ Logoworks by HP Ⓒ Lion & Joy Media 3C Ⓓ Joseph Blalock Ⓒ Joseph Blalock Design Office 3D Ⓓ Glitschka Studios Ⓒ Landor Associates
4A Ⓓ BrandBerry Ⓒ Grey Lynx 4B Ⓓ Torch Creative Ⓒ CSU 4C Ⓓ Gyula Nemeth Ⓒ Jakarta International School 4D Ⓓ Akhmatov Studio Ⓒ Ju-Jitsu federation of Kazakhstan
5A Ⓓ lumo 5B Ⓓ River Designs, Inc. Ⓒ Foxhall Residential 5C Ⓓ Jon Flaming Design Ⓒ Pure Luck Farm & Dairy 5D Ⓓ Joseph Blalock Ⓒ Trophy Hunting Systems

	A	B	C	D
1				
2				
3				
4				
5				

Ⓓ = Design Firm Ⓒ = Client

1A Ⓓ Odney Ⓒ MBT's 1B Ⓓ Jerron Ames Ⓒ Arteis 1C Ⓓ R&R Partners Ⓒ MGM/Mirage 1D Ⓓ Odney
2A Ⓓ Roy Smith Design Ⓒ Grizedale Lodge 2B Ⓓ Roy Smith Design Ⓒ Grizedale Lodge 2C Ⓓ bigoodis Ⓒ Deerta 2D Ⓓ Donation Design Ⓒ Al's Wine
3A Ⓓ Alphabet Arm Design Ⓒ Josh McFadden 3B Ⓓ Joseph Blalock Ⓒ Trophy Hunting Systems 3C Ⓓ Steve DeCusatis Design Ⓒ JEG 3D Ⓓ RawRender Ⓒ wdo advertsing agency
4A Ⓓ Wissam Shawkat Design 4B Ⓓ GeniusLogo Ⓒ Mustangs 4C Ⓓ Emilio Correa Ⓒ Arteis, Inc. 4D Ⓓ Dwayne Design Ⓒ Murray State College
5A Ⓓ Elixir Design Ⓒ Vaguely Noble Horse-Keeping 5B Ⓓ Pixonal Ⓒ Stallion 5C Ⓓ Communication Agency Ⓒ Kidko 5D Ⓓ Hirschmann Design Ⓒ Tim Trapp

	A	B	C	D	
					1
					2
					3
					4
					5

Ⓓ = Design Firm Ⓒ = Client

1A Ⓓ Little Box Of Ideas Ⓒ Zia Choudhary 1B Ⓓ Impact Visual Communications Ⓒ Mooberry Winery 1C Ⓓ Rudy Hurtado Global Branding Ⓒ Siga La Vaca Restaurant 1D Ⓓ Sabingrafik, Inc. Ⓒ ECOV
2A Ⓓ Oronoz Brandesign Ⓒ Toreto 2B Ⓓ Diaconu Felix Ionut 2C Ⓓ R&R Partners Ⓒ Airwave 2D Ⓓ Odney Ⓒ Bull Run Honey
3A Ⓓ 144design Ⓒ Minot Minotauros 3B Ⓓ SGNL Studio Ⓒ Cycle Prophet 3C Ⓓ Jerron Ames Ⓒ Moovers 3D Ⓓ Design Laurels Ⓒ 4 Steer Ranch and Kennels
4A Ⓓ Ruport Ⓒ RAMO group of companies 4B Ⓓ Haller Design 4C Ⓓ HebelerGraphics Ⓒ Buffalo Books and More.com 4D Ⓓ Sabingrafik, Inc. Ⓒ Andaz Hotel, Shanghai
5A Ⓓ El Paso, Galeria de Comunicacion Ⓒ MASCOMPANY 5B Ⓓ Joseph Blalock Ⓒ Texas Early Hearing Detection and Intervention 5C Ⓓ Rudy Hurtado Global Branding Ⓒ WildSmart 5D Ⓓ pandabanda Ⓒ pandabanda design

A B C D

1

2

3

4

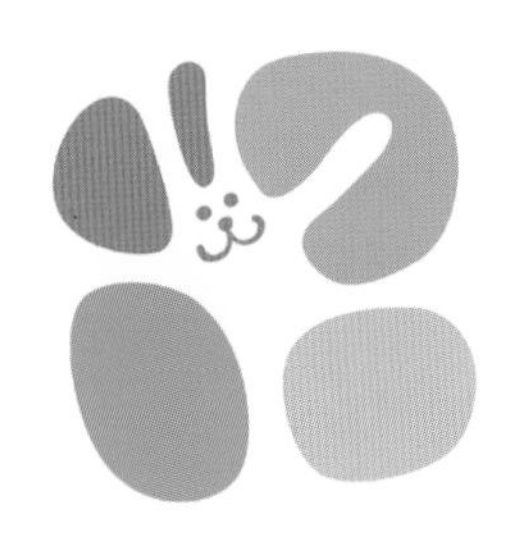

5

Ⓓ = Design Firm Ⓒ = Client

1A Ⓓ Ink Tycoon Ⓒ Coventry Bears 1B Ⓓ Glitschka Studios Ⓒ Gere Donovan Creative 1C Ⓓ A.D. Creative Group Ⓒ Rocky Mountain College 1D Ⓓ Rudy Hurtado Global Branding Ⓒ WildSmart
2A Ⓓ Dotzero Design Ⓒ Kate Sokoloff 2B Ⓓ LOGOSTA Ⓒ NB-Tsuzuki 2C Ⓓ Murillo Design, Inc. Ⓒ redGizmo Interactive 2D Ⓓ Graphic Granola Ⓒ Red Rabbit Cooperative Bakery
3A Ⓓ MINE Ⓒ Peachpit Press 3B Ⓓ Mattson Creative 3C Ⓓ VGreen Design Ⓒ BlackHare Studio 3D Ⓓ Mattson Creative Ⓒ Crazy Hare
4A Ⓓ Tribambuka Ⓒ Roger - toy warehouse 4B Ⓓ Rikky Moller Design Ⓒ HV Communications 4C Ⓓ Jerron Ames Ⓒ Arteis 4D Ⓓ Alphabet Arm Design Ⓒ Loot
5A Ⓓ TheNames Ⓒ Nashe Mesto 5B Ⓓ Fernandez Design Ⓒ Briar Chapel 5C Ⓓ Studio Ink Ⓒ Sweetlabs 5D Ⓓ Kuharic Matos Ltd. Ⓒ Tomislav Rukavina

A B C D

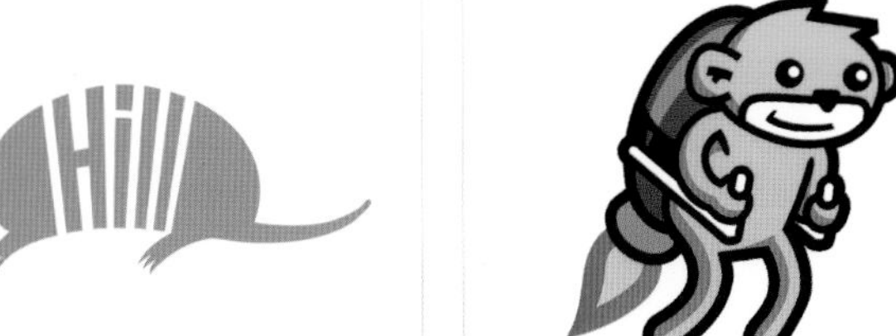

1

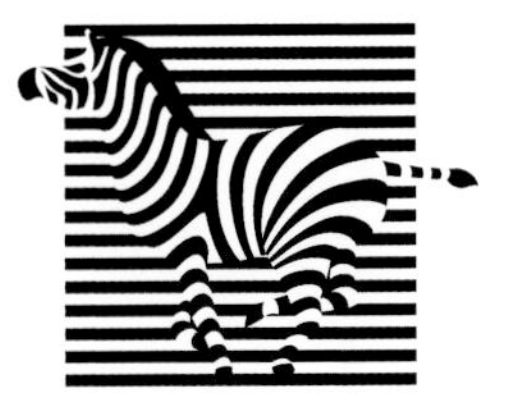

2

3

4

BIOLOGY
DAY

5

Ⓓ = Design Firm Ⓒ = Client

1A Ⓓ dandy idea Ⓒ Hill Elementary PTA 1B Ⓓ concussion, llc Ⓒ WDS Logistics 1C Ⓓ Glitschka Studios Ⓒ Angry Porcupine Design 1D Ⓓ Hulsbosch Ⓒ Tourism Australia
2A Ⓓ MT Estudio Ⓒ zebra producciones 2B Ⓓ Brandburg Ⓒ Double Brand 2C Ⓓ Komprehensive Design Ⓒ Pink Rhino Kids 2D Ⓓ Logo Design Works Ⓒ OwynCo
3A Ⓓ instudio Ⓒ P. Ruppert 3B Ⓓ Mircea Constantinescu Ⓒ enormail 3C Ⓓ RONODESIGN Ⓒ Elefante 3D Ⓓ Sunshinegun Ⓒ Oasis
4A Ⓓ Oxide Design Co. Ⓒ Cultures East 4B Ⓓ Red Clover Studio Ⓒ Airtex Design Group 4C Ⓓ California Baptist University Ⓒ Western Center for Paelontology 4D Ⓓ 01d Ⓒ Open Alliance
5A Ⓓ Braue: Brand Design Experts Ⓒ Apr1l Magazine 5B Ⓓ R&R Partners Ⓒ Busch Entertainment 5C Ⓓ Lunar Cow Ⓒ IMATA 5D Ⓓ Lunar Cow Ⓒ Six Flags Great Adventure

James Beard Foundation Identity Redesign

Simplissimus, New York City, New York

JAMES BEARD FOUNDATION

Simplissimus designed a new logo for the James Beard Foundation that balances playfulness with sophistication.

Heralded as the "dean of American cookery" by the *New York Times* in 1954, James Beard is the reason America is one of the forerunners in global gastronomy today. Beard wrote dozens of seminal cookbooks and established the James Beard Cooking School in 1955. Upon his death thirty years later, the James Beard Foundation was formed in the school's famed Greenwich Village location in the pursuit of keeping Beard's joyous relationship with good food alive.

The New York design shop Simplissimus had been working with the Foundation for more than ten years and suggested creating a new brand identity in time for its twenty-fifth anniversary in the fall of 2011. The resulting logo design and other applications capture the combination of eminence and humor that Beard himself embodied.

"The Foundation, like its namesake, has a serious mission to celebrate and nurture America's culinary past and present, but it also has a whimsical side, throwing fantastic galas and events throughout the year," says Simplissimus Creative Director Scott Meola. "We wanted to capture this celebratory feeling but not let it overwhelm the importance of the organization, or the man."

As they began work on the logo design, the team made an exciting discovery: The word *eat* could be formed from the foundation name. Not only is the word at the core of everything the organization stands for, but visually it also could provide the perfect fulcrum on which to balance the wit and elegance of the logo. It also presented a useful element for future branding applications.

The word *eat* nudged them toward a type-only solution with *eat* highlighted in color. They opted for the Knockout Ultimate Middleweight typeface by Hoefler & Frere-Jones. But the name is a long one and wouldn't be clearly visible at small sizes. At first the designers were convinced the type had to sit on one line, making the word too spread out to be immediately accessible.

That's when Simplissimus realized they had to stack the name. Meola describes this as the "Eureka!" moment. By playing with the negative space and administering some detailed kerning, the letters fell into place. And with the black-and-silver color scheme, the inspiration of the Foundation's twenty-fifth anniversary was gracefully integrated into the design.

The new identity has been implemented throughout a year of festivities and gives shape to the new James Beard Foundation website, collateral such as business cards, letterhead, and envelopes, as well as signage, marketing materials, and T-shirts.

The logo sits nicely on business cards. The silver EAT *hints at the Foundation's twenty-fifth anniversary, which occasioned the new identity.*

A | B | C | D

LOGO SEARCH

Keywords **Nature**

Type:  Symbol  Typographic  Combo ◉ All

1

2

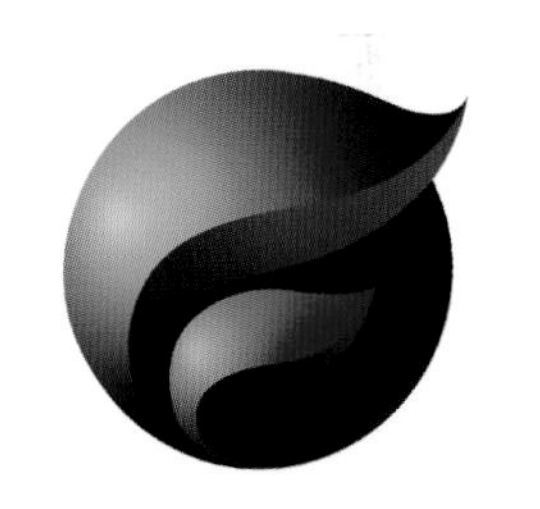

3

4

5

Ⓓ = Design Firm Ⓒ = Client

1C Ⓓ petervasvari.com Ⓒ St. Julian's Rowing Club 1D Ⓓ Flight Deck Creative Ⓒ Diana O'Quinn DDS
2A Ⓓ A.D. Creative Group 2B Ⓓ Motiv Design Ⓒ Leaf & Ladle Soup & Salad Kitchen 2C Ⓓ Type08 Ⓒ Eco-Logic Systems 2D Ⓓ O'Hare Design Ⓒ Greg Newell-WSI
3A Ⓓ hatchmarks 3B Ⓓ Piotr Ciesielski Ⓒ Dominican Republic Ministry of Tourism 3C Ⓓ Absolu communication marketing Ⓒ Les 3 Monts - Réserve écologique de la Serpentine-de-Coleraine 3D Ⓓ Shubho Roy Ⓒ Exflora, LLC
4A Ⓓ Almosh82 Ⓒ Scientific Conservation 4B Ⓓ maria guarracino Ⓒ GSW Worldwide 4C Ⓓ Creative United Ⓒ Jantzen development 4D Ⓓ Hollis Brand Culture Ⓒ Serosun Farms
5A Ⓓ Ryan Ford Design Ⓒ Cereplast 5B Ⓓ Denis Aristov Ⓒ Ministry of Commerce of Perm Region 5C Ⓓ Helius Creative Advertising Ⓒ Four Seasons Landscaping 5D Ⓓ Rikky Moller Design Ⓒ Woodmont Cabinetry

A B C D

1

2

bioregions

3

GOLDEN
STAR
TEA CO

4

5

Ⓓ = Design Firm Ⓒ = Client

1A Ⓓ AtelierLKS Ⓒ Precise Cut Landscaping 1B Ⓓ Ishan Khosla Design Ⓒ Ten Sages (Avasara) 1C Ⓓ Strange Ideas 1D Ⓓ Logo Design Works Ⓒ HerbalCentre
2A Ⓓ Webcore Design Ⓒ Bioregions 2B Ⓓ Milou Ⓒ amari 2C Ⓓ Kuznetsov Evgeniy I KUZNETS Ⓒ My book 2D Ⓓ Sebastiany Branding & Design Ⓒ UTR
3A Ⓓ Elixir Design Ⓒ Golden Star Tea Company 3B Ⓓ Woods Creative Ⓒ The Orchard 3C Ⓓ HABERDASHERY Ⓒ inVentiv Health 3D Ⓓ HELOHOLO Ⓒ Yedynka
4A Ⓓ jsDesignCo. Ⓒ Japan relief effort 4B Ⓓ Limeshot Design Ⓒ Inspiration Exchange 4C Ⓓ Tactical Magic Ⓒ Temple Israel Synagogue 4D Ⓓ Sarah Rusin / Graphic Design Ⓒ Robyn Linn
5A Ⓓ Communication Agency Ⓒ Parfemka 5B Ⓓ jamjardesign Ⓒ TULIP Digital Ink 5C Ⓓ Paul Black Design Ⓒ Mary Kay Cosmetics 5D Ⓓ Nikita Lebedev

A B C D

BLOSSOM PHOTO

1

2

3

4

5

Ⓓ = Design Firm Ⓒ = Client

1A Ⓓ Matto 1B Ⓓ Sunday Lounge Ⓒ Weathervane Farm 1C Ⓓ Go Welsh Ⓒ Royer's Flowers & Gifts 1D Ⓓ The Infantree Ⓒ Mayor's Office of Special Events
2A Ⓓ Yury Akulin | Logodiver Ⓒ Flowers & People 2B Ⓓ Jerron Ames Ⓒ Arteis 2C Ⓓ 01d Ⓒ Bouquetville 2D Ⓓ mmplus creative Ⓒ sahitya agri corpora
3A Ⓓ Principals Pty Ltd. Ⓒ Principals 3B Ⓓ Idea Girl Design Ⓒ Earthborn 3C Ⓓ Voov Ltd. Ⓒ Zena beauty + med center 3D Ⓓ Plum Ⓒ Whitney Oaks Care Center
4A Ⓓ Nikita Lebedev 4B Ⓓ Willoughby Design Group Ⓒ Lavender & Sage 4C Ⓓ bryon hutchens | graphic design Ⓒ Wonder Tree Child Development Center(s) 4D Ⓓ DBDA Ⓒ Wiki Sym
5A Ⓓ Emu Design Studio Ⓒ The OtiumGroup 5B Ⓓ HELOHOLO Ⓒ Octava Capital 5C Ⓓ Nectar Graphics Ⓒ Deer Haven Farms B&B 5D Ⓓ VANESSA FOGEL DESIGN Ⓒ darling cellars

A B C D

1

2

3

4

5

Ⓓ = Design Firm Ⓒ = Client

1A Ⓓ HebelerGraphics Ⓒ The Corporate Mind 1B Ⓓ Rossignol & Associates Design Ⓒ Willowbank- School of Restoration Arts 1C Ⓓ Stitch Design Co. Ⓒ Schermer Pecans 1D Ⓓ Elixir Design Ⓒ From the Fields'
2A Ⓓ 3 Advertising, LLC Ⓒ Dixon's Apple Orchard 2B Ⓓ Graphic Moxie, Inc. 2C Ⓓ TheNames Ⓒ FMG 2D Ⓓ Sebastiany Branding & Design Ⓒ Fazenda Santa Helena
3A Ⓓ DOXA Ⓒ The Roan Group 3B Ⓓ Made By Thomas Ⓒ Spice Mountain 3C Ⓓ DOXA Ⓒ LifeSource, Inc. 3D Ⓓ Keith Russell Design Ⓒ Tacoma German Language School
4A Ⓓ instudio 4B Ⓓ Jerron Ames Ⓒ Arteis 4C Ⓓ Diann Cage Design Ⓒ Branch Communications 4D Ⓓ re:play
5A Ⓓ Marcos Calamato Ⓒ onetreeink 5B Ⓓ SANDIA, Inc. Ⓒ Timberline Tree Sprayings & Fertilizing 5C Ⓓ SANDIA, Inc. Ⓒ Timberline Tree Sprayings & Fertilizing 5D Ⓓ Siah Design Ⓒ Armadillo Christmas Bazaar

A	B	C	D	
				1
				2
				3
				4
				5

Ⓓ = Design Firm Ⓒ = Client

1A Ⓓ Gina Malsed Ⓒ Meals on Wheels of Boulder 1B Ⓓ Almosh82 Ⓒ Nature's Bliss 1C Ⓓ DOXA Ⓒ Orchard Park Capital 1D Ⓓ Miller Creative, LLC Ⓒ Olli Salumeria Americana
2A Ⓓ Jerron Ames Ⓒ Arteis 2B Ⓓ ARTENTIKO Ⓒ Pinetree Dental Centre 2C Ⓓ Tone Graphic Design Ⓒ Hamann Carpentry 2D Ⓓ One up
3A Ⓓ Coloryn Studio Ⓒ Honeyoaks 3B Ⓓ Brandon Winckler Design, Inc. Ⓒ Tim Carter Marketing 3C Ⓓ rizen creative co. Ⓒ Harvest Homes 3D Ⓓ The Brand Agency Ⓒ LandCorp
4A Ⓓ Anderson Mraz Design Ⓒ Entrada 4B Ⓓ Jerron Ames Ⓒ Green Path Garden Supply 4C Ⓓ Shay Isdale Design Ⓒ Heights Lumber and Supply - Harker Heights, Texas 4D Ⓓ R&R Partners Ⓒ Las Vegas Convention & Visitors Authority
5A Ⓓ Matchstic Ⓒ Kanakuk 5B Ⓓ Niedermeier Design Ⓒ Southern Utah Wilderness Alliance 5C Ⓓ Toledo Area Metroparks Ⓒ Metroparks of the Toledo Area 5D Ⓓ A.D. Creative Group Ⓒ DNC

A B C D

1

2

3

4

5

Ⓓ = Design Firm Ⓒ = Client

1A Ⓓ Conover Ⓒ Boulderscape, Inc. 1B Ⓓ Oxide Design Co. Ⓒ Josh Davies for Denver City Council 1C Ⓓ William Homan Design Ⓒ Big Sky on the Fly 1D Ⓓ Tran Creative Ⓒ Priest Lake Race
2A Ⓓ twentystar Ⓒ Cellular Recycler 2B Ⓓ moter 2C Ⓓ Strange Ideas 2D Ⓓ Larkef Ⓒ Develuper
3A Ⓓ entz creative Ⓒ FSI Energy Services, Inc. 3B Ⓓ deili Minsk Ⓒ Belarusian Oil Trading House 3C Ⓓ Wissam Shawkat Design Ⓒ Zee 3D Ⓓ Enter98 Ⓒ Hungarian Canoe Federation
4A Ⓓ Helix Design Communications Ⓒ Pristine Ponds 4B Ⓓ McGuire Design Ⓒ Crystal's Resort & Hospitality 4C Ⓓ Jerron Ames Ⓒ Arteis 4D Ⓓ Jerron Ames Ⓒ Marketsplash
5A Ⓓ Ryan Cooper Ⓒ Mindful Life 5B Ⓓ Blue Clover Ⓒ Rackspace Hosting 5C Ⓓ Schisla Design Studio Ⓒ America's Central Port 5D Ⓓ Alf Design Ⓒ Cloud Call

	A	B	C	D	
					1
					2
					3
					4
					5

Ⓓ = Design Firm Ⓒ = Client

1A Ⓓ AtelierLKS Ⓒ Land & Coastal Services 1B Ⓓ Brandburg Ⓒ Brandburg 1C Ⓓ Nikita Lebedev 1D Ⓓ Diseño Porfavor Ⓒ Fundación de apoyo a la juventud
2A Ⓓ Sol Consultores Ⓒ Terrafertil 2B Ⓓ Jerron Ames Ⓒ Arteis 2C Ⓓ Jodi Bearden Ⓒ Sunview 2D Ⓓ Johnson & Sekin Ⓒ stitches under the sun
3A Ⓓ United by Design Ⓒ Earthmedia 3B Ⓓ Sean Heisler Ⓒ New Sky Productions 3C Ⓓ Steve Cantrell Ⓒ New Earth Wood & Marketing 3D Ⓓ Type08 Ⓒ Eco Love Cafe
4A Ⓓ Jerron Ames Ⓒ Arteis 4B Ⓓ S2N Design Ⓒ Paper Moon Films 4C Ⓓ Logoworks by HP Ⓒ Magic by the Moon 4D Ⓓ Marina Rose Ⓒ Nysa
5A Ⓓ Paradox Box Ⓒ Brunen 5B Ⓓ Steve Cantrell Ⓒ Cancun Destinations 5C Ⓓ Sabingrafik, Inc. Ⓒ Civita 5D Ⓓ Sebastiany Branding & Design Ⓒ Boiaba

Casa dei Curiosi
Logo Design

Breno Bitencourt, Bauru, Brazil

Alessio Mosca is an acting teacher in Rome, Italy. In 2011, he founded Casa dei Curiosi, a school that provides adult classes in acting and theater. In order to reach a wider audience of potential students, Mosca wanted to build an online identity. He found the work of Sao Paulo–based designer Breno Bitencourt online and liked it. This is how a designer in Brazil came to breathe life into a theater school in Italy.

"Alessio is a big fan of Brazilian music, and I have my roots in Italian culture, so it was very easy to create a bond of friendship with him," explains Bitencourt. "Overall, I believe that this kind of relationship magnifies the work. It allows me to explore the client's needs with greater intensity and find material not only for inspiration, technique, and strategy, but also the feeling and emotion to develop the project."

Bitencourt was given the opportunity to design the identity from a blank slate, although Mosca did outline which attributes he wanted it to convey: quality, diversity, creativity, body language, freedom, movement, color, and emotion—all aspects of the practice of acting. The designer immersed himself in research for a few weeks, in the world of theater and performance. He wanted to understand what those abstract qualities of performance are—what exactly Mosca meant when he said "creativity, movement, and freedom"—which he could express through the logo.

Because the identity would appear primarily online, Bitencourt could play all he wanted with color gradations and tone; however, after the creation is complete he makes sure that what he has produced can still work in both black-and-white and one color. He followed a few different ideas for the logo, one of which entailed two geometric theater masks overlapping, one red and one blue.

The chosen route drew from Bitencourt's love of color and sinuous, organic lines. Making several drafts, he crafted the shape of a body with its leg up and arms outstretched so that it appears to be taking flight.

"If it's a real-life object you are drawing, then it would make sense to draw it with hard lines and a restricted color palette," admits Bitencourt. "I on the other hand love curves, variation in line, and experimentalism." The chosen design is as much about the abstract qualities of acting as it is a depiction of what a student at the school might physically do.

Designer and client selected the final logo together. It has a sensitivity that the other options do not have, and at the same time it says exactly what Mosca wanted to say. A body taking flight and releasing its creativity captures the essence of what Casa dei Curiosi is all about.

Breno Bitencourt's logo for the Casa dei Curiosi theater school is as much about the abstract qualities of acting as it is a depiction of what a student might physically do.

A B C D

LOGO SEARCH

Keywords: Shapes

Type: Symbol   All

1

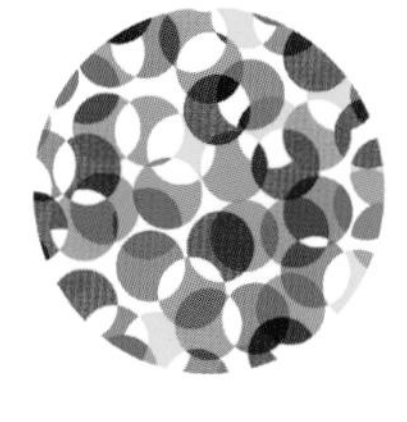

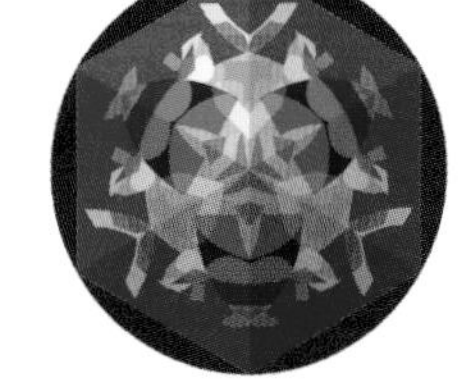

2

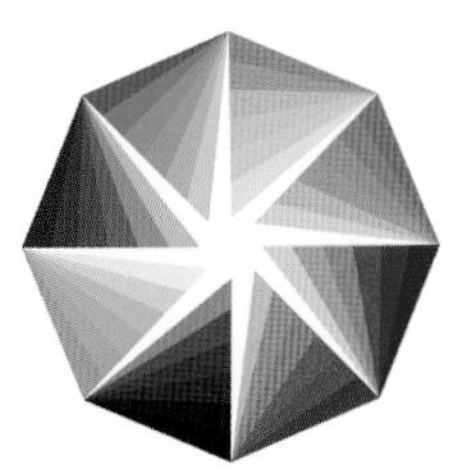

3

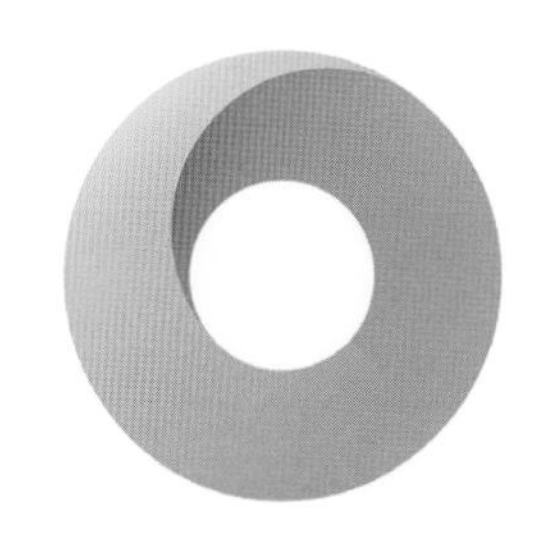

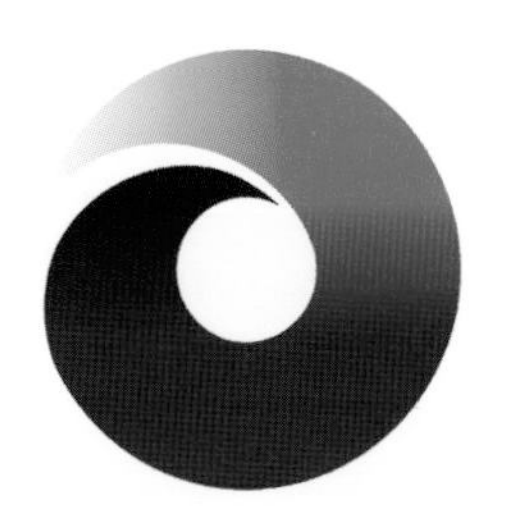

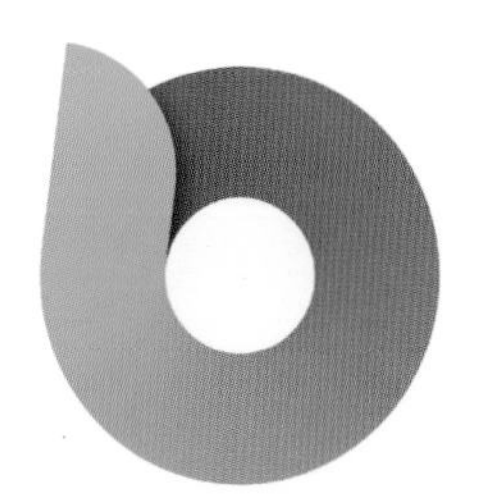

4

5

D = Design Firm C = Client

1C D TheNames C Sfera 1D D Sibley Peteet C CLS Partners

2A D Paraphernalia Design C Academy of Makeup 2B D Shay Isdale Design C AXON 2C D 36creative C Vibrant Villages 2D D Sol Consultores C Metrix Networks

3A D TD2 C SINED 3B D BrandBerry C Addrian 3C D artslinger C Courtney Lynn Photography 3D D Intrinsic Design C Center for Integrative Therapy

4A D Gardner Design C ReLive 4B D Hulsbosch C Woolworths Limited 4C D binocle C Bibliothèque Forum Meyrin 4D D Hulsbosch C Woolworths Limited

5A D demasijones C Aerosolar 5B D Bonsai Media C The BlueField Group 5C D Aldasbrand C Fidupais 5D D Corporate Movement C CorporateGroupBuy

	A	B	C	D
1		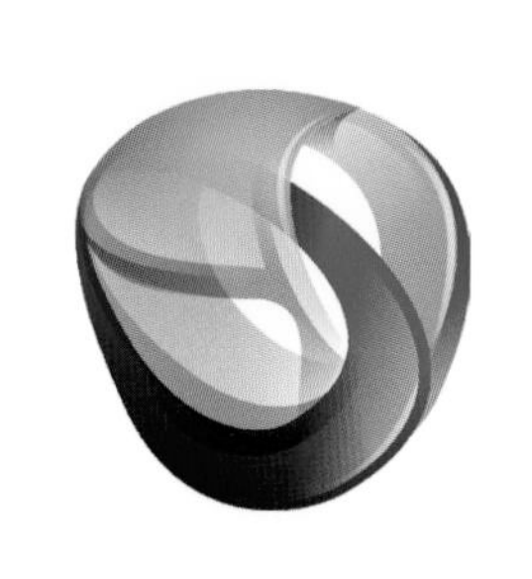		
2				
3				
4	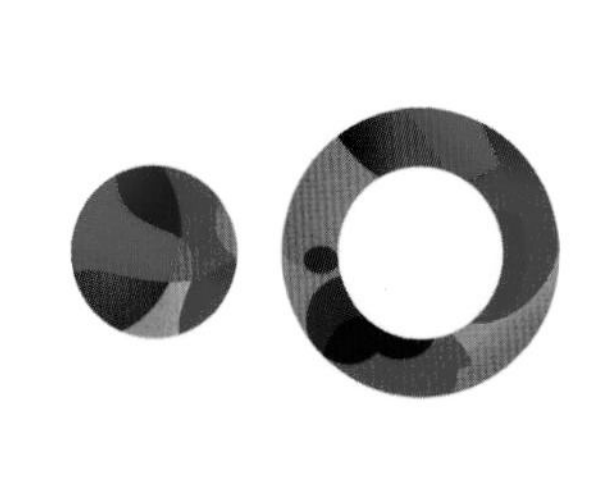			
5		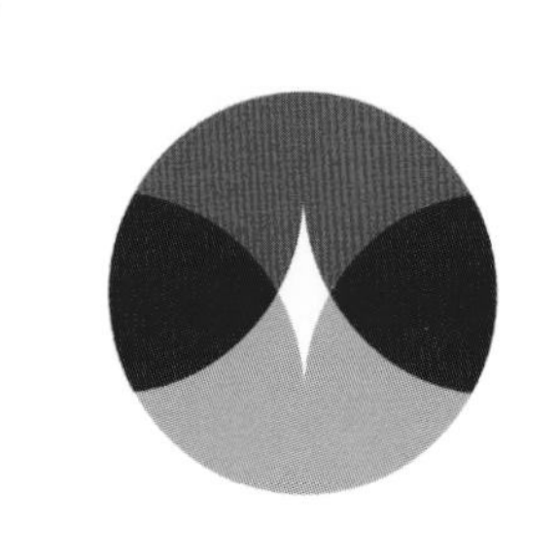		

Ⓓ = Design Firm Ⓒ = Client

1A Ⓓ Higher Ⓒ Voscast 1B Ⓓ stanovov Ⓒ seonika 1C Ⓓ Black Velvet Design Ⓒ Procter & Gamble Crailsheim 1D Ⓓ Visua Ⓒ Australian Paper
2A Ⓓ Travis Quam Ⓒ Energy Solutions 2B Ⓓ Art Machine 2C Ⓓ Kerry F. Williams Design Ⓒ Medtech 2D Ⓓ Anthony Lane Studios Ⓒ Muslim Philanthropy Network
3A Ⓓ Sol Consultores Ⓒ ARC 3B Ⓓ AtelierLKS Ⓒ Thrive 3C Ⓓ lumo 3D Ⓓ 903 Creative, LLC Ⓒ Richmond Residential Services, Inc.
4A Ⓓ Andrei Bilan 4B Ⓓ Arsenal Design, Inc. Ⓒ Aperature Optical Sciences 4C Ⓓ Bitencourt 4D Ⓓ Sunshinegun Ⓒ Oasis Group
5A Ⓓ XCLV / Superheroes Ⓒ NC:Group 5B Ⓓ Absolu communication marketing Ⓒ Corporation du Centre culturel de Drummondville 5C Ⓓ Just Creative Design Ⓒ Jacob Cass 5D Ⓓ Studio Z Ⓒ Max-Planck-Institut

	A	B	C	D	
			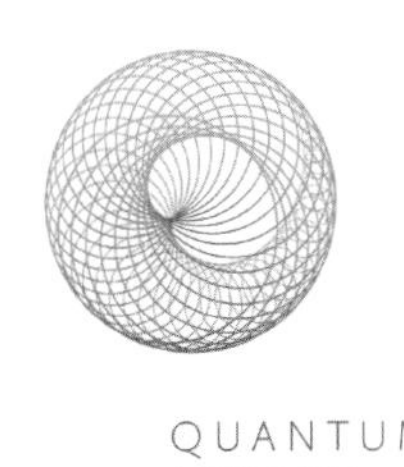		1
					2
					3
					4
					5

Ⓓ = Design Firm Ⓒ = Client

1A Ⓓ The Martin Group Ⓒ Global Fellowship 1B Ⓓ BlueBossa Design e Comunicação Ⓒ Supervisao Financeira 1C Ⓓ Hand dizajn studio Ⓒ Quantum Virtus 1D Ⓓ Petra Dietlein Ⓒ Cicle Tech 2A Ⓓ DOXA Ⓒ Walton Arts Center 2B Ⓓ Misign Visual Communication Ⓒ doloMitici 2C Ⓓ Sunday Lounge Ⓒ Moonstone Ventures, LLC 2D Ⓓ Hayes Image Ⓒ Eco Stock 3A Ⓓ Jolt Ⓒ Affinity Communication 3B Ⓓ Phanco Design Studio Ⓒ Mid India Christian Mission 3C Ⓓ Conyers Design, Inc. Ⓒ Orchestrate Hospitality 3D Ⓓ Type08 Ⓒ Naturvolt 4A Ⓓ M Jones Design Ⓒ Sustainable Business Incubator 4B Ⓓ Orn Smari | Design Ⓒ Menja 4C Ⓓ A3 Design Ⓒ International Business Council 4D Ⓓ Diagram Ⓒ Neinver Polska 5A Ⓓ Logoholik Ⓒ http://ethicalstudios.com 5B Ⓓ Graphic design studio by Yurko Gutsulyak Ⓒ Olena Zubkova 5C Ⓓ TheNames Ⓒ Transportnie sistemy 5D Ⓓ Almosh82 Ⓒ synka

	A	B	C	D
1				
2				
3		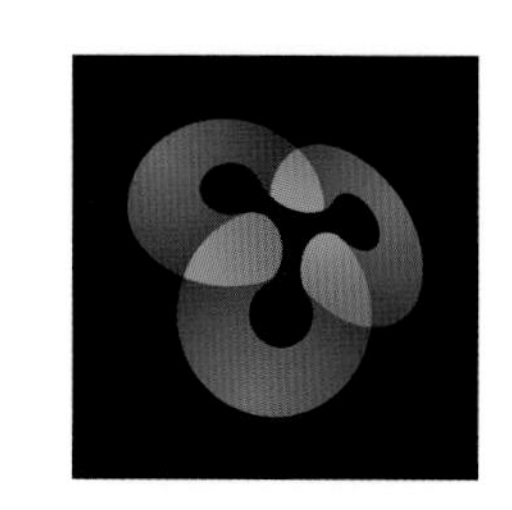		
4				
5			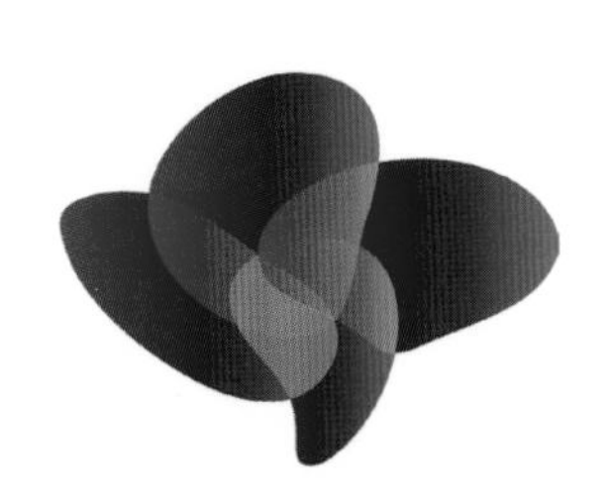	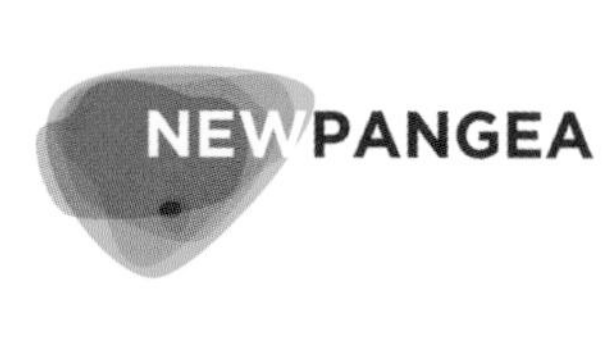

Ⓓ = Design Firm Ⓒ = Client

1A Ⓓ Indicate Design Groupe Ⓒ Summit Series 1B Ⓓ Larkef 1C Ⓓ Sebastiany Branding & Design Ⓒ Gellus 1D Ⓓ McGuire Design Ⓒ Crystal's Resort & Hospitality
2A Ⓓ Willoughby Design Group Ⓒ Cerner 2B Ⓓ Cubic Ⓒ Tulsa Performing Arts Center 2C Ⓓ BBMG Ⓒ The Jewish Education Project 2D Ⓓ BHAGdesign Ⓒ Infinites Music Corp
3A Ⓓ Jan Vranovsky Ⓒ Visualscream 3B Ⓓ Almosh82 3C Ⓓ BrandBerry Ⓒ Artive 3D Ⓓ stanovov
4A Ⓓ FLOVEY Ⓒ Himpunan Kimia Indonesia 4B Ⓓ ZEBRA design branding Ⓒ Faza 4C Ⓓ Burocratik Design Ⓒ MEDISIMLAB 4D Ⓓ Envision Creative Group Ⓒ Mobile Health
5A Ⓓ Liquid Agency Ⓒ Amyris 5B Ⓓ Firestarter Ⓒ Printman 5C Ⓓ FMedia Studios Ⓒ MediaMarkt 5D Ⓓ jsDesignCo. Ⓒ GSW - program ID

A	B	C	D	
			 	1
				2
				3
			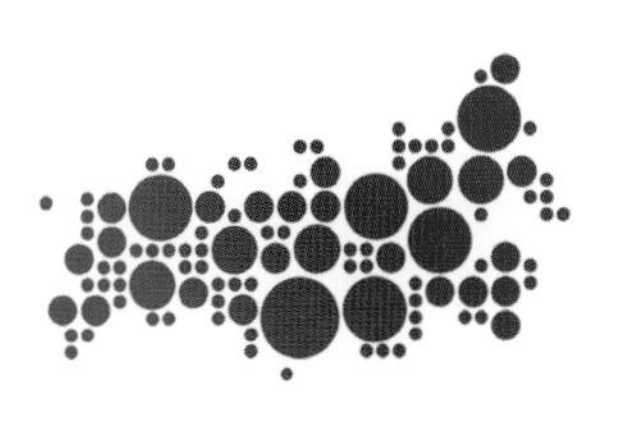	4
				5

Ⓓ = Design Firm Ⓒ = Client

1A Ⓓ RedEffect 1B Ⓓ Sabet Ⓒ Change Pals 1C Ⓓ Momentum 18 Ⓒ Laing Dermatology & Skin Cancer Center 1D Ⓓ Creative Squall Ⓒ Inspirus/Diamond H
2A Ⓓ RJ Thompson Ⓒ Flavor Spark 2B Ⓓ Matto Ⓒ FotoSkrydis.lt 2C Ⓓ Marketing with a Flair Ⓒ Serene Dental 2D Ⓓ Karl Design Vienna Ⓒ Bertha Benz Challenge
3A Ⓓ Vox One Ⓒ Green Ground Transport 3B Ⓓ Croak Design Ⓒ Expertprint 3C Ⓓ Gizwiz Studio Ⓒ Network Control 3D Ⓓ Brandburg Ⓒ Suniberia Travel
4A Ⓓ BrandBerry Ⓒ Inward Shores Media 4B Ⓓ BrandBerry Ⓒ Idealogy 4C Ⓓ HELOHOLO Ⓒ Yedynka 4D Ⓓ notamedia Ⓒ Ministry of Regional Development of the Russian Federation
5A Ⓓ Kneadle, Inc. Ⓒ Mukumu 5B Ⓓ Jerron Ames Ⓒ Tom & Jerron 5C Ⓓ Range Ⓒ Oregon Surf 5D Ⓓ Logo Design Works Ⓒ Australian Oceanographics

	A	B	C	D
1				
2				
3				
4				
5		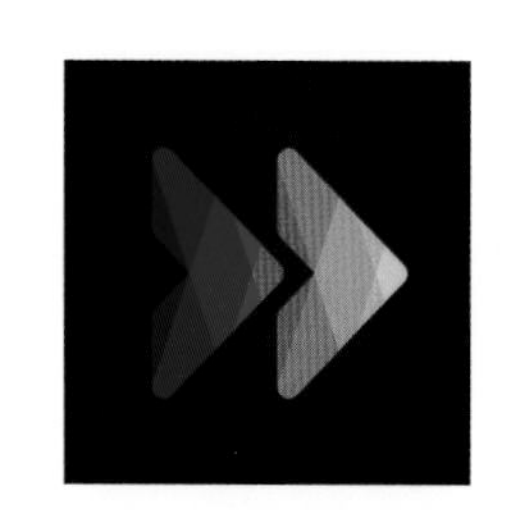		

Ⓓ = Design Firm Ⓒ = Client

1A Ⓓ Alexander Wende Ⓒ xinfini 1B Ⓓ Absolu communication marketing Ⓒ Arc de vie - docteurs en chiropratique 1C Ⓓ Type08 Ⓒ Concrete Fab 1D Ⓓ Rise Design Branding Inc. Ⓒ Lushine Foods 2A Ⓓ Dept of Energy Ⓒ Spiral 9 2B Ⓓ SANDIA, Inc. Ⓒ Spectware 2C Ⓓ CSK Stategic Marketing Group, Inc. Ⓒ Focus on the Family 2D Ⓓ Handoko Tjung Design Ⓒ MARC 3A Ⓓ The BrandingHouse Ⓒ Summit Search Solutions 3B Ⓓ A Ginger Snaps 3C Ⓓ Red Thinking Ⓒ NVFS 3D Ⓓ Vladimir Isaev Ⓒ Telecom Trade company 4A Ⓓ Kommunikat Ⓒ CCA 4B Ⓓ Jeremy Slagle Design Ⓒ Kinetic Climbing Gym 4C Ⓓ Gizwiz Studio Ⓒ Seven Harvest International 4D Ⓓ Damian Dominguez Ⓒ T. B. Group 5A Ⓓ Sebastiany Branding & Design Ⓒ PepsiCo 5B Ⓓ BlueBossa Design e Comunicação Ⓒ Leggero Email Marketing 5C Ⓓ Interbrand Sampson Group Ⓒ Commercial Bank of Africa 5D Ⓓ Benedict Sato Design Ⓒ Australian Petroleum Industry Contractors and Suppliers Association

A	B	C	D	
				1
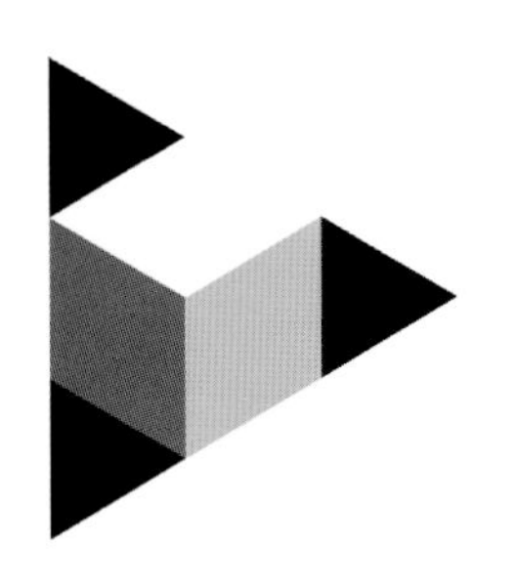				2
				3
				4
	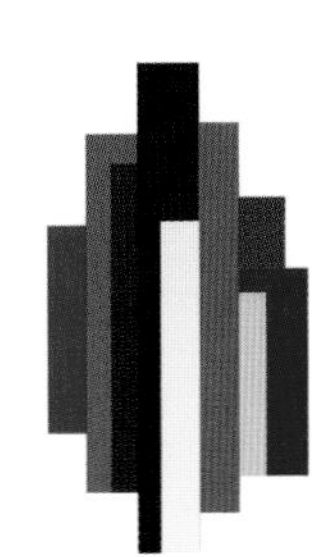			5

Ⓓ = Design Firm Ⓒ = Client

1A Ⓓ Sabet Ⓒ Walmart 1B Ⓓ Steve Kelly Design Ⓒ Acumen Advertising 1C Ⓓ Made By Thomas Ⓒ Spice Mountain 1D Ⓓ Sean Heisler Ⓒ Katapult Design
2A Ⓓ Gardner Design Ⓒ D Construction 2B Ⓓ Molly Eckler Graphic Arts Ⓒ Bio-Remediation Int'l 2C Ⓓ Yury Akulin | Logodiver Ⓒ Goal4Life 2D Ⓓ Yury Akulin | Logodiver Ⓒ Goal4Life
3A Ⓓ Logoworks by HP Ⓒ Camden Central Mosque & Communities Centre 3B Ⓓ Hulsbosch Ⓒ Woolworths Limited 3C Ⓓ Fernandez Design Ⓒ Wheatman Insurance 3D Ⓓ Greteman Group Ⓒ Wichita Area Technical College
4A Ⓓ Zther Design Studio 4B Ⓓ Mattson Creative Ⓒ El Montecito School 4C Ⓓ The Infantree Ⓒ The Infantree 4D Ⓓ HELOHOLO Ⓒ Octava Capital
5A Ⓓ Creative Suitcase Ⓒ KUT Radio 5B Ⓓ Communication Agency Ⓒ Property magazine 5C Ⓓ Diagram Ⓒ Deptak Projekt P2 5D Ⓓ The Pink Pear Design Company Ⓒ My Arts Kansas City

A B C D

1

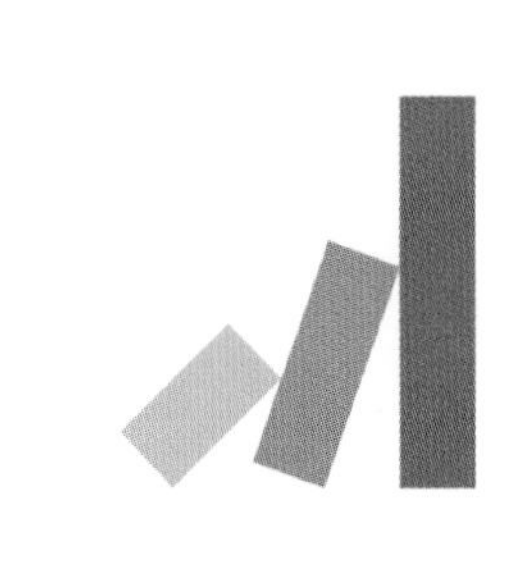

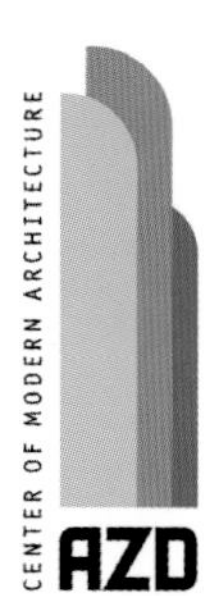

2

3

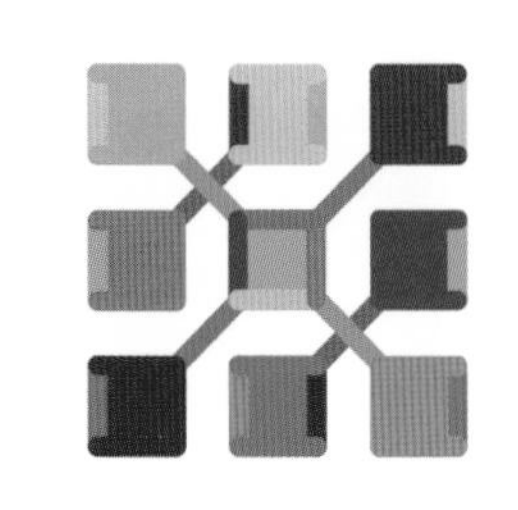

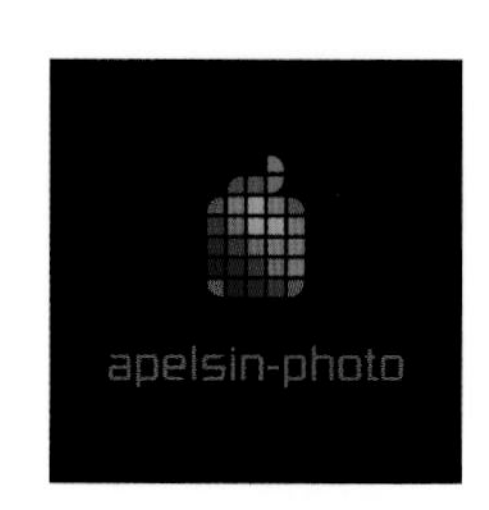

4

5

Ⓓ = Design Firm Ⓒ = Client

1A Ⓓ Eggra Ⓒ Shtepia Botuese Shkupi 1B Ⓓ Mission Minded Ⓒ OneJustice 1C Ⓓ Akhmatov Studio Ⓒ AZD-Centre of Modern Architecture 1D Ⓓ Type08 Ⓒ Iconik
2A Ⓓ Denis Aristov Ⓒ The government of Perm region 2B Ⓓ entz creative Ⓒ Flick Studios 2C Ⓓ Hollis Brand Culture Ⓒ Formulatin PR 2D Ⓓ Schisla Design Studio Ⓒ Tempest Med
3A Ⓓ Communication Agency Ⓒ Baza 3B Ⓓ Rise Design Branding, Inc. Ⓒ Deeko Convenience store 3C Ⓓ Longshot Creatifs Ⓒ DOHPE 3D Ⓓ Nikita Lebedev
4A Ⓓ Alexander Wende Ⓒ SimPlus.com 4B Ⓓ BBDO NY Ⓒ Gender Equality Project 4C Ⓓ Innereactive Media Ⓒ Amplify 4D Ⓓ Indicate Design Groupe Ⓒ ARCA
5A Ⓓ Pear Design Ⓒ Icon Building Group 5B Ⓓ Absolu communication marketing Ⓒ Lortie construction 5C Ⓓ estudiotres Ⓒ Stage Equity Partners 5D Ⓓ Infinite Scale Design Group Ⓒ Utah Center for Architecture

A B C D

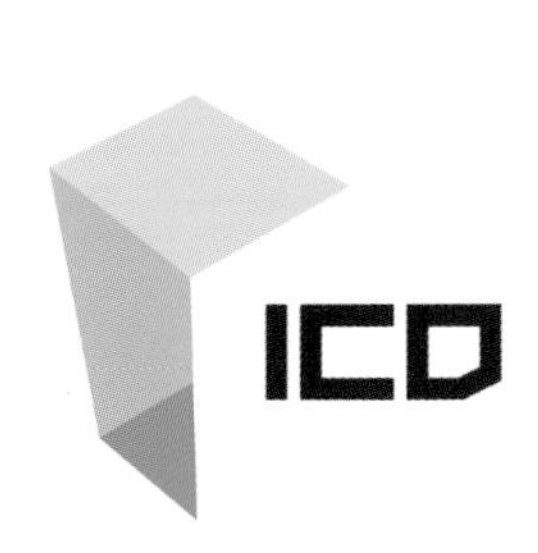

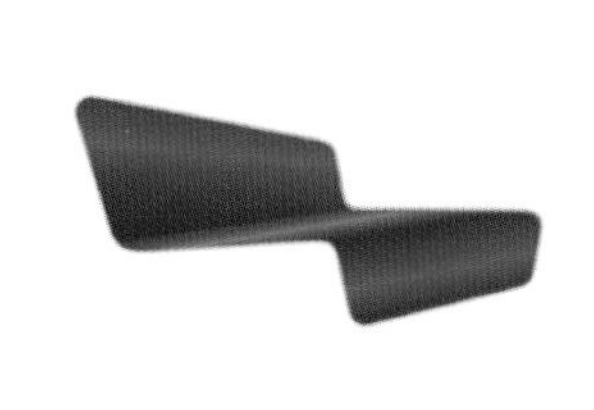

1

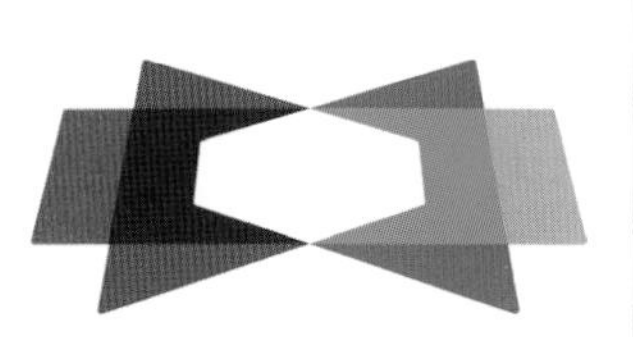

2

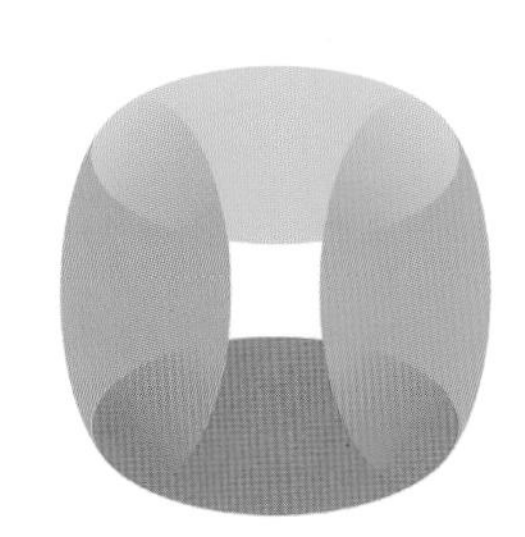

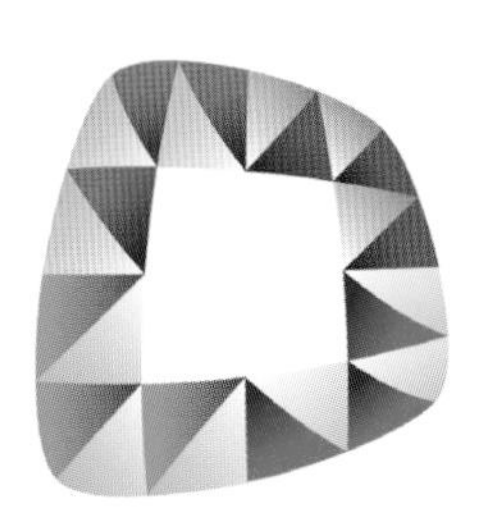

3

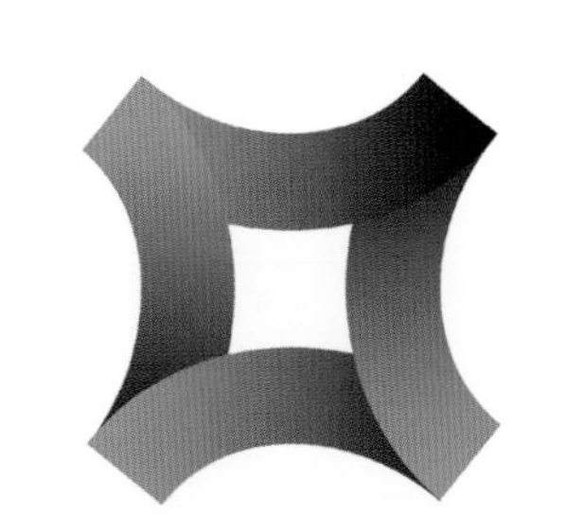

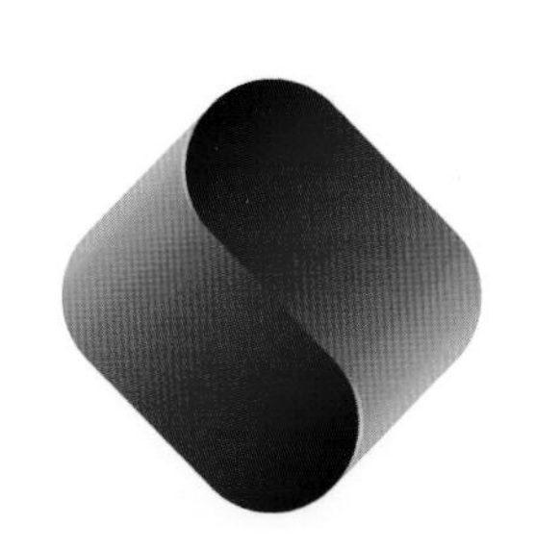

4

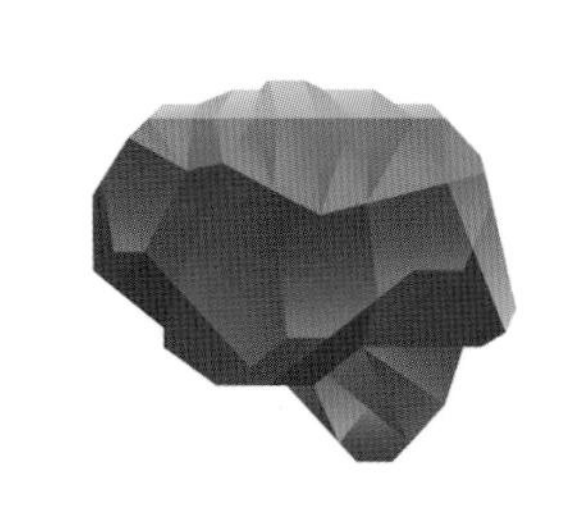

5

Ⓓ = Design Firm Ⓒ = Client

1A Ⓓ Extension Ⓒ Innovative Construction & Development 1B Ⓓ Hollis Brand Culture Ⓒ Eat. Drink. Sleep. 1C Ⓓ stan can design Ⓒ Design Matters 1D Ⓓ koxa design Ⓒ Face Decor
2A Ⓓ TPG Architecture 2B Ⓓ Tema Semenov Ⓒ Inform Security 2C Ⓓ Tema Semenov Ⓒ Inform Security 2D Ⓓ Gardner Design Ⓒ LEDA Alliance
3A Ⓓ Communication Agency Ⓒ Ferratum bank 3B Ⓓ RedEffect Ⓒ ScreenVu 3C Ⓓ Communication Agency Ⓒ Volume Media 3D Ⓓ Logoholik Ⓒ vibrantdrive.com
4A Ⓓ Qing Li Design Ⓒ Morgan Lewis 4B Ⓓ Makespace 4C Ⓓ Axiom Design Partners Ⓒ Resource Development Group 4D Ⓓ Floris Design Ⓒ SHM Language Services
5A Ⓓ Elua Ⓒ Braincode 5B Ⓓ Meir Billet Ltd. Ⓒ Dani Hakim Agency 5C Ⓓ re:play Ⓒ American Council for the Blind Ohio 5D Ⓓ Brandient Ⓒ Patria Credit

Menu Cover Depot
Identity Design

Jacob Cass, Just Creative Design, New York City, New York

The online company Menu Cover Depot provides a one-stop source where restaurants around the world can shop for, customize, and purchase their menu covers. But like any startup, at first the business did not have a name. Jacob Cass, the founder of Just Creative Design in New York (he hails originally from Sydney, Australia) worked with the company to design its brand identity from the ground up.

The first step was to settle on a company and domain name that was self-explanatory as well as functional on an international level, while still standing out among competitors like MenuCoverman.com and TheMenuShop.com, to name only two. They came upon Menu Cover Depot, which also worked well as a URL, and deciding this was the right route, the design process could begin.

"Because the brand's positioning called for a rather generic name, we decided we needed a unique, strong, memorable mark to help the business project itself," says Cass.

There were important guidelines to follow: The logo had to work both online and in print, and in both environments convey trust, friendliness, quality, and strength. The brand's position was neither "discount depot" nor was it high end, so they had to steer clear of looking cheap or luxurious. After many explorations and revisions, the concept of an *M* mark was chosen and then refined. The circle head floats just high enough above it so that the mark can also be read as a menu.

Color was key to the identity because of the need for both simplicity and recognizability. Cass scoured dozens of competitive examples from the restaurant-supply industry then narrowed the choice down to just a few combinations, using them in context to see how well they worked together. "The dark red proved to be the most successful as it is robust without screaming for too much attention," says Cass. "It is also an industry classic."

In selecting the typeface, Cass's strategy was to sample different fonts in application. Which one did the best job of appearing clear and simple while still reminding viewers of the very human act of ordering from a restaurant? After many trials, the team settled on Proxima Nova for its clean, geometric feel and humanistic proportions.

Menu Cover Depot, complete with brand name and logo, launched in early 2012.

Jacob Cass's logo design for Menu Cover Depot works online and in print, and conveys both friendliness and strength in each environment.

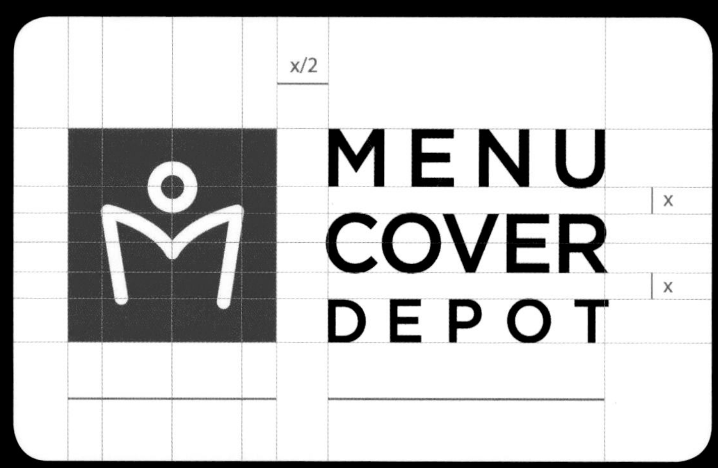

The eventual solution took some detailed kerning of the stacked name to align the letters and give them breathing room, as in the mark itself.

	A	B	C	D	
	LOGO SEARCH Keywords: Symbols Type: ◯ Symbol ◯ Typographic ◯ Combo ◉ All  				1
	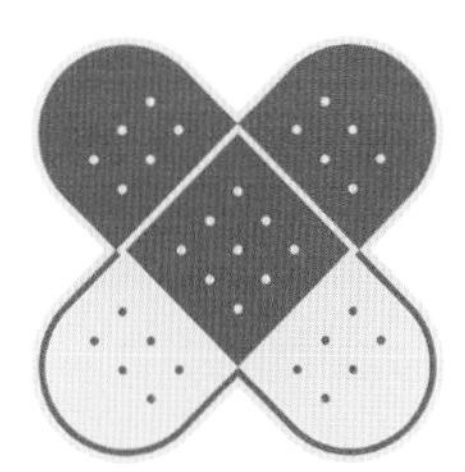				2
					3
					4
					5

Ⓓ = Design Firm Ⓒ = Client

1C Ⓓ jsDesignCo. Ⓒ Japan relief efforts 1D Ⓓ TBWA\Chiat\Day
2A Ⓓ 3 Advertising, LLC Ⓒ New Day New Mexico 2B Ⓓ Lowercase a: Design Studio Ⓒ Fight Plaque Give Back 2C Ⓓ Gardner Design Ⓒ EmberHope 2D Ⓓ Gardner Design Ⓒ EmberHope
3A Ⓓ Device Ⓒ Vital 3B Ⓓ Studio Rayolux Ⓒ LifeCenter Northwest 3C Ⓓ Akhmatov Studio Ⓒ ZhanMedClinic 3D Ⓓ Sputnik Design Partners, Inc. Ⓒ YMCA Canada
4A Ⓓ Higher Ⓒ Somatic Vision 4B Ⓓ Pretty Pollution Ⓒ iheartu 4C Ⓓ Strange Ideas 4D Ⓓ Traction Ⓒ S.H.A.R.E.
5A Ⓓ Akhmatov Studio Ⓒ Happynest.kz 5B Ⓓ TheNames Ⓒ Tvoya Para 5C Ⓓ Erwin Bindeman Ⓒ Jonathan Endersby 5D Ⓓ Brittany Phillips Design Ⓒ Fayetteville Public Library

	A	B	C	D
1				
2				
3				
4				
5	 			

Ⓓ = Design Firm Ⓒ = Client

1A Ⓓ Kuznetsov Evgeniy | KUZNETS Ⓒ My book 1B Ⓓ Strange Ideas 1C Ⓓ Samuel Nunez Design Ⓒ Bedside books 1D Ⓓ O'Hare Design Ⓒ WYSO Public Radio
2A Ⓓ Just Creative Design Ⓒ Menu Cover Depot 2B Ⓓ CAPSULE Ⓒ Read Indeed 2C Ⓓ Sean Heisler Ⓒ Ezra Millstein 2D Ⓓ Wall-to-Wall Studios Ⓒ Grow Pittsburgh 3B Ⓓ rjd creative Ⓒ American Modular 3C Ⓓ Joseph Blalock Ⓒ Raising Texas 3D Ⓓ Red Rooster Group Ⓒ America-Israel Chamber of Commerce
4A Ⓓ Murillo Design, Inc. Ⓒ KGB Texas 4B Ⓓ Hulsbosch Ⓒ Caltex Australia 4C Ⓓ Jerron Ames Ⓒ Arteis 4D Ⓓ Ninet6 Ltd.
5A Ⓓ Logorado 5B Ⓓ Pinkerton Design Ⓒ Texas Prime Cleaners 5C Ⓓ The Joe Bosack Graphic Design Co. Ⓒ Souther Stars Youth Hockey 5D Ⓓ Insight Design Ⓒ Our Gifted Kids

	A	B	C	D	
	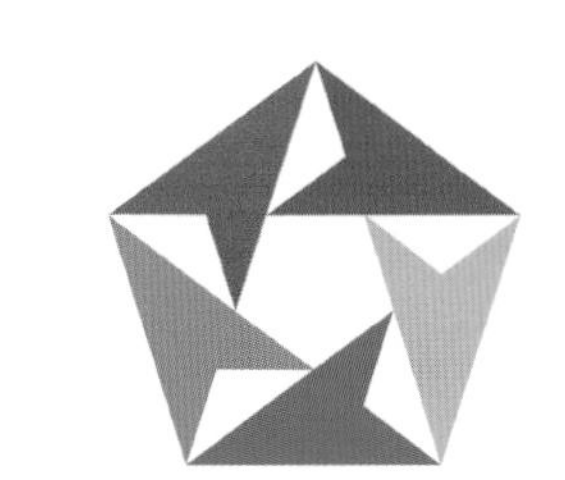			 	1
					2
					3
					4
					5

Ⓓ = Design Firm Ⓒ = Client

1A Ⓓ BFive branding & identity Ⓒ Kuznetsov 1B Ⓓ alekchmura.com Ⓒ StudioMC2 1C Ⓓ Karl Design Vienna Ⓒ Braunhofer Visions 1D Ⓓ Gardner Design Ⓒ WFI
2A Ⓓ Gardner Design Ⓒ ReLive 2B Ⓓ Gardner Design Ⓒ EmberHope 2C Ⓓ Howerton+White Ⓒ Viega 2D Ⓓ Kuznetsov Evgeniy I KUZNETS Ⓒ Ots
3A Ⓓ Fixation Marketing Ⓒ Lutheran World Relief 3B Ⓓ R&R Partners Ⓒ Envision EMI 3C Ⓓ Alf Design Ⓒ Fire Armor 3D Ⓓ Church Logo Gallery
4A Ⓓ Sean Heisler Ⓒ Conceptual Exploration 4B Ⓓ Double A Creative Ⓒ Christian Carpentry 4C Ⓓ TD2 Ⓒ SINED 4D Ⓓ Dickerson Ⓒ Healing Touch
5A Ⓓ Sean Heisler Ⓒ iPracticeMD 5B Ⓓ Bitencourt 5C Ⓓ Lodge Design Ⓒ Re 5D Ⓓ Rocket Science Ⓒ Rocket Science

A B C D

1

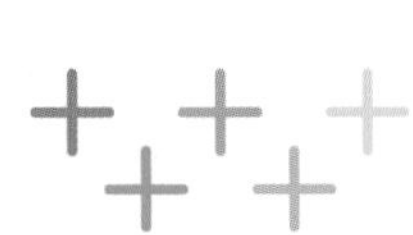

2

UBQ360 ™

3

4

5

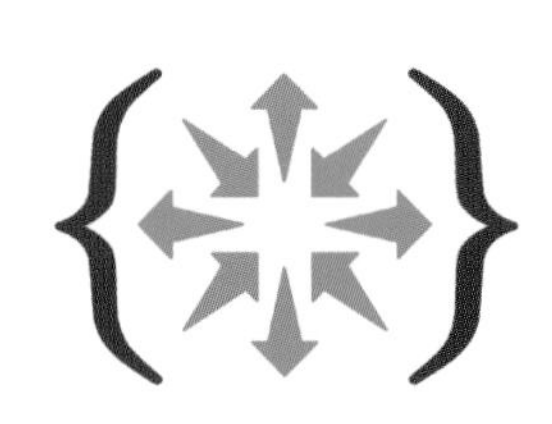

Ⓓ = Design Firm Ⓒ = Client

1A Ⓓ Anthony Lane Studios Ⓒ Webadelic 1B Ⓓ Glitschka Studios Ⓒ Northwest Church 1C Ⓓ Maks Shvahin [Polar] 1D Ⓓ Sarah Petty
2A Ⓓ Sunday Lounge Ⓒ Ubiquity Group 2B Ⓓ Studio Ink Ⓒ Chalk and Talk 2C Ⓓ Dickerson 2D Ⓓ Chicken Leg Studio Ⓒ Secure Risk Solutions
3A Ⓓ entz creative Ⓒ Ideonomia 3B Ⓓ FLOVEY Ⓒ Meet Sheet 3C Ⓓ Rise Design Branding, Inc. Ⓒ Tagschools Canada 3D Ⓓ Tema Semenov Ⓒ Profilink
4A Ⓓ TheNames Ⓒ Exio 4B Ⓓ TypeOrange Ⓒ Furrs Communications 4C Ⓓ Lockheed Martin Ⓒ Lockheed Martin 4D Ⓓ Webcore Design Ⓒ ClickPlant
5A Ⓓ Riza Cankaya Ⓒ Murat Muzaffer 5B Ⓓ Karl Design Vienna Ⓒ Karl Design Vienna 5C Ⓓ Gerren Lamson Ⓒ Counterpoint Consulting 5D Ⓓ Denis Aristov Ⓒ The government of Perm region

Institute of Scientific Animal Communication (ISAC) Identity Design

Dragon Rouge China, Hong Kong

ISAC (Institute of Scientific Animal Communication) is an organization that contributes scientific research to the field of animal communication in the pursuit of building harmonious relationships between animals and their human families. It offers pet owners services they are unlikely to find anywhere else, such as animal consultations and communication courses.

A modern-day Dr. Dolittle, ISAC's founder, animal communicator Thomas Cheng, "talks" to all sorts of animals through telepathy. "It is the instinctive language that all animals, including mankind, are born with but gradually forget as urban lives involve more and more verbal communication," says Cheng.

When it came time to create a brand identity for the organization, however, Cheng needed to use more than telepathy. He hired Dragon Rouge China to design a logo and identity system that conveyed the practical as well as esoteric qualities of the services he provides.

Says Belinda Lau, creative director, "When we first discussed this project with the client, we thought, what an amazing idea, but isn't it just too 'good' to be true?" The team studied Cheng's book, website, press, and volunteering case studies. "Despite what some might call the myth of telepathy, what we could clearly see was a person who devotes himself to animal caring and delivers a message of respecting animals in daily urban life."

Dragon Rouge mapped out the core value and commitment of ISAC as the basis of its identity development. The challenge was to highlight ISAC as a scientific and professional institution while also conveying the natural, instinctual mind connection between animals and human beings. The team decided the identity had to be about language barriers and cultivating a sense of animals' understanding and heart. Themes of "togetherness" and "sharing" rose to the top of a list of key elements.

The solution emerged from a circular layout, solid in shape and delicate in its look and feel. A heart shape anchors ISAC's mission of trust and understanding in the design, extending fine lines—branches, veins, symbolic lines of communication—that meet a white dot at the point of the brain in each animal outline.

The logo Dragon Rouge China designed for the Institute of Scientific Animal Communication in Hong Kong plays with the color effects of overlapping animal forms to express the brand's message of embracing and respecting animals.

A palette of earthy, natural tones—lilac, sky blue, turquoise, navy, brown, and orange—add friendliness and subtlety. The team reworked the color scheme many times, adjusting each shade until it was just right. The combination had to be lively and attention grabbing, yet modest at the same time. The solution plays with the effects of overlapping the animal shapes, which also expresses the brand's message of embracing and respecting animals.

The logo has been applied to the ISAC Hong Kong website, the organization's Facebook page, and its business card design. It illustrates what ISAC is all about: connecting animals and humans in a decent and direct way.

A B C D

1

LOGO SEARCH

Keywords: Arts

Type: ◯ Symbol ◯ Typographic ◯ Combo ◉ All

2

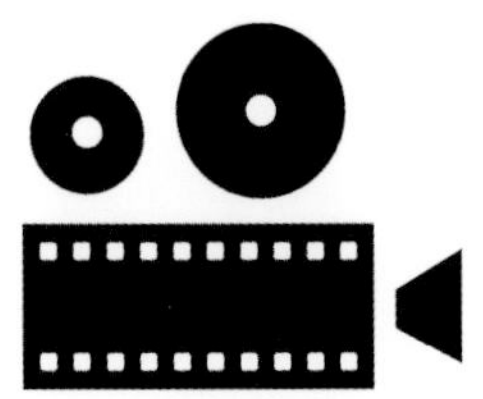

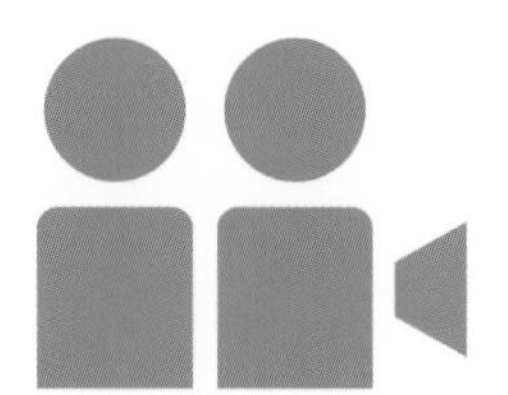

3

4

5

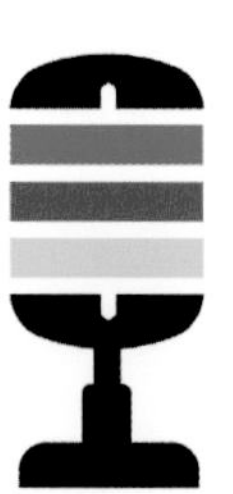

Ⓓ = Design Firm Ⓒ = Client

1C Ⓓ Design Nut Ⓒ Reel Affirmations Film Festival 1D Ⓓ Kuznetsov Evgeniy | KUZNETS Ⓒ sarafan media
2A Ⓓ Communication Agency Ⓒ Bioskop 2B Ⓓ Double A Creative Ⓒ Codecs.com 2C Ⓓ Siah Design Ⓒ Joseph Hobbs 2D Ⓓ Type08 Ⓒ Cake Film
3A Ⓓ Yury Akulin | Logodiver Ⓒ Viva Art 3B Ⓓ Swanson Russell Ⓒ Great Plains Regional Medical Center 3C Ⓓ Mattson Creative 3D Ⓓ Jordahl Design Ⓒ Video Traffic Masters
4A Ⓓ 01d Ⓒ HotLab 4B Ⓓ Anthony Lane Studios Ⓒ Kellie Rae Photography 4C Ⓓ Oronoz Brandesign Ⓒ Xitle 4D Ⓓ Cubo Ⓒ Gobierno de Aragon
5A Ⓓ R&R Partners Ⓒ Valley Metro 5B Ⓓ Tim Frame Design Ⓒ REDCAST 5C Ⓓ Gyula Nemeth Ⓒ Cloud Deck 5D Ⓓ McGuire Design Ⓒ Ink Talk Radio

A B C D

1

2

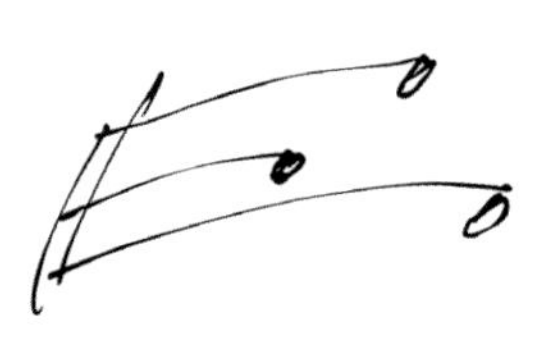

3

4

5

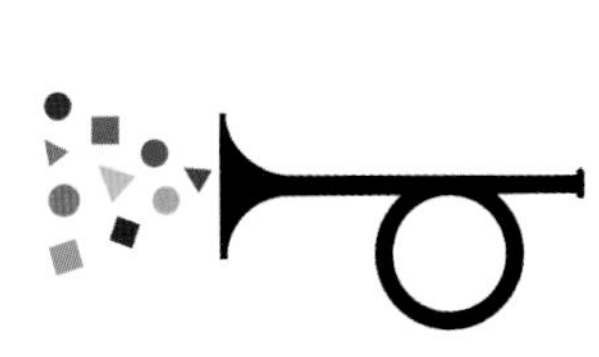

Ⓓ = Design Firm Ⓒ = Client

1A Ⓓ Alphabet Arm Design Ⓒ Adam Levy 1B Ⓓ Josue Zapata Ⓒ Bobby Duran 1C Ⓓ The Brand Agency Ⓒ Perth Zoo 1D Ⓓ Ikola designs... Ⓒ Don G Lee & Associates
2A Ⓓ lumo 2B Ⓓ DBDA Ⓒ Smellslikepop.com 2C Ⓓ Michael Lashford Design Ⓒ Beans For Bands 2D Ⓓ Headshot brand development Ⓒ eva
3A Ⓓ fuszion Ⓒ Wolf Trap Foundation for the Performing Arts 3B Ⓓ angryporcupine*design Ⓒ School of Rock Foundation 3C Ⓓ Gardner Design Ⓒ Pauline Reese & Blake Behrns 3D Ⓓ Niedermeier Design Ⓒ fivefreesongs.com
4A Ⓓ Gardner Design Ⓒ Pauline Reese, Blake Behrns 4B Ⓓ Chris Rooney Illustration/Design Ⓒ MOG 4C Ⓓ Schwartzrock Graphic Arts Ⓒ Hawley High School 4D Ⓓ lumo
5A Ⓓ TheNames Ⓒ Ohotnik 5B Ⓓ Lienhart Design Ⓒ Trumpet Social Media 5C Ⓓ DL Creative Ⓒ Cheltenham Township 5D Ⓓ Zande+Newman Design Ⓒ Bike Easy

A B C D

1

2

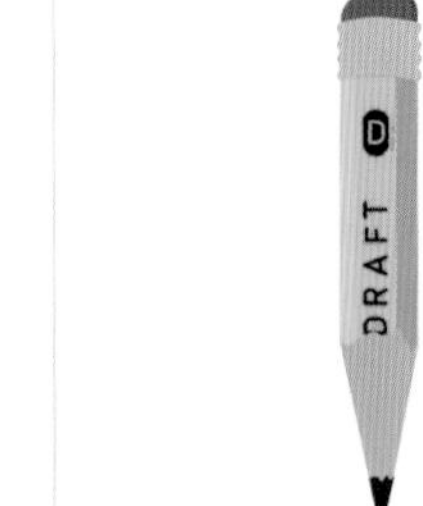

3

4

5

Ⓓ = Design Firm Ⓒ = Client

1A Ⓓ TOKY Branding+Design Ⓒ Opera Theatre of Saint Louis 1B Ⓓ Jerron Ames 1C Ⓓ Jon Flaming Design Ⓒ KERA/National Public Radio Radio 1D Ⓓ Range Ⓒ Highland Park Cafeteria
2A Ⓓ reaves design Ⓒ inkd 2B Ⓓ DOXA Ⓒ Wordbuilders 2C Ⓓ Emilio Correa Ⓒ Arteis 2D Ⓓ Sean Heisler Ⓒ Sean Heisler
3A Ⓓ Jan Vranovsky Ⓒ Homework Paradise 3B Ⓓ Matto Ⓒ mgdes.com 3C Ⓓ Swink Ⓒ Threadian 3D Ⓓ Hole in the Roof Ⓒ yarnivore
4A Ⓓ Vistaprint 4B Ⓓ Marjoram Creative Ⓒ Palmetto Threads 4C Ⓓ Logo Design Works Ⓒ Hand Pick 4D Ⓓ Matto
5A Ⓓ Brandburg Ⓒ Double Brand / MTP 5B Ⓓ Marchhouse design Ⓒ Hall interiors 5C Ⓓ Alescar Ortiz Ⓒ 3D, Design and Digital Development 5D Ⓓ bigoodis Ⓒ Difference design

A B C D

LOGO SEARCH

Keywords: Miscellaneous

Type: Symbol Typographic Combo All

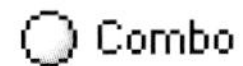

1

FISHERMANHAT
productions

PERCIVAL
PRINT & PACKAGING

KING CHEMICAL

2

DISCOVER

3

4

5

Ⓓ = Design Firm Ⓒ = Client

1C Ⓓ Sally Says Ⓒ Sweet and Sexy Food Co. 1D Ⓓ POLLARDdesign Ⓒ Kill Pillow
2A Ⓓ Double A Creative Ⓒ Fisherman Hat Productions 2B Ⓓ Dessein Ⓒ Percival Print and Packaging 2C Ⓓ Karl Design Vienna Ⓒ Karl Design Vienna 2D Ⓓ Visual Lure, LLC Ⓒ King Chemical
3A Ⓓ RDQLUS Creative Ⓒ Expeditiously Delicious 3B Ⓓ Strange Ideas 3C Ⓓ Rick Carlson Design & Illustration 3D Ⓓ Double A Creative Ⓒ Goeni Eyewear
4A Ⓓ Matto 4B Ⓓ Matto 4C Ⓓ Swanson Russell Ⓒ Nebraska Children's Home Society 4D Ⓓ Damian Dominguez Ⓒ AVON PRODUCTS
5A Ⓓ 01d Ⓒ The Science of Sleep 5B Ⓓ Studio Ink Ⓒ Sweetlabs 5C Ⓓ Muhina Design Ⓒ Rost school of managers 5D Ⓓ Strange Ideas

A B C D

1

2

3

4

5

Ⓓ = Design Firm Ⓒ = Client

1A Ⓓ Oscar Morris Ⓒ Texas Department of Agriculture 1B Ⓓ Virginia Patterson Design Ⓒ Small Electric Appliance Museum 1C Ⓓ EAT Advertising and Design, Inc. Ⓒ Christal Highland 1D Ⓓ Gardner Design Ⓒ Target
2A Ⓓ Oscar Morris Ⓒ The City of Austin 2B Ⓓ Hayes Image Ⓒ Infoxicated Promotions 2C Ⓓ Type08 Ⓒ Buffalo Web Design 2D Ⓓ Mindgruve Ⓒ A Dog's Life Pet Resort
3A Ⓓ Hirschmann Design Ⓒ Bonnie Parsons 3B Ⓓ lumo 3C Ⓓ Riggs Partners Ⓒ Tree, LLC 3D Ⓓ Gardner Design
4A Ⓓ Vistaprint 4B Ⓓ Roy Smith Design Ⓒ RSD 4C Ⓓ DL Creative 4D Ⓓ Karl Design Vienna Ⓒ Haendlerbund Leipzig
5A Ⓓ Kommunikat 5B Ⓓ entz creative Ⓒ Unibox 5C Ⓓ sposato design & illustration Ⓒ Tyler School of Art 5D Ⓓ RONODESIGN Ⓒ Comcare

Box Frites
Logo Design

Eric Baker Design, New York City, New York

Much was praised about Citi Field, the new Mets ballpark that opened in Flushing Meadows, New York, in April 2009—especially the food. The renowned Big Apple restaurateur Danny Meyer and his Union Square Hospitality Group were asked to develop food concepts for the venue, so the appearances of his ever-successful Shake Shack and Blue Smoke restaurants were a given. But the team also debuted two new concepts for the park itself: Box Frites and El Verano Taqueria. Box Frites was Meyer's answer to one of sports' fans biggest food cravings: french fries.

Eric Baker, founder of Eric Baker Design in New York, had collaborated with Meyer and his team on many projects before Citi Field, and there was indeed a common feel that tied the restaurant identities together. "The idea for each entity is separate, but we strive to have a similar aesthetic: simple, clean, and appropriate," explains Baker. "We avoid trendy and shoot for what's real and true."

There is a practical reason for simplicity in the case of a chain-restaurant logo, and even more so when that restaurant exists in a stadium: The logo has to be readily identifiable. The Box Frites mark would appear on everything from menu boards to packaging to large-scale neon signs, and it had to get across in each of these applications.

"When we begin a project like this, we look at the words very carefully, looking for a letter or shape that we might begin to play with," says Baker. The *X* in *BOX* stood out to him early on, especially with the use of the type family Champion, designed by Jonathan Hoefler, and he began to study how it might be visually incorporated into a box of fries.

The solution, Baker says, was a happy accident. Meyer is very involved in the design process of his identities and so the back-and-forth really helped the logo to emerge.

Since its unveiling at Citi Field, Box Frites, along with the other three USHG concepts, has popped up at Nationals Park in Washington, DC, and will be appearing at other sports and entertainment venues in the future. The food itself has reaped rave reviews, and Baker is pleased with how well the logo has done its job of being simple, clean, and most certainly appropriate in each new context.

Above: Eric Baker's final logo design for Box Frites emerged out of the X in BOX, with help from the typeface Champion by Jonathan Hoefler.

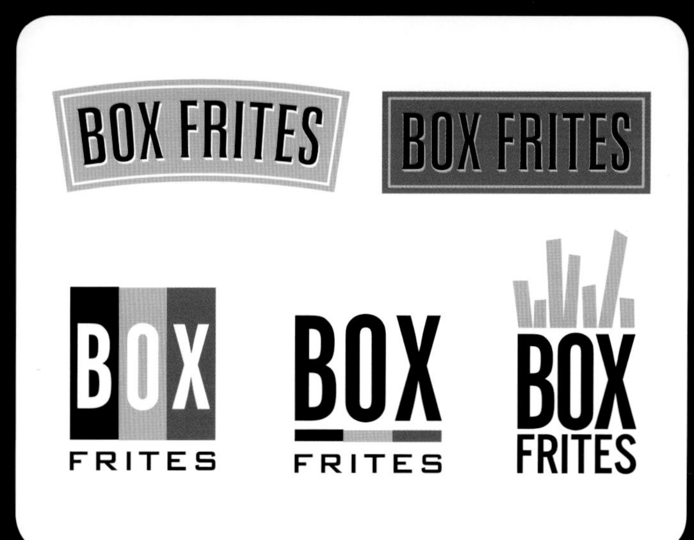

Right: Baker explored other routes before homing in on a french-fry X. The result, he says, was a "happy accident."

	A	B	C	D
1	**LOGO SEARCH** Keywords: Food Type: Symbol Typographic Combo All 			
2				
3				
4				
5				

Ⓓ = Design Firm Ⓒ = Client

1C Ⓓ daverawlins.com Ⓒ Cafe Aroma Macomb Illinois 1D Ⓓ Sommese Design Ⓒ The Gallery Cafe
2A Ⓓ Joanna Malik Ⓒ Art Cafe 2B Ⓓ Logoworks by HP Ⓒ Carrie's Cafe 2C Ⓓ RONODESIGN Ⓒ RB COFF 2D Ⓓ RONODESIGN Ⓒ Organizze Coffee
3A Ⓓ Jerron Ames 3B Ⓓ Laurel Black Design, Inc. 3C Ⓓ Type08 Ⓒ Tea Break 3D Ⓓ Gyula Nemeth Ⓒ Pötti Mugs 4A Ⓓ Corporate Image Design & Marketing Ⓒ Black Kettle Tearooms
4B Ⓓ Richards Brock Miller Mitchell & Associates Ⓒ Winewood 4C Ⓓ Webster Design Associates, Inc. Ⓒ Webster Design 4D Ⓓ genarodesign Ⓒ Marioli Mexican Gourmet (proposed)
5A Ⓓ Type08 Ⓒ Wine Kingdom 5B Ⓓ Marjoram Creative Ⓒ Woop Woop Wine & Dine Club 5C Ⓓ Strange Ideas 5D Ⓓ Somerset Ⓒ Providence Cafe

A B C D

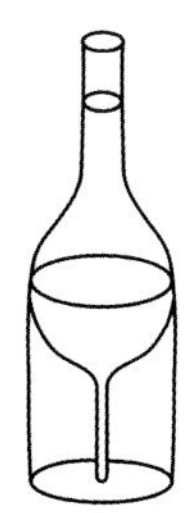

1

2

3

4

5

Ⓓ = Design Firm Ⓒ = Client

1A Ⓓ Sommese Design Ⓒ Dante's Restaurants 1B Ⓓ Type08 Ⓒ Bubalo Wines 1C Ⓓ Kraftwerk Design, Inc. Ⓒ Terravant Wine Company 1D Ⓓ 01d Ⓒ Chianti Wine Bar
2A Ⓓ Banowetz + Company, Inc. Ⓒ The Hilton Anatole Hotel 2B Ⓓ Stebbings Partners Ⓒ Children's Hosptial Boston 2C Ⓓ QUIQUE OLLERVIDES Ⓒ Molotov 2D Ⓓ moter
3A Ⓓ Bidwell ID Ⓒ Blatant Brewery 3B Ⓓ The Robin Shepherd Group Ⓒ Jacksonville Zoo and Gardens 3C Ⓓ Sunday Lounge Ⓒ Guadalupe Brewing Co. 3D Ⓓ Roy Smith Design Ⓒ Further
4A Ⓓ 3 Advertising, LLC Ⓒ RockTops 4B Ⓓ R&R Partners Ⓒ Phil 4C Ⓓ Turner Duckworth Ⓒ The Coca-Cola Company North America 4D Ⓓ Sunday Lounge Ⓒ Vino Salida, LLC
5A Ⓓ Taylor Vanden Hoek Ⓒ Verdoni's 5B Ⓓ Esparza Advertising 5C Ⓓ Richards Brock Miller Mitchell & Associates Ⓒ Central Market 5D Ⓓ Shawn Wideman Ⓒ Sin Noir

	A	B	C	D
1				
2				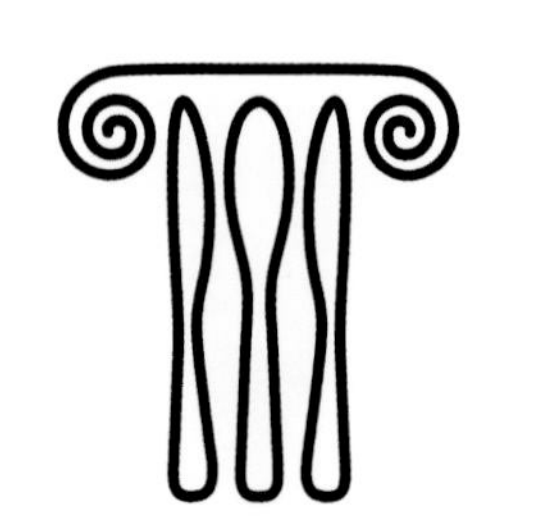
3				
4			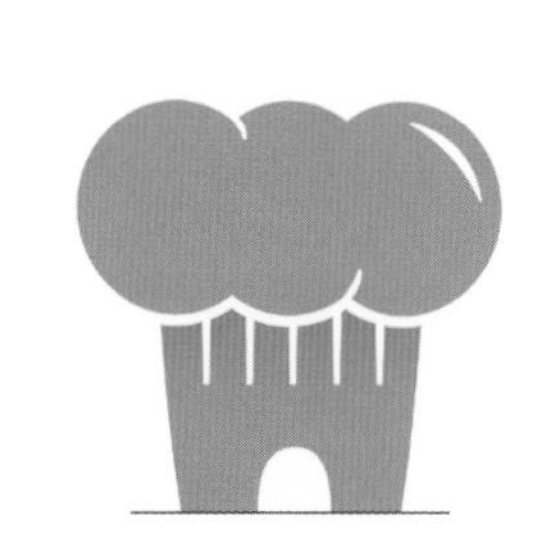	
5				

Ⓓ = Design Firm Ⓒ = Client

1A Ⓓ Strange Ideas 1B Ⓓ Damian Dominguez Ⓒ Tony's Organic Food 1C Ⓓ Aibrean's Studio Ⓒ Made 2 Order Software 1D Ⓓ Dotzero Design Ⓒ Lucia
2A Ⓓ Gardner Design 2B Ⓓ ORFIK DESIGN Ⓒ Daily Diet 2C Ⓓ DL Creative Ⓒ Smachno! Restaurant 2D Ⓓ Stanislav Topolsky Ⓒ The French culinary academy
3A Ⓓ genarodesign Ⓒ ART + BAKING 3B Ⓓ RONODESIGN Ⓒ Hokkaido Milk 3C Ⓓ ilogo.pl Ⓒ Centrum Zaopatrzenia Barat 3D Ⓓ Shawn Castle Ⓒ Yogurt Twists/Hare Communications
4A Ⓓ Art Machine 4B Ⓓ Art Machine Ⓒ cakespray 4C Ⓓ Joanna Malik Ⓒ Yumvy home cooking made easy 4D Ⓓ J Burwell Mixon Design Ⓒ Peace, Love & Desserts Bakery
5A Ⓓ Elua Ⓒ Burger 5B Ⓓ Stevaker Design Ⓒ Five Points Pizza 5C Ⓓ 01d Ⓒ Rollolo 5D Ⓓ Webcore Design Ⓒ Say Cheese Photography

	A	B	C	D
1				
2				
3				
4				
5				

Ⓓ = Design Firm Ⓒ = Client

1A Ⓓ Michael O'Connell Ⓒ Museum of Contemporary Art Jacksonville 1B Ⓓ Indicate Design Groupe Ⓒ Dachshund Bavarian Restaurant 1C Ⓓ Wall-to-Wall Studios Ⓒ Hank's Haute Dogs 1D Ⓓ Sunday Lounge Ⓒ Guadalupe Brewing Co. 2A Ⓓ Sequence Ⓒ Chipotle 2B Ⓓ QUIQUE OLLERVIDES Ⓒ Carrot Skateboards 2C Ⓓ Odney 2D Ⓓ Kruhu Ⓒ Rooster's Beak Bar & Kitchen 3A Ⓓ Type08 Ⓒ Bite Spokane 3B Ⓓ Strange Ideas 3C Ⓓ Avenueva Ⓒ Nutrition Council of Cincinnati 3D Ⓓ Hulsbosch Ⓒ Woolworths Supermarkets 4A Ⓓ IDEGRAFO Ⓒ Panere 4B Ⓓ Denis Aristov Ⓒ KS-Stroy 4C Ⓓ LONI DBS Ⓒ Domaine Vrabci 4D Ⓓ Sunday Lounge Ⓒ Weathervane Farm 5A Ⓓ RJ Thompson Ⓒ H.J. Heinz Company 5B Ⓓ Studio Ink Ⓒ Thirst Studios 5C Ⓓ Rubber Design Ⓒ Sulo Foods 5D Ⓓ k.elbizri Ⓒ Pomegranate Private Kitchen

A B C D

1

LOGO SEARCH

Keywords  

Type: ◯ Symbol ◯ Typographic ◯ Combo ◉ All

2

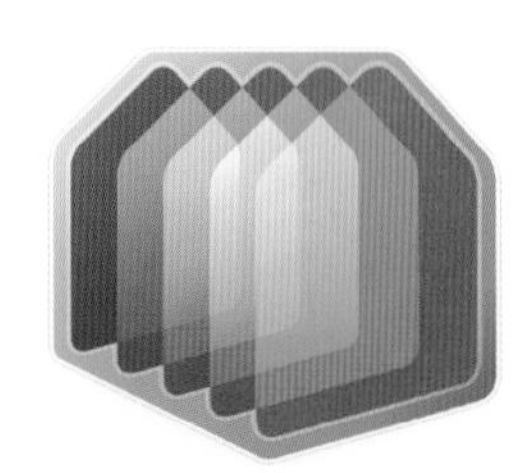

3

4

5

Ⓓ = Design Firm Ⓒ = Client

1C Ⓓ Brandburg Ⓒ Double Brand / UMWW 1D Ⓓ Pavone Ⓒ Excel Homes
2A Ⓓ Fernandez Design Ⓒ Briar Chapel 2B Ⓓ Brandon Winckler Design, Inc. Ⓒ Tim Carter Marketing 2C Ⓓ Reghardt 2D Ⓓ Bitencourt Ⓒ Bruno Scatolin
3A Ⓓ Strange Ideas 3B Ⓓ HELOHOLO Ⓒ Octava Capital 3C Ⓓ Swanson Russell Ⓒ AGP 3D Ⓓ Moller Creative Group Ⓒ The Room Stylists
4A Ⓓ 12 punktov 4B Ⓓ THINKMULE Ⓒ Black Book Gallery 4C Ⓓ Fernandez Design Ⓒ Mi Rancho 4D Ⓓ California Baptist University Ⓒ The Rustik Frog
5A Ⓓ SGNL Studio Ⓒ Farmhouse Delivery 5B Ⓓ Jon Flaming Design Ⓒ Pure Luck Farm & Dairy 5C Ⓓ Velocity Vectors Ⓒ Allenbrooke Farms 5D Ⓓ Clark Creative Ⓒ Bluegrass BBQ

A B C D

1

THE PALLADIUM
AT THE CENTER FOR THE PERFORMING ARTS

2

3

4

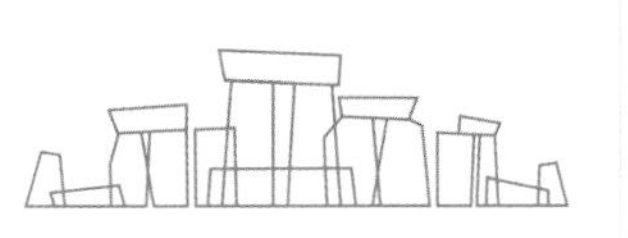

5

Ⓓ = Design Firm Ⓒ = Client

1A Ⓓ Gardner Design 1B Ⓓ Ullman Design Ⓒ Alliance Industries 1C Ⓓ Alphabet Arm Design Ⓒ Old City Restoration Company 1D Ⓓ Rossignol & Associates Design Ⓒ The Distillery Historic District
2A Ⓓ Imaginaria Ⓒ Hotel New Yorker 2B Ⓓ Fernandez Design Ⓒ The Palladium 2C Ⓓ TheNames Ⓒ EGF 2D Ⓓ McGuire Design Ⓒ City Voice
3A Ⓓ re:play Ⓒ American Council for the Blind Ohio 3B Ⓓ R&R Partners Ⓒ Academy of Hospitality and Tourism 3C Ⓓ The Collaboration Ⓒ Highwoods Properties 3D Ⓓ Insight Design Ⓒ GOOGOO Wonderland
4A Ⓓ back2basics media Ⓒ Clarion Fire Protection Solutions 4B Ⓓ [2 one 5] Creative Ⓒ North Broad Living 4C Ⓓ Tim Frame Design Ⓒ TOWNE BAKERY 4D Ⓓ Red Rooster Group Ⓒ Urban Bloom
5A Ⓓ 12 punktov Ⓒ Capital City Brokers 5B Ⓓ DOXA Ⓒ Brand Villages 5C Ⓓ cresk design Ⓒ Mystery Islands 5D Ⓓ Elua Ⓒ Department of Real Estate

A B C D

1

2

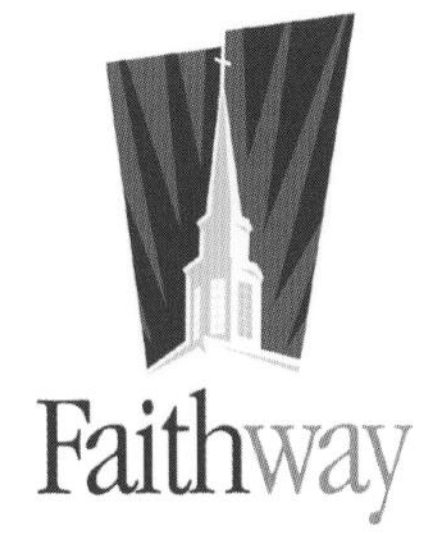

3

4

5

Ⓓ = Design Firm Ⓒ = Client

1A Ⓓ Dez Propaganda Ⓒ Goldsztein Cyrela 1B Ⓓ Imaginaria Ⓒ Zukali Mexican Gourmet 1C Ⓓ 01d Ⓒ Pivburg 1D Ⓓ Gardner Design Ⓒ TowerHawk
2A Ⓓ One up Ⓒ Co Hotels 2B Ⓓ Dirty Design Ⓒ Whiteladies Picture House 2C Ⓓ North Star Marketing Ⓒ Faithway 2D Ⓓ Allegra_East Ⓒ Kennebunkport Marina
3A Ⓓ Nikita Lebedev 3B Ⓓ Mattson Creative 3C Ⓓ SGNL Studio Ⓒ Skylin 3D Ⓓ RONODESIGN Ⓒ Tokyo Yaki
4A Ⓓ Elixir Design Ⓒ Castor Architecture 4B Ⓓ Shay Isdale Design Ⓒ Federal Select 4C Ⓓ Rikky Moller Design Ⓒ Alamo City Handmade 4D Ⓓ Eric Mower & Associates Ⓒ Destiny USA
5A Ⓓ A Blue Moon Arts, LLC 5B Ⓓ Travers Collins & Company Ⓒ Counsel Financial Services 5C Ⓓ Anonymous Art Ⓒ Jawl Corporation 5D Ⓓ Gardner Design Ⓒ College Hill Neighborhood Association

A B C D

LOGO SEARCH

Keywords: Transportation

Type: ○ Symbol ○ Typographic ○ Combo ◉ All

1

2

3

4

5

(D) = Design Firm (C) = Client

1C (D) Fuelhaus Brand Strategy + Design 1D (D) Prejean Creative (C) Lafayette Consolidated Government
2A (D) Roy Smith Design (C) World Moto 2B (D) Hip Street 2C (D) Elua (C) Cars Collection 2D (D) Nikita Lebedev
3A (D) Lunar Cow (C) Squad Car 37 3B (D) Hole in the Roof (C) Real Jeep Parts 3C (D) Thrillustrate (C) Freemont Street Experience 3D (D) Tasty Concepts (C) Rabbit Restaurant
4A (D) DOXA (C) Simmons Foods 4B (D) SGNL Studio (C) Farmhouse Delivery 4C (D) Soulsight (C) Waukegan Township Art Bus 4D (D) Type08 (C) Buffaleaux Coffee
5A (D) Double A Creative (C) NONSTOP 5B (D) Hexanine (C) Plastic Highway 5C (D) 13THFLOOR (C) Hot Wheels, Mattel, Inc. 5D (D) Gardner Design (C) I Bike Douglas

A B C D

1

2

3

4

5

Ⓓ = Design Firm Ⓒ = Client

1A Ⓓ The Key Ⓒ Bicycle Network Victoria 1B Ⓓ Damian Dominguez Ⓒ Webcontent Group 1C Ⓓ reaves design 1D Ⓓ Double A Creative Ⓒ Ventus Custom Cycles
2A Ⓓ Hellofolio s.r.o. Ⓒ Hungarian Cyclist Club 2B Ⓓ Webster Design Associates, Inc. Ⓒ Omaha's Henry Doorly Zoo 2C Ⓓ Sol Consultores Ⓒ Incluyendo Mexico 2D Ⓓ Mattson Creative
3A Ⓓ Creative Suitcase Ⓒ Hopfields 3B Ⓓ MINE Ⓒ Bun Mee, llc 3C Ⓓ 01d Ⓒ Mototema.ru 3D Ⓓ Double A Creative Ⓒ Little Gravity
4A Ⓓ Anonymous Art Ⓒ Michael Kelly 4B Ⓓ Banowetz + Company, Inc. Ⓒ Ronald McDonald House of Dallas 4C Ⓓ Banowetz + Company, Inc. Ⓒ Ronald McDonald House of Dallas 4D Ⓓ Elua Ⓒ Kira Rozanov
5A Ⓓ Logorado 5B Ⓓ 01d Ⓒ I Love toys 5C Ⓓ Timber Design Company Ⓒ The Orkestra Projekt 5D Ⓓ Helius Creative Advertising Ⓒ Rocket Readers

A B C D

1

2

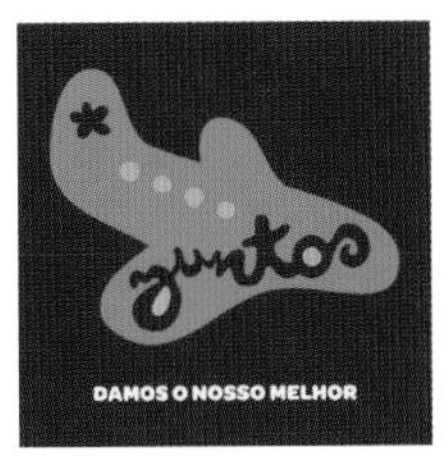

3

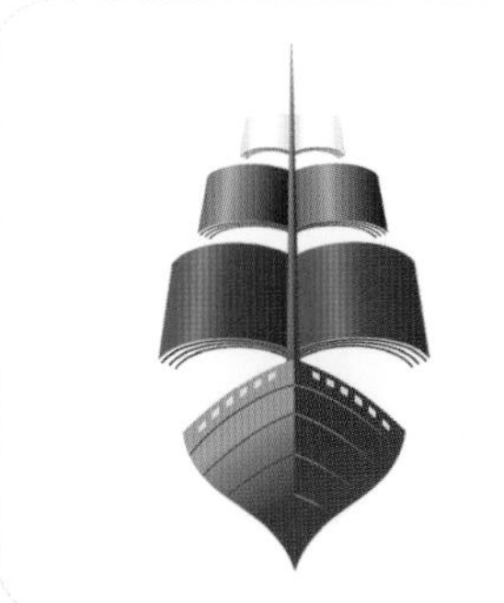

4

5

(D) = Design Firm (C) = Client

1A (D) Studio Rayolux (C) Astrowright 1B (D) Gardner Design 1C (D) Big Communications (C) Jacksonville International Airport 1D (D) Thomas Cook Designs (C) Tailwind Aviation
2A (D) The Brandit (C) Hangar 24 Craft Brewery 2B (D) Double A Creative (C) Double A Creative 2C (D) Dunham Design, Inc. (C) American Airlines 2D (D) The Brandit (C) Hangar 24 Brewery
3A (D) born 3B (D) Funnel Design Group (C) C.E. Page Airport 3C (D) The Design Farm (C) Susan Moran 3D (D) Fernandez Design (C) Phoenicia Specialty Foods
4A (D) Oronoz Brandesign 4B (D) Jerron Ames (C) Arteis 4C (D) Traction (C) Michigan State University 4D (D) Denis Aristov (C) Caspian Expo
5A (D) Sunday Lounge (C) Pack & Paddle 5B (D) Chris Rooney Illustration/Design (C) WETA 5C (D) Greenhouse Studio (C) Sonar App 5D (D) Dotzero Design (C) Dotzero

index

You can access a fully searchable database of logos featured in this and all other *LogoLounge* books by purchasing a membership to www. logolounge.com. With your membership, you can search for logos by keyword, client, or design firm name, client industry, or type of mark, and get designer credits and contact information for each logo as well. The database is always growing: in fact, your membership also allows you to upload an unlimited number of your own logos, each of which will be considered by our judges for inclusion in upcoming *LogoLounge* books.

directory

[2 one 5] Creative
USA

01d
Belarus
+375 29 660 12 28
www.01d.ru

12 punktov
Russia
+7 903 006 31 52
www.12pt.ru

1310 Studios
USA
704-375-2471
www.1310studios.com

13THFLOOR
USA
949-429-3055
www.13thfloordesign.com

13thirtyone Design
USA
715-531-0125
www.13thirtyone.com

144design
USA
612-708-7004
www.144design.com

20nine
USA
218-267-1791

3 Advertising, LLC
USA
505-293-2333
www.whois3.com

343 Creative
USA
212-213-2294
www.343creative.com

343 RLP sports marketing
USA
201-981-0705

36creative
USA
603-969-8548

3906 Design
USA
910-620-2542
www.3906design.com

3x4 Design Studio
Iran

903 Creative, LLC
USA
434-774-5164
www.903creative.com

A Blue Moon Arts, LLC
USA
918-742-3136
www.abluemoonarts.com

A Ginger Snaps
USA
850-501-7768
www.agingersnaps.com

A.D. Creative Group
USA
406-248-7117
www.adcreativegroup.com

A3 Design
USA
704-568-5351
www.athreedesign.com

Absolu communication marketing
Canada
819-752-8888
www.absolu.ca

Acute Cluster Ltd.
Thailand
6685 810 0002
www.acutecluster.com

addicted2be
Bulgaria
+359 895 688 684
www.behance.net/addicted2be

Aibrean's Studio
USA
937-684-7156
www.studio.aibrean.com

Airtype Studio
USA
336-793-4437
www.airtypestudio.com

akapustin
Russia
+7 9167538141
www.akapustin.ru

Akhmatov Studio
Kazakhstan
77051826068

Alama Marketing & Design
UAE
97144345309
www.3alama.com

Aldasbrand
Columbia
www.aldasbrand.com

alekchmura.com
Poland
+48 0 792 370 107
www.alekchmura.com

Alescar Ortiz
Dominican Republic
8098564229
www.alescarortiz.com

Alexander Wende
Germany
www.behance.net/AlexWende

Alf Design
Malaysia

Allegra_East
USA

Allegro Design
USA
503-827-0169
www.allegro-design.com

Almosh82
India
www.almosh82.com

Alphabet Arm Design
USA
617-451-9990
www.alphabetarm.com

Anagraphic
Hungary
+36 1 202 0555
www.anagraphic.hu

Anderson Mraz Design
USA
509-624-4029

Andrei Bilan
Romania
40742147660

Anemone Design
USA
202-351-1153
www.anemonedesign.com

angryporcupine*design
USA
435-655-0645
www.angryporcupine.com

Anna Kovecses
Hungary
003620 4288714
www.annakovecses.com

Anonymous Art
Canada
250-704-0456
www.anonymousart.ca

Anoroc Agency, Inc.
USA
919-821-1191

Anthony Lane Studios
USA
www.012485.com

Arsenal Design, Inc.
USA
401-848-0064
www.arsenaldesign.com

Art Machine
Germany
+49 030 31 50 56 66
www.julianhrankov.com

ARTENTIKO
Poland
793338001
www.artentiko.com

artslinger
Canada
780-884-2242
www.artslinger.ca

Artsmith Communications
Canada
780-424-2621
www.artsmith.ca

Asgard
Russia
79219322216
www.asgard-design.com

AtelierLKS
USA

atom
UK
07963 745 630
www.atomcreate.com

Austin Logo Designs
USA
512-705-1710
www.austinlogodesigns.com

Avenueva
USA
214-770-9985
www.avenueva.com

Axiom Design Partners
Australia
618 9381 6270
www.axiomdp.com.au

b2 kreativ
USA
908-247-2142
www.b2kreativ.com

back2basics media
USA
www.back2basicsmedia.com

Bad Feather
USA
646-484-8314
www.badfeather.com

bailey brand consulting
USA
610-940-9030

Bailey Lauerman
USA
402_514_9416

Balazs Vekes
Hungary
36302920115
www.vekes.bz

BalazsCreative
USA
216-906-9599
www.balazscreative.com

BANG
Mexico
+52 1 81 8378 1578
www.bangbang.mx

Banowetz + Company, Inc.
USA
214-823-7300 ext. 100
www.banowetz.com

Baris Atiker
Turkey

BASIS
USA
970-231-9921

BBDO NY
USA
212-459-5000

BBMG
USA
www.bbmg.com

Beganik Strategy + Design
USA
651-488-7900
www.beganik.com

Benedict Sato Design
Australia
03 9809 0484
www.benedictsato.com

Benjamin Della Rosa Graphic Design
USA
916-508-7557
www.benjamindellarosa.com

BenKandoraDESIGN
USA
760-333-8133
www.benkandoradesign.com

bethvansistine
UK
7791211167

BFive branding & identity
Russia
79272166799
www.bfive.ru

BHAGdesign
South Africa
2145004690

Bidwell ID
USA
413-585-9387
www.bidwellid.com

Big Communications
USA
205-322-5646
www.bigcom.com

bigoodis
Russia
9236464866
www.ivanbobrov.com

binocle
Switzerland
41227851104
www.binocle.ch

Bitencourt
Brazil
www.brenobitencourt.com

Bittersweet Design Boutique
USA
512-574-8517
www.designbybittersweet.com

Black Box Studio
USA
864-660-9415

Black Velvet Design
Switzerland
www.blackvelvet-design.com

Blue Clover
USA
210-223-5409
www.blueclover.com

Blue Orange
Ireland
+353 86 398 2337
www.blueorange.ie

Blue Sky Design
USA
210-344-4644

BlueBossa Design e Comunicação
Brazil
www.bluebossa.art.br

BluesCue Designs
Philippines
639173262583
www.bluescue.com

bob neace graphic design, inc.
USA

Bonsai Media
Australia
0411 776 459
www.bonsaimedia.com.au

Boost Marketing
USA
800-689-6751

born
Portugal

Boss Creative
USA
210-568-9677

The Brand Agency
Australia
61893224433
www.brandagency.com.au

Brand Agent
USA
214-979-2047

BRAND BROTHERS
France
+33 1 83 62 43 92

brand renew design
South Africa
7216859310

BrandBerry
Russia
89171091522
www.brand-berry.ru

Brandburg
Poland
512693936

Brandcentral
Ireland

BrandExtract
USA

Brandient
Romania
+40 212308173
www.brandient.com

The BrandingHouse
USA
828-350-9077
www.thebrandinghouse.com

The Brandit
USA
910-508-9938

BRANDiT.
Lebanon
9613406276

Brandmor
Romania
40723450094
www.brandmor.ro

Brandon Winckler Design, Inc.
USA
612-229-0868

Braue: Brand Design Experts
Germany
+49.471.983820
www.braue.info

Brian Buirge Design
USA

BRIGGS
Canada
www.briggsstrategy.com

Brittany Phillips Design
USA
479-225-1001

Brook Hagler
Canada

bryon hutchens | graphic design
USA
310-621-0677

Burocratik Design
Portugal
351239711403
www.burocratik.com

Burst! Creative Group
Canada
604-662-8778

Caliber Creative, LLC
USA
214-741-4488
www.calibercreative.com

Caliente Creative
USA
512-627-2607
www.calientecreative.com

California Baptist University
USA
951-343-4675

Candor Advertising
USA
614-309-9333
www.candorad.com

CAPSULE
USA
612-374-4525
www.capsule.us

Carol Gravelle Graphic Design
USA
805-383-2773
www.carolgravelledesign.com

Carrmichael Design
USA
312-226-0755

Cassandra Smolcic
USA
724-216-3259

Causality
USA
888-999-5592

Chapa Design
USA
608-333-7446
www.chapadesign.com

Char Davidson Design
USA
206-550-6342

Che Woo Design
USA
312-772-4391
www.chewoodesign.com

Chicken Leg Studio
USA
254-338-2052

Chris Gorney Design
USA
612-805-1949
www.chrisgorney.com

Chris Rooney Illustration/Design
USA
www.looneyrooney.com

Chris Trivizas | Design
Greece
302109310803
www.christrivizas.eu

Church Logo Gallery
USA
760-231-9368
www.churchlogogallery.com

Clark & Co.
USA
360-903-5954

Clark Creative
USA
912-233-1160
www.clarkcreativedesign.com

Clay Wiese
USA
402-341-2846
www.andersonpartners.com

The Clear Agency
USA
727-489-2332

C-moll Design
Russia
www.c-moll.spb.ru

co:lab
USA
860-951-7782
www.colabinc.com

Colin Saito
USA
562-682-4292
www.colinsaito.com

The Collaboration
USA
816-474-3232
www.the-collaboration.com

Collaboration Reverberation
USA
619-501-3392
www.thecrstudio.com

Coloryn Studio
USA
912-596-7644

COLOSSAL
USA
214-742-9800

Communication Agency
Slovakia
421907915937
www.communicationagency.com

concussion, llc
USA
817-336-6824 ext. 207

Conover
USA
619-238-1999
www.studioconover.com

Conyers Design, Inc.
USA
515-255-3939
www.conyersdesign.com

Copilot Creative
USA
719-633-5000
www.copilotcreative.com

Corporate Image Design & Marketing
Australia
+61 3 9855 2499
www.cidesign.com.au

Corporate Movement
USA

CPR + Partners
USA
504-304-8461

Craft Creation and Design, LLC
USA
404-643-9682

CREACTIS
China
+41 32 481 21 73
www.creactis.ch

creative space
USA
907-632-5782

Creative Squall
USA
214-244-5011

Creative Suitcase
USA

The Creative Underground
USA
954-415-3561

Creative United
Denmark
+45 8676 0010
www.creativeunited.dk

creativefire
USA
214-850-7637
www.creativefiredesign.com

cresk design
The Netherlands
31615286911
www.cresk.nl

Cricket Design Works
USA
608-255-0002
www.cricketdesignworks.com

Croak Design
UK
1143601117

CSK Stategic Marketing Group, Inc.
USA
719-434-5250

Csordi
Hungary
+36 20 326 1446
www.csordi.hu

Cubic
USA
918-587-7888
www.cubiccreative.com

Cubo
Spain
+34 976 203 398

DAIS
Australia
+61 7 3216 0990
www.dais.com.au

Damian Dominguez
Dominican Republic
8098755301

Dana Rocha
Brazil
55 41 85145413
www.tabadesign.com.br

dandy idea
USA
512-627-9103
www.dandyidea.com

Dara Creative
Ireland
00 353 1 672 5222
www.daracreative.ie

dark horse productions
USA

daverawlins.com
USA
309-830-0209

Davina Chatkeon Design
USA
818-953-7143
www.davinachatkeon.com

DBDA
USA
www.dbdastudio.com

dee duncan
USA
316-204-3873
www.deeduncan.com

DeGraf Design
USA
573-216-3465

deili Minsk
Belarus
+375 29 508 31 98
www.deili.by

Deksia
USA
515-318-7171
www.deksia.com

Delikatessen
Germany
49-40-3508060
www.delikatessen

Dell
USA

demasijones
Australia
+618 8212 9065
www.demasijones.com

Demographic, Inc.
USA
773-301-2816

Denbo Design
USA
205-777-1692

Deney
Turkey
902164287997
www.deney.com.tr

Denis Aristov
Russia
+7 908 2553131
www.denisaristov.com

Dept of Energy
USA
206-910-0288
www.deptofenergy.com

The Design Farm
USA
325-665-3369

Design Hovie Studios, Inc.
USA
206-783-8600
www.hovie.com

Design im Barockhaus
Germany
+ 49 7543 913149
www.barockhaus.de

Design Laurels
USA
424-229-1737
www.designlaurels.com

Design Nut
USA
301-942-2360
www.designnut.com

design ranch
USA
816-472-8668

designproject
USA
312-379-8656
www.designprojectweb.com

DesignUnion
USA
815-494-7363
www.designunion.co

Dessein
Australia
61.8.9228.0661
www.dessein.com.au

Device
UK
+ 44 208 896 0626
www.devicefonts.co.uk

Dez Propaganda
Brazil
55 51 21011010
www.dezpropaganda.com.br

Di Vision Creative Group
USA
212-533-3009
www.divisioncreativegroup.com

Diaconu Felix Ionut
Romania

Diagram
Poland
48618862079
www.diagram.pl

Diann Cage Design
USA
314-503-4001
www.dianncage.com

Dickerson
USA
817-207-9009

Dirty Design
UK
+44 117 9273344
www.dirtydesign.co.uk

Disciple Design
USA
901-386-4299

Diseño Porfavor
Mexico

DL Creative
USA

dmDesign
USA
512-750-9956
www.dmdesigninc.com

Doc4
USA
479-879-7950
www.doc4design.com

Donation Design
USA
608-279-3365
www.donationdesign.com

Dotzero Design
USA
503-892-9262
www.dotzerodesign.com

Double A Creative
USA
402-960-6553
www.doubleacreative.com

Doug Barrett Design
USA
407-716-5086
www.dougbarrett.com

Doug Beatty
UK
+44 079 603 007 12

Down With Design
USA

DOXA
USA
479-582-2695

Dragon Rouge China Limited
China
+852 2512 1340

DTM_INC
The Netherlands
075 635 52 46

Duffy & Partners
USA
612-548-2333
www.duffy.com

Dunham Design, Inc.
USA
214-373-4994

Dwayne Design
USA
918-938-8342

EAT Advertising and Design, Inc.
USA
816-505-2950

ecVisualMedia
USA
www.ecvisualmedia.com

EDC Studio
USA
816-520-3821
www.edcstudio.net

Eggra
Mexico
38970390144
www.eggra.com

El Paso, Galeria de Comunicacion
Spain
0034 91 594 22 48
www.elpasocomunicacion.com

Elevation
USA
804-780-2300
www.elevationadvertising.com

elina frumerman design
USA
415-652-2184

Elixir Design
USA
415-834-0300

Elua
Russia
+7 920 742
www.elua.ru

Emilio Correa
Mexico
52 55 5712 7910
www.emiliographics.com

Emu Design Studio
USA
630-587-4033
www.emudesign.com

encompus
USA
619-294-3295

Enter98
Hungary
36-30-4644648
www.enter98.blogspot.com

entz creative
Singapore
+65 62554353
www.entzcreative.com

Envision Creative Group
USA
512-292-1049
www.envision-creative.com

Eric Mower & Associates
USA
716-880-1418
www.mower.com

Eric Rob & Isaac
USA
501-978-4543

Erwin Bindeman
South Africa
27790982068
www.erwin.co.za

Esparza Advertising
USA
505-765-1505

Essex Two
USA
773-489-1400
www.sx2.com

estudiotres
USA
619-865-8603
www.estudiotres.com

Ewert Design
USA
503-692-5513
www.ewertdesign.com

ex nihilo
Belgium
0032 65 62 25 58
www.exnihilo.be

Extension
Australia
+61 3 9699 4334
www.extensionco.com

Eytan Schiowitz Design
USA
347-279-6257
www.eytanschiowitz.com

Face.
Mexico
+52 81 8356 1001
www.designbyface.com

Faduchi Group
Canada
289-813-0813
www.faduchigroup.com

fallindesign
Russia

FBA (Foxtrot Bravo Alpha)
USA
512-637-8999
www.foxtrotbravoalpha.com

Fernandez Design
USA
512-619-4020
www.fernandezstudio.com

Fezlab
USA
www.fezlab.com

ffsako
Brazil
www.ffsako.com

Field Branding & Design
USA
www.wearefield.com

Fierce Competitors
USA
203-506-0030

Filip Komorowski
Poland
600337232
www.behance.net/komorowski

Firefly Branding Boutique
Romania
40724504938
www.firefly.ro

Firestarter
Romania
0040 368 88 10 25
www.firestarter.ro

Fixation Marketing
USA
240-207-2009
www.fixation.com

Fleishman Hillard
USA
314-982-9149

Flight Deck Creative
USA
214-534-9468
www.flightdeckcreative.com

Florin Negrut
Romania
+40 742 302 054

Floris Design
Spain
666229869
www.florisvoorveld.com

FLOVEY
Indonesia
www.flovey.com

FMedia Studios
Romania
40741082656
www.vladfiscutean.com

Focus Lab, LLC
USA
912-228-5211

Forthright Strategic Design
USA
415-205-4466
www.forthrightdesign.com

Fuelhaus Brand Strategy + Design
USA
619-574-1342
www.fuelhaus.com

Fugasi Creative
USA
512-497-7284
www.fugasicreative.com

Funnel Design Group
USA
405-840-7006
www.funneldesigngroup.com

fusecollective
Poland
+48 888501301
www.behance.net/koralgol

fuszion
USA
703-548-8080
www.fuszion.com

FutureBrand
Australia
+61 3 9604 2777
www.futurebrand.com.au

FutureBrand BC&H
Brazil
55 11 38211166
www.futurebrand.com

Gabe Re
USA
303-618-6309
www.gabere.com

Gardner Design
USA
316-691-8808
www.gardnerdesign.com

Gavula Design Associates
USA
www.gavuladesign.com

GDNSS
USA
212-866-1449
www.gdnss.com

Gehring Co.
USA
512-474-2882

genarodesign
USA
210-508-0225
www.genarodesign.com

THE GENERAL DESIGN CO.
USA
202-640-1842
www.generaldesignco.com

GeniusLogo
Serbia
+381 64 2 655433
www.geniuslogo.com

Gerren Lamson
USA
210-854-8699
www.gerrenlamson.com

Gilah Press + Design
USA
410-366-3330

Gina Malsed
USA
303-990-1517

giographix
USA
866-702-3747
www.giographix.com

Gizwiz Studio
Malaysia
604 228 9931
www.logodesigncreation.com

Glad Head
Ukraine

Glitschka Studios
USA
971-223-6143
www.glitschka.com

Go Welsh
USA
717-898-9000
www.gowelsh.com

Grabelnikov
Ukraine
+38 097 6561551
www.grabelnikov.com

graham yelton creative, llc
USA

Graphic design studio by Yurko Gutsulyak
Ukraine
380674465560
www.gstudio.com.ua

Graphic Granola
USA
512-436-8222
www.graphicgranola.com

Graphic Moxie, Inc.
USA
910-256-8990
www.graphicmoxie.com

Green Ink Studio
USA
415-203-4164
www.greeninkstudio.com

Green Jays Communications
USA
317-410-5312
www.greenjaysonline.com

Green Olive Media
USA
404-815-9327

Greenhouse Studio
USA
904-356-8630
www.gogreenhouse.com

GregScottDesign
USA

Greteman Group
USA
316-263-1004
www.gretemangroup.com

Gröters Design
Germany
+49 (0) 8142 6523987
www.groeters.de

Gyula Nemeth
Hungary
36 20 429 2019
www.seadevilworks.blogspot.com

H2 Design of Texas
USA
512-650-8821
www.hoyth.com

HABERDASHERY
USA
614-302-2154
www.haberdasherydesign.com

HALFNOT indesign
Indonesia
6221 9126 0562
www.halfnotindesign.com

Haller Design
USA
480-390-8722

Hand dizajn studio
Croatia
38512333489
www.hand.hr

Handoko Tjung Design
Indonesia
www.handokotjung.daportfolio.com

HAPI
USA
602-326-5457
www.livehapi.com

hatchmarks
USA
484-410-4285

Hayes Image
Australia
(03) 52672567
www.hayesimage.com.au

Headshot brand development
Ukraine
380443830041
www.headshot.ua

HebelerGraphics
USA
716-908-7257
www.hebelergraphics.com

Heins Creative, Inc.
USA
406-248-9924
www.heinscreative.com

Heisel Design
USA
941-922-0492
www.heiseldesign.com

Helius Creative Advertising
USA
801-673-4199
www.heliuscreative.com

Helix Design Communications
Canada

Hellofolio s.r.o.
Hungary
00 36 30 267 66 65
www.hellofolio.net

hellozacharnold
USA
636-208-2361
www.hellozacharnold.com

HELOHOLO
China
8613811611402
www.heloholo.com

Hexanine
USA
773-293-7068
www.hexanine.com

High Bandwidth
USA
972-479-9707
www.highbandwidth.com

Higher
Belarus

Hip Street
USA
651-226-5799
www.hipst.com

Hirschmann Design
USA
303-449-7363

Hole in the Roof
USA
254-756-1200
www.holeintheroof.com

Hollis Brand Culture
USA
619-234-2061
www.hollisbc.com

Honey Design
Canada
519-679-0786
www.honeydesign.ca

Hosanna Yau
Hong Kong

Howerton+White
USA
316-262-6644
www.howertonwhite.com

Hue Studio
Australia
61 3 94158380
www.huestudio.com.au

Hulsbosch
Australia
0413 746 000
www.hulsbosch.com.au

Idea Girl Design
USA
310-623-2288

IDEGRAFO
Romania
+40 742 959 457
www.idegrafo.com

Identivos
USA
www.identivos.com

Ikola designs...
USA
763-533-3440

ilogo.pl
Poland

Imaginaria
USA
214-725-8744
www.imaginariacreative.com

Impact Media Design
UK
0845 867 6580
www.impactmediadesign.co.uk

Impact Visual Communications
Canada
250-824-0011

Indicate Design Groupe
USA
415-422-0339
www.indicatedesign.com

The Infantree
USA
717-394-6932
www.theinfantree.com

INFECCION VISUAL
Mexico
(52) 91166406
www.infeccionvisual.com

inferno
USA
901-278-3773

Infinit
USA

Infinite Scale Design Group
USA
801-363-1881

Ingenia Creative
USA
619-438-5287
www.ingeniacreative.com

Ink Tycoon
USA
864-990-8493

Inky Lips Letterpress
USA

Innereactive Media
USA
616-682-9370
www.innereactive.com

inServ Worldwide
USA
614-543-6753
www.inserv-worldwide.com

Insight Design
USA

insight design
USA
956-580 1544

instudio
Lithuania
+370 652 43028
www.instudio.lt

Interbrand Sampson Group
South Africa
3+27 (0) 11 783 9595
www.interbrand.com

Intrinsic Design
USA

invectra, inc.
USA
281-882-3885

iQ, inc.
Canada
416-481-1175

Ishan Khosla Design
India
91-11-32927419
www.ishankhosladesign.com

Itchy Illustration
USA

J Burwell Mixon Design
USA
662-323-5975
www.cargocollective.com/jburwellmixon

J Fletcher Design
USA
843-364-1776
www.jfletcherdesign.com

J.D. Gordon Advertising
USA

Jacob Tyler Creative Group
USA
619-573-1061
www.jacobtyler.com

jamjardesign
Lebanon
+961 3 385885
www.jamjardesign.com

Jan Vranovsky
Czech Republic
www.visualscream.net

Jane Kelley
USA

Javier Garcia Design
USA
650-235-5686
www.javiergd.com

Jeremy Honea
USA
405-315-4764
www.sweetashonea.com

Jeremy Slagle Design
USA
614-804-6234

Jerron Ames
USA
801-636-7929

jo
USA
718-496-5983
www.jofolio.com

Joanna Malik
Poland
www.joannamalik.pl

Jodi Bearden
USA
559-434-6100
www.balldesign.com

The Joe Bosack Graphic Design Co.
USA
215-766-1461
www.joebosack.com

Johnson & Sekin
USA
972-567-1301

Jolt
Australia
+61 7 3216 0656
www.joltstudio.com.au

Jon Flaming Design
USA
972-235-4880
www.jonflaming.com

Jon Kay Design
USA
352-870-8438

Jordahl Design
USA
320-226-4190
www.jordahldesign.com

Joseph Blalock
USA
512-689-1345
www.josephblalock.com

josh higgins design
USA
619-379-2090
www.joshhiggins.com

Josue Zapata
USA
210-251-9250
www.josuezapata.com

Joy Renee Design
USA
952-200-0794
www.joyrenee.com

JSCameron Design
USA
503-313-6572

jsDesignCo.
USA
614-353-6412

Junebug Design
Canada
204-889-0254
www.junebugdesign.ca

Just Creative Design
USA
www.justcreativedesign.com

Justin Ardrey
USA
870-217-3980
www.justinardrey.com

k.elbizri
USA
415-516-2344

Kahn Design
USA
760-944-5574
www.kahn-design.com

kaimere
UAE
971505512868
www.kaimere.com

Kantorwassink
USA
616-233-3118

Karl Design Vienna
Austria
43-1-208 66 53
www.karl-design-logos.com

Kastelov
Bulgaria
359886034151
www.kastelov.com

Keith Russell Design
USA
206-817-4249
www.keithrusselldesign.com

Kelley Nixon
USA
512-878-1182

Kendall Creative Shop, Inc.
USA
214-827-6680

Kerry F. Williams Design
USA
415-722-7149
www.kerryfwilliams.com

Kevin Archie Design
USA

The Key
Australia
+61 423 011 409
www.pausefest.com.au

Kiku Obata & Company
USA
314-505-8414
www.kikuobata.com

Klik
Poland
48501149883
www.klik-dizajn.pl

Kneadle, Inc.
USA
714-441-1157

Kommunikat
Poland
602820318
www.kommunikat.pl

Komprehensive Design
USA
215-620-7375

Kongshavn Design
Norway
4790090902
www.kongshavndesign.no

Koodoz Design
Australia
61 3 9421 2291
www.koodoz.com.au

koxa design
USA
415-797-8086

Kraftwerk Design Inc.
USA
805-785-0589
www.kraftwerkdesign.com

Kruhu
USA
706-496-7887

Kuharic Matos Ltd.
Croatia
00385 1 3770377
www.kuharicmatos.hr

Kuznetsov Evgeniy | KUZNETS
Russia
79101517929
www.kuznets.net

La Roche College
USA
412-779-7665

Laboratorium
Croatia
00385 1 606 1512

Lance LeBlanc Design
USA
www.lanceleblanc.com

Larkef
The Netherlands
31614052314
www.larkef.com

Laura Bardin Design
USA

Laurel Black Design, Inc.
USA
360-457-217
www.laurelblack.com

Lefty Lexington
USA
608-225-9892

Lemon Design Pvt Ltd.
India
912064782278
www.lemondesign.co.in

Leo Burnett
USA
612-242-5138

Lienhart Design
USA
312-738-2200
www.lienhartdesign.com

Lifeblue Media
USA
972-984-1899
www.lifeblue.com

Limelight Advertising & Design
Canada
905-885-9895
www.limelight.org

Limeshot Design
Australia

LIOBmedia
USA

Lippincott
USA
212-521-0010
www.lippincott.com

Liquid Agency
USA
408-850-8833
www.liquidagency.com

Little Box Of Ideas
Australia
61424962505
www.lboi.co

Lockheed Martin
USA
972-358-8150

Lodge Design
USA

Logo By Design
Australia
+61 8 8212 5259

Logo Design Works
USA
216-373-0612
www.logodesignworks.com

Logoholik
Serbia
914 595 6926
www.logoholik.com

Logoidentity.com
USA
908-665-6878
www.logoidentity.com

Logorado
Turkey
905427186318
www.logorado.com

LOGOSTA
Japan
www.logosta.com

Logoworks by HP
USA
800-210-7650
www.logoworks.com

Longshot Creatifs
USA

LONI DBS
Slovenia
38631419688
www.loni.si

The Loomis Agency
USA
832-723-7716

LOWE
Colombia
57 1 6058000

Lowercase a: Design Studio
USA
210-413-8219
www.lowercasea.com

LPA
USA
503-614-1545

Lumino
Australia
61 7 3251 2600
www.lumino.com.au

lumo
Canada
204-745-7420
www.golumo.com

Lunar Cow
USA
800-594-9620 ext. 12
www.lunarcow.com

M Jones Design
USA
908-204-9752

Made By Thomas
Belgium
0498 21 94 53
www.madebythomas.com

Magic Identity
USA
201-951-7760
www.magicidentity.com

Magnetic Creative
USA
951-506-2444

Makespace
USA
502-257-2520

Maks Shvahin [Polar]
Russia
+7(915)196
www.shvahin.ru

Marchhouse design
New Zealand
0064 21 246 9990
www.marchhousedesign.com

Marcos Calamato
USA
408-515-9678
www.marcoscalamato.com

mardi.be
Belgium
02 543 44 52

maria guarracino
USA
614-284-9997

Marina Rose
UK
448454300243
www.marinarose.co.uk

Marjoram Creative
USA
404-843-1990
www.marjoramcreative.com

Marketing with a Flair
USA
602-374-4923
www.marketingwithaflair.com

Marlin
USA
417-885-4530
www.marlinco.com

The Martin Group
USA
716-853-2757
www.martingroupmarketing.com

Matchstic
USA
404-446-1511
www.matchstic.com

Matias Fiori & Juan Pablo Sabini
Uruguay
59899376670
www.matiasfiori.com

Matt Lehman Studio
USA
615-504-2454
www.mattlehmanstudio.com

Mattel, Inc.
USA
310-252-3114

Matto
Lithuania
37062832493
www.brandmatto.com

Mattson Creative
USA
949-651-8740
www.mattsoncreative.com

McDill Associates
USA

McGuire Design
USA

MDG
USA
508-429-0755
www.thinkmdg.com

Mediascope
Romania
40766412151

Meir Billet Ltd.
Israel
972-3-5627577

Melissa Ott Design
USA
412-804-8116

Messenger
Canada
416-536-4129

Michael Lashford Design
USA
415-519-6627
www.michaellashford.com

Michael O'Connell
USA
904-705-4437

Michael Patrick Partners
USA
650-327-3185

Miller Creative, LLC
USA
732-905-0844
www.yaelmiller.com

milou
Poland
48664771121
www.milou.com.pl

Mindgruve
USA

MINE
USA
415-647-6463
www.minesf.com

Mircea Constantinescu
Romania

Misign Visual Communication
Italy

Mission Minded
USA
415-680-5864
www.mission-minded.com

mitchel design, inc.
The Netherlands
www.mitcheldesign.com

MKJ Creative
USA
215-997-2355
www.mkjcreative.com

mmplus creative
Indonesia
62-341-362371

Modern Species
USA
206-659-5930
www.modernspecies.com

moko creative
Australia
0418 213 805
www.moko.com.au

Moller Creative Group
USA
www.mollercreative.com

Molly Eckler Graphic Arts
USA
707-829-7900
www.mollyeckler.com

Momentum 18
USA
www.momentum18.com

Momentum Worldwide
USA
314-646-6285
www.momentumww.com

Mootto Studio
Poland
www.moottostudio.com

Morillas
Spain

morninglori Graphic Design
USA

moter
Australia
www.moter.com.au

Motif Creative Design
Australia
439750013
www.motifcreativedesign.com.au

Motiv Design
Australia
+61 8 8363 3833
www.motiv.com.au

Movement, Inc.
USA

Mrs Smith
South Africa
27117774075
www.mrssmith.co.za

MT Estudio
Mexico

Muhina Design
Russia
+7(3412) 52
www.muhinadesign.ru

Murillo Design, Inc.
USA
210-248-9412
www.murillodesign.com

Nectar Graphics
USA
503-472-1512
www.nectargraphics.com

The Netmen Corp
Argentina
5411-4776-3684
www.thenetmencorp.com

Neutra Design
USA
508-789-9511
www.neutra-design.com

Newhouse Design
USA
406-600-6532

Niedermeier Design
USA
206-351-3927

Nikita Lebedev
Russia

Nikosey Design, Inc.
USA
818-704-9993
www.tomnikosey.com

Ninet6 Ltd.
UK
7765670144
www.ninet6.com

Noriu Menulio
Lithuania
37067113180
www.noriumenulio.lt

North Star Marketing
USA
336-229-6610

notamedia
Russia
+7 (495) 995
www.notamedia.ru

oakley design studios
USA
971-221-5023
www.oakleydesign.com

Odney
USA
701-527-0819
www.odney.com

O'Hare Design
USA
513-897-0933
www.oharedesign.com

ohTwentyone
USA
972-646-0021
www.ohtwentyone.com

Oleg Peters
Russia
+7 915 434 07 42
www.yarvu.ru

One Man's Studio
USA
617-874-6334
www.onemansstudio.com

One up
Romania
004 0722 616 739
www.one-up.ro

OrangeRoc
USA
808-792-3077

ORFIK DESIGN
Greece
306932909191
www.orfikdesign.com

origo branding company
USA
614-784-0020
www.origobranding.com

Orn Smari | Design
Iceland
+354 863 8765
www.ornsmari.net

Oronoz Brandesign
Mexico
6142598591
www.alanoronoz.com

Oscar Morris
USA
512-293-5954
www.oscarmorris.com

Overhaul
Jordan
962 6 4616544
www.overhaul.jo

Oxide Design Co.
USA
402-344-0168
www.oxidedesign.com

p11creative
USA
714-641-2090

Padilla Speer Beardsley
USA
612-455-1769

pandabanda
Russia
www.pandabanda.com

Paradigm New Media Group
USA
314-621-7600
www.pnmg.com

Paradox Box
Russia
79177519251
www.paradoxbox.ru

Paraphernalia Design
Australia
4 1617 3462

Patten ID
USA
517-627-2033

Paul Black Design
USA
214-537-9780
www.paulblackdesign.com

Pavone
USA
717-234-8886

Pear Design
USA
312-498-1147

Peter Vasvari
Hungary
+36 209 349 873
www.petervasvari.com

Petra Dietlein
Germany
+49 176 78 23 83 46
www.park13.de

Phanco Design Studio
USA
www.phancodesign.com

The Pink Pear Design Company
USA
816-519-7327
www.pinkpear.com

Pinkerton Design
USA
817-335-7465

Piotr Ciesielski
Poland
www.behance.net/soaroe

Pixonal
Egypt

Plenty Creative
USA
616-233-9222
www.plentycreative.com

Plum
USA
916-624-6230

POLLARDdesign
USA
503-246-7251
www.pollarddesign.com

Poppyseed Creative
USA
806-799-6630

The Potting Shed
UK
01481 727699

Powell Allen
UK
+44 (0)20 7401 8971

Prejean Creative
USA
337-593-9051
www.prejeancreative.com

Pretty Pollution
Australia
+61 2 9954 4477

Principals Pty Ltd.
Australia
+61 9251 3833
www.principals.com.au

Proof Advertising
USA
512-345-6658

PUSH Branding and Design
USA
515-288-5278
www.pushbranding.com

PUSH Creative
USA
801-990-0691

Q
Germany
49-611-181310
www.q-home.de

Qing Li Design
USA

Qualita Design
Brazil
+55 41 30221702
www.qualitadesign.com.br

QUIQUE OLLERVIDES
Mexico
52 55 5616 0595
www.ollervides.com

R&R Partners
USA
702-228-0222

R3M1X3D
USA
407-283-7369

Range
USA
214-744-0555
www.rangeus.com

Raul Plancarte
Mexico
9811441558

RawRender
Turkey
905326838809
www.kemalhayit.com

RDQLUS Creative
USA
www.rdqlus.com

re:play
USA
937-461-6560
www.nicelyreplayed.com

reaves design
USA
773-552-2040
www.wbreaves.com

Red Clover Studio
USA
206-683-2314

Red Design Consultants
Greece
30-210-8010003

Red Rooster Group
USA
212-673-9353

Red Thinking
USA
703-283-4700
www.redthinkingllc.com

redeemstrategic
Indonesia
628122011528
www.redeemstrategic.com

RedEffect
Greece

Redhead Design Studio
USA
517-853-3681

Refinery Design Company
USA
563-584-0172

Reghardt
South Africa
+2783 5664688
www.reghardt.com

Rene Rutten Design & Digital
The Netherlands

Richard Baird Ltd.
Czech Republic
7931131587
www.richardbaird.co.uk

Richards & Swensen
USA
801-532-4097

Richards Brock Miller Mitchell & Associates
USA
214-987-6500
www.rbmm.com

Rick Carlson Design & Illustration
USA
919-604-1912
www.rcarlsondesign.com

Rickabaugh Graphics
USA
614-337-2229
www.rickabaughgraphics.com

Riggs Partners
USA

Rikky Moller Design
USA
210-410-3021
www.rikkymoller.com

Riordon Design
Canada
905-339-0750
www.riordondesign.com

Rise Design Branding, Inc.
China
86-533-3118581
www.clevay.com

River Designs, Inc.
USA
406-370-5063
www.riverdesigns.com

Riza Cankaya
Turkey
+90 216 5655897

rizen creative co.
USA
208-938-9598

RJ Thompson
USA
412-779-7665
www.whatiszola.com

rjd creative
USA
602-712-9020
www.rjdcreative.com

The Robin Shepherd Group
USA
904-359-0981

Rocket Science
USA
513-398-1700
www.rocket201.com

Rocketman Creative
USA
858-663-5082
www.rocketmancreative.com

RONODESIGN
Thailand
66 86 9937197
www.ronodesign.blogspot.com

Roskelly, Inc.
USA
401-683-5091
www.roskelly.com

Rossignol & Associates Design
Canada
416-588-9094

Roy Smith Design
UK
+44 (0)7767 797525
www.roysmithdesign.com

RP Public Relations
USA
419-241-2221

Rubber Design
USA
415-626-2990
www.rubberdesign.com

Rudy Hurtado Global Branding
Canada
416-525-2210
www.rudyhurtado.com

Rule29
USA
630-262-1009
www.rule29.com

Ruport
Russia
+7 861 277
www.ruport.ru

Ruth
USA
206-505-6550

Ryan Cooper
USA
303-917-9911
www.visualchili.com

Ryan Ford Design
USA
714-794-9645
www.liquisoft.com

S Design, Inc.
USA
405-608-0556
www.sdesigninc.com

S2N Design
USA
901-830-9837
www.s2ndesign.com

S3design studio graficzne
Poland
+48 515 250 599

Sabet
USA
949-705-9960
www.sabet.com

Sabingrafik, Inc.
USA
760-431-0439
www.tracysabin.com

Sally Says
USA
312-315-5760
www.sallysays.com

Samuel Nunez Design
USA
210-386-3103

SANDIA, Inc.
USA
719-473-8900

Sarah Petty
USA
214-460-4521

Sarah Rusin / Graphic Design
USA
765-532-3746
www.sarahrusin.com

Savacool Secviar Brand Communications
USA
858-342-7709
www.savacoolsecviar.com

Schisla Design Studio
USA
314-553-9500

Schwartzrock Graphic Arts
USA
952-994-7625
www.schwartzrock.com

Scott Oeschger
USA
610-457-3188
www.scottoeschger.com

Scott Pridgen Design Co
USA

Sculpt Communications
Australia
www.sculptcommunications.com.au

Sean Heisler
USA
402-917-6100
www.seanheislerdesign.com

Sebastiany Branding & Design
Brazil

Second Street Creative
USA
317-426-9799
www.2ndcreative.com

Sequence
USA

Sergey Shapiro
Russia
+7 962 969 2114
www.fromtheska.ru

the serif design
USA

serrano design
USA

Seth Cable Design
USA
714-813-1391

SGNL Studio
USA
405-514-5158
www.thesgnl.com

Sharisse Steber Design
USA
615-945-1099
www.sharissedesign.com

Shawn Castle
USA
205-690-0072
www.shawncastle.com

Shawn Meek
USA
210-382-9091

Shawn Wideman
USA
334-782-3496
www.shawnwideman.com

Shay Isdale Design
USA
512-968-7767

Shine Advertising
USA
608-442-7373

Shubho Roy
India
919734736748
www.rarh.in

Siah Design
Canada
406-290-0088
www.siahdesign.com

Sibley Peteet
USA
512-473-2333
www.spdaustin.com

Signifly
Denmark
22765174
www.signifly.com

SivierolNahas
USA
646-369-2280

Skye Design Studios
USA
910-814-7546
www.skyedesignstudios.com

Smart! Grupo Creativo
Argentina
www.smartgc.com.ar

Smyers Design
USA
202-329-7038
www.smyersdesign.com

Sol Consultores
Mexico
(011) (525) 56586300
www.solconsultores.com.mx

Somerset
USA
256-772-3435

Sommese Design
USA
814-353-1951

Soulsight
USA
847-681-4444

Sparkfly Creative
USA
www.sparkflycreative.com

sposato design & illustration
USA
845-365-1940

Sputnik Design Partners, Inc.
Canada
416-537-1637
www.sputnikart.com

Square Feet Design
USA
646-237-2828

stan can design
USA

Stanislav Topolsky
Ukraine
380677453618

stanovov
Russia
+7 904 375 8021
www.stanovov.ru

Starlight Studio
USA

Stebbings Partners
USA
508-699-7899
www.stebbings.com

Steele Design
USA
415-922-2804
www.briansteeledesign.com

Stevaker Design
USA
423-385-5989
www.stevaker.com

Steve Biel Design
USA
262-439-9423
www.stevebiel.com

Steve Cantrell
USA
954-574-0601

Steve DeCusatis Design
USA
215-840-0880
www.stevedecusatis.com

Steve Kelly Design
UK
+44 (0)7966 270339
www.stevekellydesign.com

Stiles Design
USA
512-633-9247
www.brettstilesdesign.com

Stitch Design Co.
USA
843-722-6296

Strange Ideas
USA
402-479-224
www.baileylauerman.com

Studio Absolute
USA
541-280-6836
www.studioabsolute.com

Studio French
USA
404-409-0628
www.studiofrench.com

Studio Ink
Australia
+61 35441 5991
www.studioink.com.au

Studio Rayolux
USA
206-353-1385

Studio Z
Brazil

Sudduth Design Co.
USA
512-236-0678
www.sudduthdesign.com

Sullivan Higdon & Sink
USA
316-263-0124
www.wehatesheep.com

Sunday Lounge
USA
719-207-4616
www.sundaylounge.com

Sunshinegun
South Africa
+27 11 234 8191
www.sunshinegun.co.za

Surface 51
USA
217-356-1300

Swanson Russell
USA
402-437-6400
www.swansonrussell.com

Swink
USA
608-442-8899
www.swinkinc.com

Synsation Graphic Design
Australia
+61(0)293652826
www.synsation.com.au

TEDDYSHIPLEY
USA
704-649-4659
www.theodoreshipley.com

Tactical Magic
USA
901-722-3001
www.tacticalmagic.com

Tactix Creative
USA
480-225-1480
www.tactixcreative.com

Tad Carpenter
USA
913-302-1019
www.tadcarpenter.com

Talal Obeid
Kuwait
+965 9614371

Tallgrass Studios
USA
785-842-9696
www.tallgrassstudios.com

Tandem Design Agency
USA
231-946-4804
www.tandemthinking.com

TAPHOUSE GRAPHICS
USA
888-988-5646
www.taphousegraphics.com

Tasty Concepts
USA
202-337-3930

Taylor Vanden Hoek
USA
616-745-1650

TBWA\Chiat\Day
USA
626-755-6275
www.tbwa.com

TD2
Mexico
5552920188

Tema Semenov
Russia
www.frontdesign.ru

Ten26 Design Group, Inc.
USA
847-650-3282
www.ten26design.com

TheNames
Russia
+7 495 5006000
www.thenames.ru

Theory Associates
USA
415-904-0995
www.theoryassociates.com

THINKMULE
USA
303-718-2914
www.thinkmule.com

Thoburn Design & Illustration, LLC
USA
540-247-3124
www.thoburnillustrations.com

Thomas Cook Designs
USA
919-274-1131
www.thomascookdesigns.com

Threds
USA
865-525-2830
www.threds.com

Thrillustrate
USA
503-999-4263
www.shanecawthon.carbonmade.com

Tielemans Design
USA
702-946-5511
www.tielemansdesign.com

Tim Frame Design
USA
614-598-0113
www.timframe.com

Timber Design Company
USA
317-213-8509
www.timberdesignco.com

Today
Belgium
+32 496 08 66 85
www.brandingtoday.be

TOKY Branding+Design
USA
314-534-2000
www.toky.com

Toledo Area Metroparks
USA
419-407-9735

Tomasz Politanski Design
Poland
+48 515 23 23 04
www.politanskidesign.com

Tone Graphic Design
USA

Torch Creative
USA
972-874-9842
www.torchcreative.com

Totem
Ireland
+353 58 24832
www.totem.ie

TPG Architecture
USA
212-536-5205
www.tpgarchitecture.com

Traction
USA
517-482-7919
www.projecttraction.com

Traction
USA
513-579-1008
www.teamtraction.com

Traina Design
USA

Tran Creative
USA
208-664-4098
www.tran-creative.com

Travers Collins & Company
USA
716-842-2222

Travis Quam
USA

Tribambuka
Russia
+7 921 3822829
www.tribambuka.com

Tribe Design, LLC
USA
713-523-5119
www.tribedesign.com

tugboat branding
Qatar
9747007571
www.tugboatbranding.net

TunnelBravo
USA
480-649-1400

Turner Duckworth
USA
415-675-7777
www.turnerduckworth.com

tuttle design
USA
612-812-9400

twentystar
USA
303-596-4134
www.twentystar.com

Ty Wilkins
USA
918-284-0462
www.tywilkins.com

Type08
Croatia
38598694174
www.type08.com

TypeOrange
USA
414-430-7030
www.typeorange.com

Ullman Design
USA

United by Design
UK

Unreal
USA
228-424-2779
www.unrealllc.com

VANESSA FOGEL DESIGN
South Africa
721096125

vanillashake media
USA
305-562-6032

Vanja Blajic
Croatia
385915188250
www.vectorybelle.com

Velocity Design Group
USA

Velocity Vectors
USA
www.velocity-vectors.com

Veneta Rangelova
Bulgaria
359888154195
www.kastelov.com

Verve Design
Australia
0410 475 855

VGreen Design
USA

Virginia Patterson Design
USA

Vistaprint
USA
781-652-6920

Visua
Australia
61 (3) 9018 7026
www.visua.com.au

Visual Lure, LLC
USA
618-622-9985
www.visuallure.com

VIVA Creative Group
USA

Vlad Boerean
Russia
79032863092

Vladimir Isaev
Russia
79217565758
www.vovaisaev.ru

VOLTAGE, LLC
USA
720-472-104

Voov Ltd.
Hungary
www.voov.hu

Vox One
USA
203-259-4554
www.voxone.com

Wall-to-Wall Studios
USA
412-232-0880

Webcore Design
UK
www.webcoredesign.co.uk

Webster Design Associates, Inc.
USA
www.websterdesign.com

Werger Design
USA
www.wergerdesign.com

WestmorelandFlint
USA
218-727-1552
www.westmorelandflint.com

Westwerk DSGN
USA
612-251-4277
www.westwerkdesign.com

Whole Brain Design
USA
505-820-0945

William Homan Design
USA
612-869-9105
www.williamhomandesign.com

Willoughby Design Group
USA
816-561-4189
www.willoughbydesign.com

Winnow Creative
USA

WinshipPhillips
USA
214-828-9699

Wise Design CG
USA

Wissam Shawkat Design
UAE
971504744130
www.wissamshawkat.com

Woods Creative
New Zealand
+64 7 575 5588

Worthen Design
USA
602-315-3921

Wox
Brazil
21 24925414
www.wox.com.br

wray ward
USA
704-332-9071
www.wrayward.com

XCLV / Superheroes
Ukraine
380503513745
be.net/konovalovxclv

XY ARTS
Australia
www.xyarts.com.au

Yatta Yatta Yatta
USA
509-996-2899

Yellow House Design, LLC
USA
919-866-0825
www.yellowhousedesign.com

yogg
USA
804-888-6380
www.landofyogg.com

Yury Akulin | Logodiver
Russia
79219577948
www.logodiver.com

Z&G
Russia
73432133345

Zande+Newman Design
USA
504-891-4526

Zapunk
UK
447523537658
www.zapunk.com

ZEBRA design branding
Russia
+7 8482 538000
www.zebradesign.ru

Zther Design Studio
USA
714-558-9990

about the authors

Bill Gardner is president of Gardner Design in Wichita, Kansas, and has produced work for Cessna, Thermos, Pepsi, Pizza Hut, Kroger, Hallmark, Cargill Corporation, and the 2004 Athens Olympics. His work has been featured in *Communication Arts, Print, Identity, Graphis, New York Art Directors,* the Museum of Modern Art, and many other national and international design exhibitions. He is the founder of LogoLounge.com and the author of *LogoLounge 1, 2, 3, 4, 5* and *6* the *LogoLounge Master Library* series, and the annual *LogoLounge Logo Trend Report.*

Anne Hellman is a freelance writer and editor. She is the co-author of *Designers on Design: Joël Desgrippes and Marc Gobé on the Emotional Brand Experience* (Rockport) and the editor of *Brandjam* (Allworth Press), *In the Pink: Dorothy Draper—America's Most Fabulous Decorator* (Pointed Leaf Press), and *Mr. Color: The Greenbrier and Other Decorating Adventures* (Shannongrove Press), among others. She is a regular contributor to the LogoLounge.com blog, Logos in the News. She lives in Brooklyn, New York.